# ALWAYS A
# CRIMSON TIDE

## PLAYERS, COACHES, AND FANS SHARE
## THEIR PASSION FOR ALABAMA FOOTBALL

### CREG STEPHENSON & KIRK MCNAIR
### FOREWORD BY MAL MOORE

TRIUMPH
BOOKS

Library of Congress Cataloging-in-Publication Data

Stephenson, Creg.
   Always a Crimson Tide / Creg Stephenson and Kirk McNair; foreword by Mal Moore.
      p. cm.
   ISBN 978-1-60078-594-8 (alk. paper)
   1. Alabama Crimson Tide (Football team)—History—Anecdotes. 2. University of Alabama—Football—History—Anecdotes. I. McNair, Kirk, 1945– II. Title.
   GV958.A4S74 2011
   796.332'640976184—dc23

                                                              2011023790

This book is available in quantity at special discounts for your group or organization. For further information, contact:

**Triumph Books**
814 North Franklin Street
Chicago, Illinois 60610
(800) 888-4741 | Fax (312) 337-1807
www.triumphbooks.com

Printed in U.S.A.
ISBN: 978-1-60078-594-8
Design and page production by Prologue Publishing Services, LLC
All photos courtesy of the University of Alabama's Paul W. Bryant Museum or Barry Fikes unless otherwise indicated

# CONTENTS

# FOREWORD

Most of us are naturally consumed with where we are. Insofar as Alabama Crimson Tide football is concerned, that means our interest in the upcoming season or the upcoming game, or maybe even about some player we are recruiting or some coach we are trying to hire.

We also look forward. We chart the players returning and the future schedule, or maybe look ahead to a game on this year's schedule that we have circled. We also need to look back, because our interest in this game and this season and in upcoming games and seasons is predicated in great part on the tradition that has been built at the University of Alabama over decades and decades, by dozens of coaches, hundreds of players, and thousands of supporters.

And what a tradition it is. The Alabama Crimson Tide is known worldwide for its football teams, its extraordinary success in the Southeastern Conference, on the national scene, and in the biggest of bowl games. It is known for its great players and coaches, and for its loyal followers as it competes for championships.

I grew up in Alabama—Dozier, Alabama—and like so many young men across this state, I was an Alabama fan because my father was an Alabama fan. He had become a fan of the Crimson Tide when the team was almost in its infancy, in the 1930s, and maybe even the 1920s.

Alabama had been fortunate to have a great coach in Wallace Wade, who took Alabama to the Rose Bowl. Alabama was the first team from the South—not just the Southeastern Conference, but the first team from the entire South—to go to the Rose Bowl.

Wallace Wade won Rose Bowl games and national championships. And then he was succeeded by Frank Thomas, who had continued success with more Rose Bowl victories and more national championships.

So the university has a great history and a great tradition. And that's what tradition is: success over a long, long period of time with contributions from a large number of people. That tradition has given the Crimson Tide a strong following, a strong base across the country. I have met people in California who became Alabama fans because their fathers and grandfathers became Alabama fans during those days of the early Rose Bowl games.

That gives us a foundation like no other team. You have to build on that foundation, and each coach who has come over those times has added to it. Certainly Coach Bryant added to it like no other. And Coach Stallings came and added another national championship, as did Coach Saban. This foundation, this strength, gives Alabama the opportunity to be a national college football power for years to come.

The feelings that Crimson Tide followers have—the genuine support this university and this athletics department have—will carry it into the future. But we have to continue to build on and support our strength. We have facilities that people can see, notably an exceptional stadium. We have an outstanding university academically, which helps us recruit the right kind of player. We have a coach who has won national championships, and he attracts the staff and the players you must have.

Mal Moore has spent most of his life at Alabama—as a quarterback, then as an assistant coach under Paul "Bear" Bryant and Gene Stallings, and finally as athletics director.

I think the University of Alabama will always be positioned to field an outstanding college football team. The state of Alabama is not a large state in population, which is a primary reason there is no pro football, no pro basketball, and no big league baseball. With no pro sports, the people of the state of Alabama support high school athletics. They love college football and high school football, so they support it. A young man growing up in this state grows up in an atmosphere where football is important.

Our good situation starts with having that type of young men in our state. And then we add to it by having a powerful name because of our tradition and success so that we can attract an outstanding player from anywhere, and so we go into surrounding states and recruit successfully. Our name and our tradition factored hugely when we were trying to attract Nick Saban to be our coach. To be a part of the great history of the Crimson Tide was important to him, and I think he also saw that he had the opportunity to build on that. Our facilities also helped attract him, because he recognized the tools were in place. As he has said, "The table was set." He had the support of our president, Dr. Robert E. Witt, and the board of trustees; and at his first A-Day Game, the spring football game in 2007, he saw the support of Crimson Tide fans as Bryant-Denny Stadium filled to capacity. Our stadium now seats more than 101,000, and every seat is filled for every game.

That was all done at a very, very awkward time in our history, and that we were able to accomplish it is a testament to the strength of Alabama football and has helped us to come out of this situation stronger and well-positioned for the future.

I am optimistic about Alabama football. We have a growing university, a university with excellent academics and leadership. Within the athletics department, we have in place the facilities and the Crimson Tide Foundation that will enable us to continue to set the pace. Alabama's history makes it a place where anyone would want to be a coach or a player, to have the opportunity to be a champion, to have the chance to be a part of the Crimson Tide tradition.

—Mal Moore

*Mal Moore played quarterback at Alabama from 1958 to 1962 and served as an assistant coach under Paul "Bear" Bryant from 1964 to 1982 and under Gene Stallings from 1990 to 1993. He has been athletics director at the university since 1999.*

# INTRODUCTION

I'M PROBABLY NOT ALONE in saying this (particularly among those reading this book), but I cried when I heard the news on the radio that Paul "Bear" Bryant had died. I was nine years old and had never seen an Alabama football game in person—and only a handful on television—but for some reason the news that the Crimson Tide's coaching icon had passed away overwhelmed me as I sat in the car with my mother waiting for my older brother to finish junior high football practice.

No one in my family attended the University of Alabama, though my grandfather and father were great admirers of the Crimson Tide football team. I grew up in Mississippi, but Crimson Tide fans among my family members and high school friends were almost as many in number as supporters of Mississippi State, Ole Miss, or Southern Mississippi.

I played football in high school to minimal acclaim, but I always loved the game and was always a decent enough writer. I knew I wanted to pursue a career in journalism, so when it came time to choose where to attend college, there really was only one choice for me.

I applied and was accepted to the University of Alabama in 1991. Bryant had been gone less than 10 years when I arrived on campus that fall, and the Gene Stallings era was just getting going.

As a student sitting in the stands at Bryant-Denny Stadium and Legion Field and with the school's student newspaper, the *Crimson White*, I got the chance to watch and cover some pretty good football teams. In my five football seasons on campus, Alabama went 45–8–1, including winning the 1992 national championship.

I covered Alabama off and on for the next decade and a half, including four years as Crimson Tide beat writer for the *Anniston Star*. It was during that time that I met and began to work closely with Kirk McNair, who conducted the bulk of the interviews with former Alabama players you'll read in this book.

We've tried to cover all the great players, teams, and events of Crimson Tide football through the years, and many times to provide firsthand accounts from the men themselves. The earliest player interviewed for this book began his Alabama career in 1929; the latest ended his in 2010.

The most well-versed among you may already have heard or read many of these stories, but we've tried to put a fresh take on what you will read here. Perhaps you will learn a thing or two in reading this book, as we certainly did in writing it. Condensing nearly 120 years of Alabama football into one volume is not an easy task, but we hope you will enjoy what we've put together. It definitely was a labor of love.

On April 27, 2011, a massive series of tornadoes hit the Southeast, including Alabama and the Tuscaloosa area. Much of the area surrounding the university was destroyed, and numerous students, residents, and Alabama fans were directly affected.

The state of Alabama and 'Bama nation have come together like never before as we rebuild and recover from the devastation. The following pages are a tribute to Alabama football fans and a celebration of what brought us together, the Crimson Tide.

—Creg Stephenson, May 2011

*chapter 1*

# COLOR IT CRIMSON: 'BAMA TRADITIONS

NO SPORT CLINGS MORE TIGHTLY to its traditions than college football, particularly in the South. And it is certainly difficult to find a college football program where tradition means more than at the University of Alabama. Here's a quick primer on Alabama football, call it Crimson Tide 101:

## THE FOOTBALL CAPITAL OF THE SOUTH

It's ironic that many of Alabama's greatest football moments and victories took place more than 40 miles from the university's campus. From the 1920s until well into the 1990s, the Crimson Tide played many of its home games—and all home contests against either Tennessee or Auburn—at Birmingham's Legion Field.

Nicknamed "the Football Capital of the South" and later "the Old Gray Lady of Graymont Avenue," Legion Field was opened in 1927 and, at its peak, could hold more than 83,000 fans, dwarfing Alabama's on-campus stadium until major expansions at Bryant-Denny Stadium in the 1980s and '90s. The stadium featured artificial turf from 1970 to 1994, but grass was replanted for use in qualifying games for the 1996 Summer Olympics soccer tournament.

The Crimson Tide was contractually obligated to play at least three home games per year at Legion Field until 1999, when the university began to move its bigger home football games back

Birmingham's Legion Field, known as "The Football Capital of the South," was the scene of many of Alabama's greatest victories and the exclusive home of the Iron Bowl from 1948 to 1988.

onto campus. Alabama played Tennessee in Tuscaloosa that season for the first time since 1930 and hosted Auburn on campus in 2000 for the first time since 1901.

Of course, Legion Field is most famous as the site of the Iron Bowl between Alabama and Auburn from 1948 to 1988. Those

41 meetings featured a true neutral site, with a 50/50 ticket split between each school. Alabama played "home" games against Auburn in Birmingham in 1990, 1992, 1994, 1996, and 1998, while the 1991 game was designated a home contest for Auburn.

Alabama played its last home game at Legion Field on August 30, 2003, a season-opening 40–17 victory over South Florida that also marked Mike Shula's debut as Crimson Tide head coach. The stadium also hosted the Alabama state high school championships for many years, but now serves primarily as the home stadium for University of Alabama at Birmingham football games.

## CLOSER TO HOME

Alabama played its earliest home football games on the university quadrangle and on other fields around and near campus, but opened Denny Stadium—named for university president George C. Denny—on the western edge of campus in 1929. The Crimson Tide routed Mississippi College 55–0 on September 28, 1929, in the first game at Denny Stadium, which then had a capacity of 12,000.

Subsequent expansions brought the stadium's capacity to 31,000 in 1946; 43,000 in 1961; and 60,000 in 1966. Artificial turf was installed in 1970, and in 1976 the Alabama legislature voted to rename the venue "Bryant-Denny Stadium" in honor of legendary coach Paul "Bear" Bryant.

The first major expansion of Bryant-Denny Stadium took place in 1988, when an upper deck was built to bring the seating capacity to 70,123. In 1998 a second upper deck was added to bring the stadium's capacity to 83,018. The north end zone was enclosed and several skyboxes were added in 2006, lifting the capacity to 92,138 and making Bryant-Denny the largest stadium in Alabama. In 2010 the south end zone was enclosed to bring the capacity to

101,821, making it the fifth-largest in college football as of the end of the 2010 season.

Alabama won 57 consecutive games at Bryant-Denny Stadium from 1964 to 1982, a streak snapped by Southern Miss in Bryant's final home game. The Crimson Tide won 20 straight at home from 2008 to 2010.

## Fight Songs, Official and Otherwise (and Those Who Sing Them)

Fight songs are nearly as old as football itself, and the Crimson Tide adopted its official song after one of the team's great early victories.

In the afterglow of Alabama's 1926 Rose Bowl victory over Washington, a contest was held on campus for students to write a fight song. The winning entry was penned by engineering student Ethelred "Epp" Sykes, who would go on to become a brigadier general in the United States Air Force.

Sykes' song, titled "Yea Alabama," was originally much longer, but includes the chorus:

*Yea, Alabama! Drown 'em Tide!*
*Every 'Bama man's behind you,*
*Hit your stride.*
*Go teach the Bulldogs to behave,*
*Send the Yellow Jackets to a watery grave.*
*And if a man starts to weaken,*
*That's his shame!*
*For Bama's pluck and grit have*
*Writ her name in Crimson flame.*
*Fight on, fight on, fight on men!*
*Remember the Rose Bowl, we'll win then.*

Bryant-Denny Stadium has undergone many renovations since it first opened as Denny Field in 1929. As of 2010, it held 101,821 fans, making it the fifth-largest stadium in college football.

*Roll on to victory,*
*Hit your stride,*
*You're Dixie's football pride,*
*Crimson Tide, Roll Tide, Roll Tide!*

Alabama's cheerleaders are among the most visible of the hundreds who make up the in-game support personnel for Crimson Tide football.

Though references to the Rose Bowl (until its 2010 BCS National Championship Game vs. Texas, Alabama hadn't played in that bowl game since 1946) and the Yellow Jackets (Georgia Tech left the Southeastern Conference in the mid-1960s) soon became outdated, the song remains a standard before, during, and after every Crimson Tide game.

Alabama has a number of unofficial fight songs, including the Lynyrd Skynyrd southern rock standard "Sweet Home Alabama." Lynyrd Skynyrd wasn't from Alabama, and the song's lyrics aren't about football, but it's been played at Crimson Tide games almost since it was first released in 1974.

Always popular with students and hard-core fans is the pre- and postgame "Rammer Jammer" chant, with its sometimes controversial lyrics "we're gonna beat the hell out of you!" or "we *just* beat the hell out of you!" The cheer—which was derived from Ole Miss' "Hotty Toddy" cheer at some point in the 1970s, after James Ferguson left that Mississippi school to become Alabama's band director—is unofficially discouraged by the school's administration and has even been banned more than once, but always seems to find its way back into the game-day routine.

Performing all those songs at one time or another has been the Million Dollar Band, Alabama's student marching band. The band—formed in the early 1920s—took its name, legend has it, from a comment by General John J. Pershing that marching bands had been "worth a million dollars" to American military forces during World War I.

Alongside the band on game day are Alabama's cheerleaders and majorette team, the Crimsonettes. Perhaps the most famous alumna of the Crimson Tide cheerleading squad is television actress Sela Ward, an Alabama cheerleader in the mid-1970s.

## IN THE PRESS BOX

Alabama football has been making major national news for more than 85 years as of 2011, and the biggest names in sports media have come to be associated with the Crimson Tide. Legendary Atlanta sportswriter Grantland Rice was an early proponent of the Crimson Tide in print, while longtime ABC sportscaster Keith Jackson called many of the team's biggest games on television.

Alabama football has also been served by a dedicated corps of in-state media, including newspaper sportswriters and columnists such as Zipp Newman, Naylor Stone, Benny Marshall, Alf Van Hoose, Bill Lumpkin, Clyde Bolton, and Jimmy Bryan of Birmingham; Jimmy Smothers of Gadsden; John Pruett of Huntsville; George Smith of Anniston; and Charles Land, Al Browning, and Cecil Hurt of Tuscaloosa. Great Crimson Tide sports information directors have included Finus Gaston, Charlie Thornton, Larry White, and this volume's coauthor, Kirk McNair.

But it is the men in the radio booth who have had the greatest and most intimate connection to Crimson Tide football. Mel Allen called games while still an Alabama student in the 1930s, before embarking on a long career as the voice of baseball's New York Yankees.

Gabby Bell and Maury Farrell were among the Crimson Tide's radio broadcasters in the 1940s and 1950s, but it was Farrell's young partner who would come to be most closely associated with Alabama football on the radio. John Forney called Alabama football games on the radio for more than 30 seasons, including all of the Paul Bryant glory years.

Eli Gold has been Alabama's football play-by-play man since 1988, a 23-season tenure (as of 2010) exceeded only by Forney's. Notable color analysts and sideline reporters in recent years have included Doug Layton, Tom Roberts, and Phil Savage, and former Crimson Tide players Ken Stabler, Jerry Duncan, and Barry Krauss.

## *Crimson Tide in Their Own Words*
# BARRY KRAUSS
### LINEBACKER, 1976–1978

At the end of the 1978 season, we had motivation and we had a second chance. A year earlier, we thought we were going to win the national championship. We had beaten Woody Hayes and a good Ohio State football team in the Sugar Bowl. We thought if Notre Dame could somehow upset Texas—which was ranked No. 1 in 1977—in the Cotton Bowl that we'd win the national championship. Notre Dame did upset Texas, but then jumped over us from fifth to first.

The next year in the Sugar Bowl we had another chance. Penn State was No. 1 in 1978, and their coach, Joe Paterno, decided to play the next-highest-ranked team, which was Alabama, in the Sugar Bowl for the national championship.

We knew we had to play another great game, and we were ready. I can remember how relaxed everyone was before the game.

Everyone played well. Tony Nathan rushed for more than 100 yards. Murray Legg had a great defensive game. Benny Perrin had a big interception. Bruce Bolton had a big touchdown catch. Lou Ikner had a punt return that took the pressure off us. As Legg said after the game, "I don't believe we were a great football team. We were a good football team, and Coach Bryant made us think we were great." And that was the difference in the game.

It came down to the goal-line stand. Don McNeal made a great play on a pass, and I think everyone came together after that. It came down to a fourth-down play. We were holding hands in the huddle. We knew everything we had worked for was at stake,

Barry Krauss (77) was the MVP of the 1979 Sugar Bowl in large part because of this fourth-down tackle at the goal line, which preserved a 14–7 victory over Penn State and gave Alabama the national championship.

particularly for the four seniors on defense. And we knew we were going to make the play.

We had just stopped a dive play, and I thought they would probably play action or sweep. But Coach Donahue made a great call for us to sell out and crash the corners. The defensive line did an incredible job of reestablishing the line of scrimmage.

So, yes, he [Mike Guman] went over the top, and I was the one who hit him. But that was because of what the defensive line had done. It was Coach Bryant's plan that the defensive line would take out the interference and let the linebackers make the play. And then Murray came in and pushed us back, keeping the back from twisting and maybe falling into the end zone. Everyone was involved. It was the epitome of Alabama defense, which was team-work at its best.

Before the game, Coach Bryant had told us he expected the game to come down to a defensive opportunity.

He always said that in a close game it would be two or three key plays that would determine the outcome. And it's the same thing in people's lives. Two or three opportunities.

Coach Bryant taught us to always be ready for the moment you can make a difference and said you never know when that time will come. We learned to condition ourselves to be ready for suc-cess. He pushed us until we felt we had nothing left and we had to dig deeper to do the job. We did that every day in practice, and so we were able to do it when the national championship was at stake.

That Penn State game was a second chance for our football team. I had a second chance with Coach Bryant. My sophomore year I wasn't happy about my place on the depth chart. And we had a quarterback who wasn't happy because they were moving him to defensive back. One night after a game, we went out and we missed curfew. It so happened that this was a night that Coach Bryant made room checks himself. I knew we were dead.

I didn't wait for him to call me. I went to see him. And I cried and apologized and begged for mercy. The quarterback didn't do anything. Coach Bryant kicked him out of the dorm and took his scholarship. He gave me a second chance. I kept my scholarship and learned a big lesson. Maybe I wasn't a model citizen, but I straightened up a lot.

My introduction to Alabama was really on the beach. I grew up in Pompano Beach, Florida, and one of my friends, Eddie Blankenship, was a big Alabama fan. We liked to toss a football around on the beach, trying to impress the girls, I'm sure. But Eddie introduced me to the wishbone offense versus the wave. What we'd do is line up in the wishbone on the shore. And when the wave came, we'd start the triple option. A wave hits at an angle so we could run the option down the sand. The fullback would dive into the wave, then the quarterback would run down the wave until he had to give it up. He'd pitch it to the halfback, who would try to dive over the wave. That kind of made me an Alabama fan.

I was being recruited by Florida, Florida State, Miami, and Georgia Tech. Alabama didn't come in until late. Miami invited me to come when Alabama was playing them in the Orange Bowl. I went to the game and thought that Alabama looked cool. And they beat Miami pretty badly, worse than the final score.

Kenny Martin was recruiting me and invited me for a visit. I went up there, and I fell in love with Alabama. I can still remember going in the locker room and standing in front of Woodrow Lowe's locker and looking at his helmet. That was awesome, because Woodrow Lowe was one of the greatest linebackers ever. I was basically done.

My signing was memorable. I had gone to our football banquet. And when I came home and opened the door, there was Coach Bryant. He had flown down, and my family knew he would be there, but I didn't. He had my scholarship, and I signed right then. Coach Bryant was not the kind of man you said no to.

I was on cloud nine, but I remember one of my best friends saying, "Why would you go to Alabama? They've got great players. You'll never get to play." And I thought, *Thanks a lot for the confidence.* Coach Bryant had promised me an opportunity, and I thought that was all I would need.

I can't begin to tell you how tough it was. It was hot and humid. Byron Braggs, a defensive tackle, nearly died of heat stroke. After that, we started getting water breaks. Even the water breaks were so disciplined. The whistle would blow, and you'd have to hustle to your spot, a hundred or more of us on one knee in one straight line, and the managers would bring the water to us.

At one practice I told our trainer, Jim Goostree, that I was going to throw up and that I should go in. I was trying to get out of practice. He told me to go over by the bushes and throw up and then to get back in the drill.

I really didn't start playing much until midway through my sophomore season when we went to Notre Dame. Somebody missed a tackle, and I went in and had a pretty good game, hitting people and making an interception. Coach Bryant started me the second half. He said for the guys who had started the game to start the second half, "except I want Krauss in there. He wants to hit someone."

I led the team in tackles in that game and again a couple of weeks later when we beat Auburn really badly.

We played UCLA in the Liberty Bowl. There was a fireworks display before the game that got me going. On the kickoff, nobody touched me, and I drilled the return guy at about the 5-yard line. Our defense was all over them, and we won big. I had an interception for a touchdown. It was probably the best game of my career.

I didn't realize at the time what I was a part of. We had great football teams at Alabama. When I got to professional football, I realized how great Coach Bryant was. The best lessons I learned were at Alabama.

There is no question that the greatest experience of my life was playing football for Coach Bryant at the University of Alabama. It is something I am very proud of and something I think about every day.

> *Barry Krauss was All-America in 1978, the year he was MVP of the Sugar Bowl for his memorable goal-line-stand tackle to preserve Bama's 14–7 win for the national championship. He was also MVP of the 1976 Liberty Bowl. He was selected to the Alabama Team of the Century. He played 10 years with the Colts and one with the Dolphins.*

## ELEPHANTS, RED AND GRAY

Alabama's earliest football teams were known as the Cadets, a nod to the school's origin as a military academy. Newspaper accounts thereafter referred to the team alternately as the "varsity" or "Crimson White."

In 1907 Hugh Roberts of the *Birmingham Age-Herald* first referred to the Alabama team as the "Crimson Tide" during a game against Auburn played in particularly muddy conditions. The nickname stuck.

"Crimson Tide" obviously does not lend itself easily to a mascot, either a live one or a human-in-costume. In about 1930 sportswriter Everett Strupper of the *Atlanta Journal* referred to the Wallace Wade's powerful Alabama team as the "Red Elephants," and Crimson Tide football has been linked to the largest of land mammals ever since.

The university used a live elephant during special events during the 1940s, and the school's elephant-dressed student mascot "Big

His face has changed over the years, but Alabama's "Big Al" remains among the most-recognizable and beloved mascots in college football.

Al" was born in 1979. Former offensive coordinator Homer Smith was known to refer to the team's offensive linemen as "pachyderms" in practice, and the Bryant-Denny Stadium staff often plays an angry elephant roar over the stadium's sound system before and during key points in games to fire up the crowd.

## HOME COOKIN'

Like any good college town, Tuscaloosa is loaded with great places to eat. And the number of restaurants and cafes with "Crimson," "'Bama," "Tide," or some other ancillary connection to the university's football team in their name is too high to count.

The most famous is Dreamland Bar-B-Que, founded by bricklayer John Bishop in 1958 in the Jerusalem Heights section of southeast Tuscaloosa. For years you could find Dreamland only in Tuscaloosa, and fans, barbecue aficionados, and newspaper and television reporters came from all over the country to sample the restaurant's distinctive pork ribs and tangy sauce (along with white bread for dipping into the sauce, that's all the original Dreamland serves).

The Bishop family began selling Dreamland franchises in the late 1990s, and the restaurant can now be found all over Alabama and surrounding states. The newer Dreamland locations even—perish the thought—serve chicken, beef, and side items.

Dreamland isn't the only good place to get a bite in or near T-town, though. There's also Archibald's, a tiny Northport barbecue smokehouse that is operated in the owner's backyard and which some argue is better than Dreamland.

In Northport, you'll also find City Café, a traditional "meat-and-three" diner that serves breakfast and lunch to thousands of patrons every week (it's not open for dinner or on weekends). Across the river from campus lies Cypress Inn, home of the best catfish on the Black Warrior River.

Back closer to campus are the Waysider, a three-room breakfast-only establishment off Greensboro Avenue, where numerous Alabama coaches and players past and present have been known to dine on the Friday before home games. In the shadows of Bryant-Denny Stadium is Rama Jama's, a breakfast and burger shack that is open year-round but often does a year's worth of business on game day.

Tuscaloosa is also well-known for its chicken wing restaurants, the most well-known being Buffalo Phil's on the University Boulevard strip west of campus and Bob Baumhower's Wings Sports Grille just across Highway 82 from the east end of campus. Baumhower, an All-America defensive tackle for the Crimson Tide in the mid-1970s, opened his first Wings in 1981 and now owns more than a dozen restaurants throughout the region.

## Immortality in Concrete

Perhaps the most recognizable structure on the Alabama campus is Denny Chimes, erected at the south end of the quadrangle in 1929 and named for longtime university president George Denny. For Crimson Tide football fans, however, Denny Chimes is also the location of the "Walk of Fame."

During a special ceremony in the spring of 1948, Alabama football captains Harry Gilmer and John Wozniak pressed their handprints and cleated footprints beneath their names in the concrete beneath the chimes. It's a tradition that continues to this day, with Alabama's permanent team captains immortalized in the pavement before each spring's A-Day intrasquad scrimmage.

"I was fortunate enough to win awards in football," former All-America cornerback Don McNeal said. "I played on two national championship teams at Alabama, and I played in two Super Bowls. But the thing I am most proud of is that I was elected captain of

Named for longtime university president George Denny and erected in 1929, Denny Chimes is not only the university's iconic symbol, but home to the Crimson Tide's "Walk of Fame."

our 1979 national championship team along with Steve Whitman. Even though I wasn't a real vocal guy, my teammates told me I was a leader. It was a great feeling to get that honor from my teammates. And when I return to the university, which I do as often as I can, I go to the quad and see all those great names around Denny Chimes—Pat Trammell, Billy Neighbors, Lee Roy Jordan, Joe Namath, Steve Sloan, Kenny Stabler, Johnny Musso, Sylvester Croom, Ozzie Newsome—and then I peek around the corner and see Don McNeal."

Alabama's team captains are generally voted on by teammates, though each head coach has different criteria for who is eligible and how many are chosen. Some coaches limit captaincy to seniors, while others open it up to the entire team.

There have been a handful of two-time captains in Alabama football history—Jarrett Johnson, Tyler Watts, Antoine Caldwell, and Rashad Johnson. Mark Barron and Dont'a Hightower were both elected captains as juniors in 2010, and will thus be eligible once again in 2011.

## EASY TO IDENTIFY

Alabama football players began wearing hard-shell style helmets in the early 1950s, and in 1957, team equipment managers began painting the players' jersey numbers on the sides of their helmets. It was a fairly common practice at the time, but by the end of the 20th century, the Crimson Tide was the only Division I college football team with numbers on the side of its helmets.

Stylized logos have become fashionable in all forms of team athletics, but the Crimson Tide's simplistic helmet numbers remain. Though perhaps understated (or even boring), the helmet numbers certainly make Alabama football players easier to identify, for both fans in the stands and watching on television.

"You might think a kid in Andrews, Texas, which is in West Texas, might never have heard about Alabama," said Shaud Williams, who played running back for the Crimson Tide in 2002 and 2003. "But I had heard stories about the Crimson Tide when I was a small child. I can remember growing up and asking my dad, 'Is the team with just numbers on the helmet playing?' I didn't know them as Alabama, just as the team that didn't have anything on its helmets but the numbers."

# Crimson Tide in Their Own Words

## SHAUD WILLIAMS

### TAILBACK, 2002–2003

You might think a kid in Andrews, Texas, which is in West Texas, might never have heard about Alabama. But I had heard stories about the Crimson Tide when I was a small child. I can remember growing up and asking my dad, "Is the team with just numbers on the helmet playing?" I didn't know them as Alabama, just as the team that didn't have anything on its helmets but the numbers.

Later I heard more about the Alabama tradition, about Joe Namath. And I watched Shaun Alexander. But it took an unusual series of events for me to play at Alabama. I am grateful every day for those events that gave me an opportunity to put on that same jersey worn by so many greats. It was an honor to play for Alabama.

I signed with Texas Tech out of high school. Spike Dykes was the head coach, and I was a running back. After my freshman year, Coach Dykes retired, and they brought in Mike Leach, who brought a new passing style of offense. I didn't feel I fit that offense. Tech released me from my scholarship, but said I couldn't go anywhere in Texas or to any other Big 12 school. Then Coach Fran got the job at Alabama. I knew him from when he had recruited me for TCU. And so I was able to go to Alabama.

I can honestly say that playing for Alabama is an honor, but I may not have seen it that way my first year. I had to sit out a year, which was the first time I had ever missed playing. And that was when Alabama had Saleem Rasheed, Kindal Moorehead, Kenny King, and Jarret Johnson. I had to go out there every day and get

Shaud Williams left Texas Tech when the Red Raiders changed from a running to a passing team and ended up as a thousand-yard rusher and team captain at Alabama.

beat up, knowing there was no chance I was going to get to play. It was tough. But that helped me, not only as a football player, but as a person. It helped me realize that there's going to be a time when I'm not playing football and not in the limelight. It was very much a humbling experience.

I was determined in spring training that year because I wanted to show I could play in the Southeastern Conference. I didn't get to touch the ball until the North Texas game in 2002, my junior year. In that game I got a few touches that boosted my confidence.

The Arkansas game was big for me. It was a night game on ESPN—always a good atmosphere. We were in Fayetteville before a full house of about eighty thousand. Our quarterback, Tyler Watts, was hurt, and it was going to be Brodie Croyle's first start. We were going to run the ball to keep the pressure off him and keep him relaxed. On the first play I went 80 yards for a touchdown.

All-in-all I had a decent year, and we had a pretty good year, finishing up 10–3. And I never sensed the change that was coming. Of course, we heard the rumors that Coach Fran was leaving. A lot of guys thought something was wrong when we were preparing for Auburn, but I never thought about Fran leaving.

I was home in Texas for a funeral when the news came that Coach Fran was going to Texas A&M. I called back, and one of my roommates said they had just gotten out of a meeting and that Coach Torbush had confirmed it. I could hardly believe it.

What upset me was that he had told us the rumors were not true, that he wasn't going anywhere. He had all the seniors convinced to stick it out through the tough times and he would stick it out with us. We were going to get through the tough times together. He hurt a lot of guys when he left like he did.

Coach Price came in and immediately put life into our football program. He made football fun again. I really thought we had a new energy with him.

We were at the football complex when they told us he was going to be fired. I put my head in my hands and wondered, *What is going to happen to us next? We bought into what coach Fran told us, and he left. Just when we bought into what coach Price told us, he gets fired. We're four months away from our senior year and we don't have a head coach.* And I started crying.

Then someone asked me if I wanted to go make a statement to media. I didn't think I was going to cry then, but I looked over at Coach Price. He had come over to us and said, "If you players ever need me, you can call me. I love each and every one of you."

My senior year was so close to being good. We had the great game with Oklahoma, which was No. 1 in the nation. Then we had the five-overtime game against Tennessee. We had near misses. We were close to being 9–4 instead of 4–9.

In the Tennessee game, I lost my temper with our offensive line. We had lost Wesley Britt early with a broken leg, but we needed people to step up. We had third-and-short, and a defensive tackle came through untouched and hit me. I was a little frustrated. Later I apologized to each guy individually for losing my temper. Most of them told me I didn't owe them an apology, but I felt I did. They were trying to do their job, just like I was.

Despite a few bumps, my whole career at Alabama was very much a positive experience. I don't regret one day I spent at The University of Alabama. Some of my best friends, who will be my best friends forever, I met at Alabama.

I was not surprised I wasn't drafted by an NFL team. A lot of teams don't want to take a chance on a small back. I just looked at it as another challenge. I knew if they would give me a chance, I would make the team.

Atlanta, Baltimore, Arizona, Dallas, and Buffalo wanted me to come in as free agent, and Buffalo seemed like the best fit. I had talked with the running backs coach [Eric Studesville] at an NFL combine, and we hit it off pretty well. He said they weren't going to draft a running back, but he was almost hoping I wouldn't get drafted because he felt like I could come in and make the team. And that's what happened.

You don't realize how special a place Alabama is until you're gone. In the NFL you may play in front sixty thousand fans, as opposed to Bryant-Denny where you have more than eighty thousand. I am very grateful I was able to be a part of the tradition and be a part of something that was so great.

*Shaud Williams played at Alabama just two years, but along with another two-year player, Derrick Pope, was captain of the 2003 Crimson Tide. He signed as a free agent with Buffalo and made the team. He was 'Bama's leading rusher in 2002 and 2003.*

## TOWER OF TERROR

It's still there on the Crimson Tide's practice field, unused but always looming. The steel tower Bryant had erected in order to give him a better vantage point from which to view football practice remains a symbol of Alabama football and a source of some horrific memories for former Crimson Tide players.

E.J. Junior, an All-America defensive end for the Crimson Tide in 1980, said Bryant came out of the tower for only four reasons: "Practice was over, some dignitary like the governor was visiting practice, someone was hurt, or he was going to chew someone out." An Alabama player who made a serious mistake on the practice field could expect a swift rebuke from Bryant, and it followed an unmistakable sound, as future All-America defensive back Mike Washington found out one day his freshman year:

I was on the scout team, and we had Johnny Musso and John Hannah and all those big guys out there. They had run a sweep, and Steve Ford, a defensive back from Tuscaloosa, was playing cornerback. Hannah hit him and broke his leg. That moved me up to corner. Here came that sweep again, and when Hannah got close to me, I gave him one of those *olé* moves like a bullfighter, getting out of the way. And Musso ran for a touchdown.

There was a chain across the steps at the top of the tower, and when Coach Bryant came down, the first thing you heard was that chain drop. We heard it and looked up, and he was coming down. And he could move. It seemed like he was going about 40 miles per hour. Everyone wondered whom he was after. I was at right corner, the farthest of anyone from him. In a minute, he had passed everyone but me. I was the only one left.

I looked at Coach Bryant coming. And I looked behind me where there was a fence separating me from the railroad tracks. And something was telling me, *You'd better hit that fence, because he's coming at you.* But I also knew if I ran, my momma and grandmother would be waiting at home, and that wasn't going to be too good, either.

He got to me and grabbed my face mask. And he was real strong. He twisted my little head like it was a pretzel. And every time he twisted he had something to say. The bottom line was that I had better get my butt in gear or I wouldn't have to run away. He would send me home. But he also told me I had too much talent to let it go to waste by wasting time in practice.

I had tears rolling down my eyes. And I know everyone who was there remembers the day. If there was ever any question about whether Coach Bryant was going to treat everyone the same way, he answered it that day.

The famed tower from which Paul "Bear" Bryant observed Alabama football practice during his days as coach still stands on the grounds of the Crimson Tide facility.

Few men other than Bryant ever went to the top of the tower. However, he did occasionally invite a favorite former player or celebrated recruit to join him during practice, as Joe Namath discovered in 1961 and recalled years later:

Coach [Howard] Schnellenberger and I flew through a terrible storm into Tuscaloosa. We got there after practice had started. I remember the movement, the crispness, a lot of players out there hustling around on both sides of the track. Coach Bryant was up in the tower. Coach Bryant said something to Coach Schnellenberger, and I couldn't understand anything he said.

Coach Schnellenberger said, "Go up there. He wants to see you."

I said, "What?"

And he repeated, this time with some urgency, "Go on up there. Coach Bryant wants to see you."

So I went up. I wasn't thinking about being on his tower, that it was an important place. It was just a matter of getting up there and thinking about getting down. And I didn't understand a word he said, except for one word, "Stud," and I didn't know what a stud was.

---

*Crimson Tide in Their Own Words*

# JOE NAMATH

## QUARTERBACK, 1962–1964

When I was a kid in Beaver Falls, Pennsylvania, my father and his friends played football pools, betting a dime or a quarter on pro games. And they'd let me pick a few games. So I'd watch the pro game on a black-and-white television set that Sunday, and I started trying to call the plays, learning from them. I was dreaming about being on a football field.

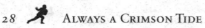

Joe Namath is one of the most celebrated players in both college and pro football. He led Alabama to a national championship and the New York Jets to the Super Bowl.

And who would have dreamed I would play on football fields for Paul Bryant, the greatest coach ever, and Weeb Ewbank, who had already coached the Baltimore Colts and Johnny Unitas to a world championship?

I learned that to be a quarterback you had to have a lot of qualities, including confidence. I always felt I could play and that I never had to talk about it. One reason was growing up the youngest child. If I played a baseball game and went 3-for-4, my brother would say, "What happened?" He wanted to know about the out.

At Alabama, the quarterback got to see Coach Bryant more than players at the other positions. One of the things I enjoyed was the walk the quarterbacks made with him the morning of every game. We'd walk down the street and talk about the game plan. On one of the first walks we made, he said, "Joe, you got the plan?"

I said, "Yeah, I think so."

"You think so?" he said. "You think so? Boy, it's time to know."

That was the last time I made that mistake.

I didn't want to go through the "A" Club initiation. I had earned my letter my sophomore year, but I didn't want to get whipped, I didn't want to get shaved. It was a pretty tough initiation.

I got a message that Coach Bryant wanted to see me, so I went to his office. He said, "I hear you're not going through 'A' Club initiation. Why not?" I told him I didn't want to go through all those things; that I had earned the letter. He said it was tradition. I still didn't want to do it. He said if I didn't go through "A" Club initiation, I couldn't be elected captain. I said okay to that, too.

Then he said, "I want you to."

I said, "Yes, sir."

You knew he was right, even when it wasn't the way you wanted it to be, or the way you saw it. He was the man. If he said, "I want you to," we all would have done it.

How did I become an Alabama football player? I was lucky.

Coach Bryant and Tom Nugent, the head football coach at Maryland, were friends, and when I failed the college boards at Maryland, I was still available. I really didn't want to go to college. I wanted to play baseball. I don't remember ever studying at home in high school. My mother had graduated from high school, but my father had finished only the third grade. When he came to America from Hungary at age 12, he went right to work. It was always work, work, work. Math came reasonably easy to me, and it's a good thing, too, because over the years I've had a great relationship with numbers.

I got by as a student. All I wanted to do was pass. Everything was football, baseball, and basketball, and the odd jobs—caddying or working for the city. So I didn't score high enough on the college boards for Maryland, although I was eligible for most schools.

There were deals out there. The first coach who ever came to my house to recruit me took me outside after he had talked to me and my family. He told me if I would sign with him that I would have a vehicle and a certain amount of money each month. I've forgotten now if it was $100 a week or $300 a month or exactly what it was, but I know at the time it was an astronomical amount. But my brother Frank said, "What kind of people do you want to be with? If they're cheating now, they will cheat you later. Or they will have you becoming a cheater."

Frank had gone to Kentucky on a football scholarship and was a catcher on the baseball team.

I heard later that Coach Nugent said that Alabama wasn't on his schedule, and that's why he called Coach Bryant. This was in August, and I was at home in Beaver Falls. The guys were already in Tuscaloosa practicing.

Coach Bryant sent Coach Howard Schnellenberger to Beaver Falls. My mother liked Coach Schnellenberger tremendously, especially when she found out he was at Kentucky when my brother

Frank was at Kentucky. She went upstairs and packed a suitcase—a small suitcase—and came back down and said, "All right, Joey. Take him, Coach."

Coach Schnellenberger and I flew through a terrible storm into Tuscaloosa. We got there after practice had started. I remember the movement, the crispness, a lot of players out there hustling around on both sides of the track. Coach Bryant was up in the tower. Coach Bryant said something to coach Schnellenberger, and I couldn't understand anything he said. Coach Schnellenberger said, "Go up there. He wants to see you." I said, "What?" And he repeated, this time with some urgency, "Go on up there. Coach Bryant wants to see you."

So I went up. I wasn't thinking about being on his tower, that it was an important place. It was just a matter of getting up there, and thinking about getting down. And I didn't understand a word he said, except for one word, "Stud," and I didn't know what a stud was.

I was one player who did not know about Coach Bryant. I didn't know about his history. I didn't know about this legacy he was working on. But one day at practice he got through to me very well and taught me a good lesson about respect and about how men need to look one another in the eye when communicating. I think that's when he and I really started to connect. At least I did.

Once in practice I was throwing passes and he was standing next to me, watching me. And for some reason I wasn't throwing a good, tight spiral. He said, "Give me the ball." And he took the ball and was manipulating it around and saying, "I think if you'll..." and he paused and said, "Oh, hell, why am I telling you about passing. You know more about it than I do." And he flipped the ball back to me.

The Vanderbilt game in my sophomore year was the only time I ever got benched for poor play. I was having a bad game and got taken out of the game in the first quarter. This was when the quarterbacks called all the plays and ran the offense from the field. Now it came after a lot of preparation with Coach Bryant and Coach Phil Cutchin and Coach Elwood Kettler, but the quarterback called all the plays.

I knew I was messing up, and that was the reason I was pulled. I went over to the sideline by the bench, took off my helmet, and threw it on the ground. I sat down on the bench with my head in my hands.

Coach Bryant came over and sat down beside me and put his arm around my shoulder. Then he put his hand on my neck and started squeezing. And it was hard, like one of my big brothers squeezing me. It told me what he thought of that kind of behavior, and how fast he'd kick my ass back to Beaver Falls, Pennsylvania, if I ever displayed that kind of selfish attitude again.

I looked Coach Bryant right in the eye—I had learned that—and told him I wasn't upset with him or the coaches. I was only upset with myself.

Coach Bryant told us early, when we were freshmen, that we would remember the tough times—the games we lost, the bad times—longer than we would remember the good. And that is true. Except for the championships, a championship game or a championship season, it is the failures you most remember.

One of my greatest disappointments came in the Orange Bowl in my last game. We had already won the national championship, but we lost to Texas in the Orange Bowl. Late in the game we had an opportunity to win, and I fouled up on the goal line. We had first and goal at the six and gained four yards on a first-down run. And I guess we gained about a yard on second and a little less than a yard on third. On fourth down we went with the surest play, a quarterback sneak. It wasn't disrespect of Texas. It was a belief that we could knock them off the ball and get it in. We were taught around here that if you couldn't blow someone out for a yard, maybe you didn't deserve it.

Over the years people have asked, "Joe Willie, did you score a touchdown against Texas?" My answer is that I did not because it was not ruled a touchdown. But I did get over the goal line. So many times over the years have I wished that I had had enough brains instead of being caught up in the situation to call time out on third down to go over to talk to the man, to talk to Coach Bryant.

But you know how lucky I am? Jim Hudson, George Sauer, John Elliott, and Pete Lammons were four of the guys on that Texas team who came to the Jets when I did and helped us win the World Championship.

The pain of losing that game was awful. But the next day I signed a contract with the Jets. The pain doesn't go right away, but signing that contract helped ease it a little.

My first season at Alabama in 1961 was frustrating because freshmen couldn't play. We sat in the stands and watched Pat Trammell lead us to the national championship. It may have been a good rule at the time for freshmen not to be able to play, but I couldn't wait to be a sophomore.

My first game as Alabama quarterback was the Georgia game in 1962. I had a terrible headache, just one of those throbbing headaches. We went out on the field, the band started playing, and my headache disappeared. I got so caught up in it that my headache just went away.

The first play of the game. I called a quarterback sneak behind Lee Roy Jordan. I just wanted to get hit to settle down. We didn't make the first down and punted. And I think we may have intercepted a pass, but on the first play after we got the ball back, Richard Williamson broke open on an out pattern, and we scored and went on to a 35–0 win.

After the game in the dressing room, we were having a big time, a lot of jubilation. And the newspaper guys came in and started interviewing us. And I heard Coach Bryant say, "Get away from the Popcorn Kid. Talk to the guys who did the winning." Well, I took a little offense at Coach Bryant calling me Popcorn Kid, and I must have showed it with my body language. I was standing next to Lee Roy, and he kind of popped me with his forearm and said not to let it bother me. Coach Bryant had a way of keeping your head on straight.

Later the *Saturday Evening Post* would write an article saying the game was fixed. Now, I was the quarterback and the quarterback called the plays. The coaches didn't call the plays.

When the article came out, we had a team meeting, and Coach Bryant read it to us. He got to the part where it said, "Georgia gained only 35 yards." He stopped and said, "That's too many yards." It was a tense situation, but that broke us up.

To be Crimson Tide is an honor because of the history and tradition. I never felt I did anything except be with a great bunch of guys. But being any part of it makes you humble because of the greatness that was there. And to be a small part of it makes you want to know about it, to learn about it. And you appreciate what other people have done.

The tradition of the university is about people. And other people associate you with your university.

I've always felt at home at the university, coming back to visit. Mal Moore is a special guy, and one of my former teammates, and that has a lot to do with my coming back more frequently in the past few years. He has made me feel welcome, inviting me to be a part of what is going on here.

And now my daughter Jessica is in school at Alabama. I have another daughter, Olivia Rose. People ask me if I want her also to go to Alabama. I tell them she's 14, and right now all I want her to be is 15. Those years, 12 to 18, are interesting, to say the least.

And I've always had some unfinished business. I had made a promise to my mother I would have a college degree. I always said I was going to do it. And then Jessica inadvertently gave me the final push. We were talking about her going to the university, and she said, "Daddy, I'll be the first one in our family to finish college."

It may have taken a beat. Not two beats. And I said, "Want to bet?"

So that's what gave me the impetus and why I'm now finishing my degree. And it's not in basket-weaving. It's not in journalism, either.

When I was a rookie in training camp, the writers from around the league would come into different training camps. We would sit in bleachers, and they would call you out to talk to the reporters. And one of them was a smart-ass. He said, "I heard you majored in basket-weaving at Alabama." I said, "Yeah, but that was pretty tough. So I dropped it and went into journalism."

I don't know if that was the right way to start out with the writers.

*Joe Namath was an All-America quarterback in 1964 and was MVP of the Orange Bowl. He and Kenny Stabler were named quarterbacks on Alabama's Team of the Century. He was a 1985 inductee into the Pro Football Hall of Fame.*

## HOUNDSTOOTH

Like most men of his generation, Paul Bryant was a hat-wearer. He wore baseball-style coaches' hats during practice and for most of his first decade with the Crimson Tide wore a brown or black fedora on the sideline during games.

During Joe Namath's contract negotiation with the New York Jets in the winter and spring of 1965, Bryant developed a friendship with Jets owner Sonny Werblin, a stylish former Hollywood talent agent. Werblin sent Bryant a houndstooth fedora as a gift, and a trademark was born.

Bryant wore a houndstooth or gingham fedora on the sideline for the remainder of his career, with a few notable exceptions. He wore no hat whenever the Crimson Tide played in the Louisiana Superdome (because his mother taught him a gentleman never wears a hat indoors), and he wore a baseball cap and parka during frigid conditions in Memphis during his final game, a 21–15 victory over Illinois in the 1982 Liberty Bowl.

Bryant's hat became a symbol of Crimson Tide football that lasted long after the coach's death in 1983. A popular sports bar in Tuscaloosa named The Houndstooth opened in 1988. And in the early 2000s, Alabama fans—particularly young women—began wearing houndstooth fedoras in the stands during games. Crimson Tide players were issued houndstooth baseball caps by the team equipment manager.

Celebrated recruits, including Andre Smith and Trent Richardson, have been known to don a houndstooth fedora when announcing their verbal commitments to the Crimson Tide on national signing day. But the popular broken-checkered pattern will remain synonymous with one man.

"One thing Coach Bryant had told me was that you had to coach with your own personality, that you couldn't be someone

Paul Bryant's houndstooth hat was a gift from New York Jets owner Sonny Werblin. It became the coach's trademark, as he wore it on the sideline for the rest of his career (but never indoors).

else," said Jimmy Fuller, an Alabama lineman in the 1960s and later an assistant coach. "But that didn't stop me from getting a houndstooth hat and leaning against the goalpost before the game. But I only did that once. That wasn't me."

## THE RV ARMADA

On September 7, 2002, Alabama played at Oklahoma, one of its first major road games outside the Southeast in years. The previous day, the *Daily Oklahoman* of Oklahoma City ran a story on the front page of its sports section headlined "Norman Conquest" about the phenomenal Crimson Tide fan traveling party that had invaded the parking lots around the Sooners' Owen Field.

While other SEC programs might boast a fleet of 20 or 30 fan-owned RVs at road games, Alabama has been known to send 200, as it did that weekend at Oklahoma. For home games, RVs often begin arriving in Tuscaloosa on *Tuesday or Wednesday afternoon*.

In 2003 lifelong Alabama fan (and *New York Times* reporter) Warren St. John released a best-selling book titled *Rammer Jammer Yellow Hammer: A Road Trip into the Heart of Fan Mania*, telling the story of the 1999 football season, when he bought a secondhand RV and followed the Crimson Tide to every game of its SEC championship–winning campaign. In the introduction to the book, St. John wrote:

> RVs completely changed the fan experience. Before, football games were circumscribed events. They took place inside a stadium on Saturdays and lasted about three hours, after which everyone went home. Logistical problems like traffic, the need for tickets, the need for…bathrooms—set games off from the rest of life. RVs blew open the experience. The event was no longer confined to three hours—it could last three days.

---

## Crimson Tide in Their Own Words

# JERRY DUNCAN

### OFFENSIVE TACKLE, 1965–1966

I was a halfback in high school, and that's what I expected to be at Alabama. It wasn't the happiest day of my life when I was moved to the offensive line. As it turned out, it was probably the best thing that ever happened to me.

The guy I have the most memories about is Howard Schnellenberger, who was my offensive line coach. I still stay in touch with him. He's athletics director at Florida Atlantic. It was a great challenge for him to take a guy like me who had been a halfback and try to make an offensive lineman out of him. And it was challenging for me, too. He was very tough, a disciplinarian of the first order. He forced you to learn good technique. And that meant a lot of preparation—practice and watching films. He was constantly trying to make you a better football player. And you also knew if you weren't doing the best you could, he was going to get the next guy.

That probably was the reason Coach Bryant chose my name when he decided to start making some awards to give players incentive to do well in spring training, which is not a very fun practice time with no game to look forward to.

In the early '70s, he started the awards, and in the first batch was the "Jerry Duncan I Like to Practice Award." I didn't know anything about it until after it was announced, and I haven't really talked to too many of the players who won it.

I've had plenty of old teammates who questioned whether any of us liked to practice, and that's a good point. I'm sure none of us enjoyed it. I guess a lot of players wonder why anyone would want to win that award. But we went about it in different ways. Some people are great players and might not have to practice as hard. Nothing ever came easy for me, and particularly after I was moved from halfback to tackle, which was done in the spring before my junior year in 1965.

I had to really focus. Sometimes I was a little banged up or I might have a headache. But I felt I still had to go. When I was playing, if I missed a couple of days of practice, there was a guy right behind me who was probably better than I was anyway, and if I gave him the opportunity, he was going to get my position. So I had to act like I enjoyed practice whether I did or not. And the truth is I did enjoy it, or at least that's the way I remember it now. Practice was tough. Coach Bryant was a taskmaster, but I think that 1964–1966 group had a lot of fun. And I guess part of the fun was going as hard as I could to let him know I wanted to play.

I don't know how I was picked out for that award over all the great players who have been at Alabama, but I'm mighty proud of it.

I was extremely fortunate to come along at the right time to have the opportunity to play for Alabama. I wasn't really a very good football player, although I was probably a decent athlete. I played at Sparta, North Carolina, a very small program with 25 or 30 guys on the team in the smallest county in the state. And I found out later that Coach Gryska was sent up to sign me without even talking to my coaches or looking at film. I never did know what Coach Bryant had heard about me. It was an extraordinary time to be given the opportunity to play for Coach Bryant and the great assistant coaches we had. It was a fantastic journey.

Back then they could sign quite a few guys. After they had taken what they wanted from the state of Alabama, they went out and got whatever else they needed. And because they could sign a large number, they could take a chance on a guy like me. And then I had to prove to Coach Bryant that he hadn't made a mistake. I think there were times that he thought he made a mistake before I finally came around and started playing.

I played with three or four great players. The rest of us were a bunch of average ragtags. But we didn't know we were average.

Coach Bryant just worked us and worked us and molded us into a unit that could play with anybody in the country.

Now some of those who were above average were our quarterbacks. It was fun to block for Steve Sloan, who looked like he was stumbling around but who was turning upfield and gaining yards. And Ken Stabler could run the option as well as anyone ever, and he could pass, too. Joe Namath was quarterback my sophomore season, so you'd say we did have some pretty good players.

And it was fun to block for them, but since I never weighed more than about 180 pounds, it would have been a lot more fun if I had been about 40 pounds heavier.

It was fun to be a part of those teams. We won the national championship in 1964 and again in 1965 and then went undefeated in 1966 while Notre Dame and Michigan State tied. But when the polls were in, we didn't get that third national championship. It was really disappointing because we thought we could beat Notre Dame or Michigan State, and we thought we had done all we could do. I'm sure I was extremely disappointed then, but looking back it's insignificant.

I have very good memories of winning the 1965 national championship because we had to beat Nebraska in the Orange Bowl to do it. We were outmanned. Nebraska had better players than we had, and they were a lot bigger than we were. That was probably the best team I ever played against. But Coach Bryant changed our offense for the game and decided to throw the ball a lot. And in those days, you could line up so that the tackle (me) was an eligible pass receiver. In fact, they would change the rule later because of the success we had. We ran three or four tackle-eligible plays, including one on the first play of the game, and we used three or four onside kicks. By the time we got to the fourth quarter,

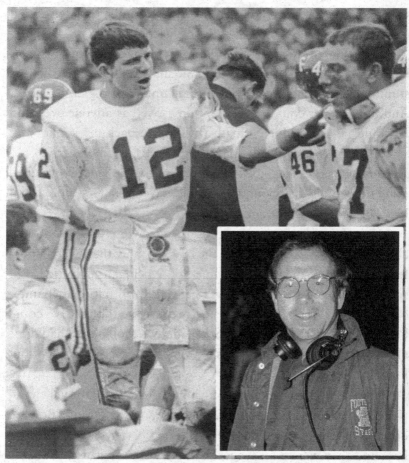

Jerry Duncan (67, on right) was a small offensive tackle whose success as an eligible receiver from the likes of Kenny Stabler (12) forced a change in college football rules. A popular player, he was equally loved as color man for 'Bama football radio broadcasts.

our offense had kept their defense on the field so long they were exhausted. We won 39–28.

It was funny. We'd win the national championship, and it was great, but there weren't any parties or parades or anything like that. Three or four days after we won one, Coach Bryant was back trying to figure out how to win it again. I've never known anyone like him. He refused to rest on his laurels.

After I graduated, I became a stockbroker in Birmingham, which I have done for 35 years. I'm sure having played at Alabama opened some doors for me. It may have closed a few by fans of other schools, but I feel that I've had an opportunity to deal with some of the finest people in the state of Alabama.

I also had another wonderful opportunity. For 24 years I was part of the Alabama football radio broadcasts, first with John Forney and Doug Layton, then with Paul Kennedy, and finally with Eli Gold. That was a pleasure and it gave me a chance to be around Coach Bryant for another 10 years.

*Jerry Duncan played on teams that won two national championships and had a record of 30–2–1. Rival coaches insisted on a rules change because of Alabama's success in using Duncan as a tackle-eligible receiver. He was later the sideline color man on Alabama radio broadcasts. He's senior vice president for UBS AG.*

## "I Like to Practice"

Spring practice can be a tedious time for college football practice, with a few weeks of hard work, but no real game-day payoff in the end. For that reason, among others, Bryant came up with a series of spring awards in 1971.

Most of the awards were named for a favorite past player of Bryant's and given to the current player who was most improved at his position. For example, the Most Improved Receiver Award was named for 1966 All-American Ray Perkins and given to future All-American Wayne Wheeler that first year.

But Bryant got creative in naming two awards. First was the Lee Roy Jordan Headhunter Award, which really needs no explanation (for the record, it was given that first year, 1971, to Robin Parkhouse).

Then there is the Jerry Duncan "I Like to Practice" Award, named in honor of the undersized but hardworking starting tackle from the 1965 national championship team. The first winner of the award was defensive back David McMakin in 1971, and other "I Like to Practice" Award winners have included Steadman Shealy (1978), Bobby Humphrey (1987), Jay Barker (1991), Ahmaad Galloway (1999), and Wallace Gilberry (2005). Recalled Duncan years later:

> I've had plenty of old teammates who questioned whether any of us liked to practice, and that's a good point. I'm sure none of us enjoyed it. I guess a lot of players wonder why anyone would want to win that award. But we went about it in different ways. Some people are great players and might not have to practice as hard. Nothing ever came easy for me, and particularly after I was moved from halfback to tackle, which was done in the spring before my junior year in 1965.
>
> I had to really focus. Sometimes I was a little banged up or I might have a headache. But I felt I still had to go. When I was playing, if I missed a couple of days of practice, there was a guy right behind me who was probably better than I was anyway, and if I gave him the opportunity, he was going to get my position. So I had to act like I enjoyed practice whether I did or not. And the truth is I did enjoy it, or at least that's the way I remember it now. Practice was tough. Coach Bryant was a taskmaster, but I think that 1964–1966 group had a lot of fun. And I guess part of the fun was going as hard

as I could to let him know I wanted to play. I don't know how I was picked out for that award over all the great players who have been at Alabama, but I'm mighty proud of it.

---

## *Crimson Tide in Their Own Words*
# LEE ROY JORDAN
### LINEBACKER AND CENTER, 1960–1962

It's funny how people can remember details of football games. I don't really remember that many. That's probably because I don't talk about them much. I have good friends who can recall minute details of games they played in, but they like to rehash them a lot so it refreshes their memories. There are a couple of plays and one game that I have heard a lot about from people who saw them.

One of those plays was after my Alabama career. In those days they had a College All-Star team play the defending NFL champions in a game at Soldier Field in Chicago. We played the Green Bay Packers and actually beat them, the last time the All-Stars beat the pros. Green Bay had a great fullback, Jim Taylor from LSU. We had a moment to meet head-on, and I drove him back, maybe for a loss. The announcers must have made a big deal out of it because so many people have told me about it.

Another play people have in their minds was against Georgia Tech. I was a center on offense. We had a pass intercepted, which meant I turned into a defender and I was chasing the guy who had intercepted the pass. Near the sideline, he just dropped the ball. Coach Bryant made something of that on his television program the next day and said, "If they stay in bounds, old Lee

Lee Roy Jordan is considered the finest linebacker in Alabama history, a College Football Hall of Fame member who set an Orange Bowl record with 31 tackles in a win over Oklahoma. He went on to a successful 14-year pro career with the Dallas Cowboys.

Roy will get them." He had a way of saying things that made people remember.

I always thought I had a pretty good memory of the Orange Bowl game at the end of our senior year. It was an important game for the seniors because we had lost one game by one point earlier in the year, but we had finished with a respectable season the way we beat Auburn and then Oklahoma. The reason I say I thought I had a good memory of that game is that I always thought they kicked a field goal just before halftime. But we won 17–0. I knew I was making a lot of tackles because I was getting sore, but I had no idea I would make 31 tackles. Our objective was to stop Joe Don Looney, which we did. And they hadn't made many turn-overs, but we got two fumbles, which helped us control the game.

I grew up in a small community, perhaps 350 people in Excel, Alabama. My family farmed. We raised about everything—cotton, corn, peanuts, and anything you could grow in a garden. And we had cattle, horses, chickens, and turkeys. We raised almost everything we ate and then hoped to have enough to sell. And everyone had responsibilities. I was taught very early about work.

I went to Excel school. I started at one end in the first grade, and went down the school through middle school or junior high, and graduated from high school at the other end of the school. Every male had to play football. If he didn't, he had a hard time in the community because we needed everyone to play 11-man football. We dressed everyone who could play from about the seventh grade on up so we'd have about 22 to 25 boys. We had a fine coach in W. C. Majors, who went on to coach at Fairhope.

I had a growth spurt between my sophomore and junior year in high school, about three inches and 31 pounds. I left a runt and came back a pretty big dude. I was one of the bigger boys, about 190 pounds. We ran the single wing, and I was a fullback and tailback.

I got my hands on the ball a lot. Jerry Claiborne was scouting a boy at W.S. Neal in Brewton, and I had a pretty good game against them as a junior. After the game, he came to the dressing room and told Coach Majors that someone would be watching me next year. And Bobby Drake Keith watched me on a regular basis as a senior. It was exciting to have college coaches watching you. I was also getting interest from Auburn and Southern Miss.

Coach Bryant had taken the job at Alabama my junior year in high school. My coach told me that Coach Bryant would like guys like me. Not necessarily the biggest, but quick and with good stamina. He said the most important thing to Coach Bryant was "want to." And that impressed me.

I was part of his second recruiting class. Billy Neighbors and Tommy Brooker and Pat Trammell were the big names in the first class, and we had guys like Bill Battle, Richard Williamson, Charley Pell, and Jimmy Wilson. It was hard work that freshman year in 1959. We were fresh meat for the varsity to practice against. But we competed against them.

We had a pretty good run in 1960, beating Georgia, Georgia Tech, and Auburn. And then in 1961 and 1962, we had about 10 shutouts. We had six in 1961. We gave up 25 points, went undefeated, and won the national championship.

Coach Bryant believed in defense. Put a kicking game and a little running game with defense and you'll win a lot. I played both ways, center on offense and linebacker on defense, and if I ever got a break, it was sitting out on offense a few series. Our defense was kind of a 5-2 that would be a 3-4 today. Darwin Holt, Ed Versprille, and I could move around to about anywhere, but I was usually one of the inside linebackers.

We had great support from Alabama fans and students. When we'd come back from away games, there would always be a nice crowd to meet us at the airport. Alabama fans had been support-ive in the bad times, and they were certainly appreciative that we were doing a good job and winning.

My first game was against Georgia in Birmingham. I had a minor injury, and it was a few days before the game that I learned I was going to start. So I started every game in my Alabama career.

I can't imagine anyone being any luckier than I was. I played in college for Coach Bryant and then in Dallas for Coach Landry, one of the top franchises in the NFL. I live and have a business in Dallas now, but spend five or six months a year in Alabama. And we're going to be retiring there to our house in Point Clear.

A year after I graduated in June 1964, I married Biddie Banks, who I had met in a biology class. Her mother was good friends with Mrs. Bryant. So we got married at Biddie's grandmother's house in Eutaw, and Dr. Frank Rose, the president of the university and one of the greatest men I've ever known, married us. Coach and Mrs. Bryant were there. Mrs. Bryant made Biddie's veil.

It may be that the best lesson I learned from Coach Bryant was to be first. If he called for a drill, I'd run over people to be first in line to do it. And that's the way I've been in everything. I didn't wait on others. I wanted to be first.

But everything I've ever done is because of a big boost I got from attending The University of Alabama. And I feel very fortu-nate that people still recognize me and think good thoughts about the teams we had. I've tried to be a good ambassador for the uni-versity because I am very proud to be an Alabama graduate.

One wonderful relationship I have had is with Gene Stallings. He was a young coach, but a very, very good one and a confident one when I was playing at Alabama. And we were so fortunate to have him with the Cowboys. We lived in the same neighborhood in Dallas, and I was very fond of his whole family. And when we beat Miami and won the national championship, I think I remember more about that game than any I played in. He is a great man, the epitome of class, a person who really cares about other people. And that couldn't have happened to a better guy.

> Lee Roy Jordan was a two-time All-American, selected Player of the Decade for the '60s, named to ESPN's all-time college team and to Alabama's Team of the Century, inducted into the College Hall of Fame in 1983, and selected for the NCAA Silver Anniversary Award in 1987.

## THE MAGIC NUMBER

There are certain uniform numbers that carry a great deal of meaning in Alabama football. Standout quarterback prospects always want No. 12, the number worn by such greats at Pat Trammell, Joe Namath, and Ken Stabler.

Any lightning-quick wide receiver or kick returner might end up in the No. 2, hearkening back to David "the Deuce" Palmer. But perhaps no jersey number in Crimson Tide history is more iconic than 54, made famous by All-America linebacker Lee Roy Jordan in the early 1960s.

Bryant would allow only a special player to wear 54, and the first man to try it on after Jordan was Paul Crane. A freshman during Jordan's senior season of 1962, Crane idolized his predecessor.

"We were going out to spring training my sophomore year, and the equipment manager gave me jersey No. 54," Crane recalled. "I was very proud to be awarded that number and put it on and went out to the practice field. When Coach Bryant saw me, he said, 'What are you doing with that number on?' It was embarrassing. I said the equipment manager had given it to me. And he said, 'Well get in there and take it off.' I turned and started back toward the dressing room, and he called to me. 'No,' he said. 'Leave it on.'"

Crane rewarded his coach's confidence, earning All-America honors himself as a senior in 1965.

---

## *Crimson Tide in Their Own Words*

# PAUL CRANE

### CENTER AND LINEBACKER, 1963–1965

When I was a freshman, Lee Roy Jordan was a senior. He was a great player. I admired him greatly, and still do. We were going out to spring training prior to my sophomore year, and the equipment manager gave me jersey No. 54, the number Lee Roy had worn and made famous. I was very proud to be awarded that number and put it on and went out to the practice field.

When Coach Bryant saw me he said, "What are you doing with that number on?" It was embarrassing. I said the equipment manager had given it to me. And he said, "Well get in there and take it off." And I think I've made Coach Bryant sound a little nicer, more subtle, than he sounded to me.

I turned and started back toward the dressing room, and he called to me. "No," he said. "Leave it on."

And that's how I got the opportunity to wear the number that Lee Roy made famous. It was an embarrassing beginning, but a thrill nonetheless and very positive. And, after me, a number of players have worn No. 54 and done very well with it.

That jersey was symbolic of what a great honor it was to play for Alabama.

Paul Crane was an All-America center and linebacker who was named SEC Lineman of the Year as Alabama won the 1964 and 1965 national championships.

Not too long ago someone gave me a little music box with the Alabama fight song. It reminded me of when I went to Alabama. I had gotten a little wind-up toy in the shape of a football that played "Yea, Alabama!" and I'd go to sleep at night listening to it. Even today, the Alabama fight song—which I think is great—means something to me. It represents my time at Alabama.

I am very appreciative for having had the opportunity of playing for Alabama and for Coach Bryant. It was a great time to be at Alabama. Because of the players we had and the coaches we had, it was a great experience.

Alabama practices were memorable in those days. We had a little three-on-three drill, three offensive linemen, a quarterback and a back or two, against three defensive players. It was in a very confined area and a high-energy situation. A coach would stand behind the defensive players and signal where the ball was to be run. The defenders couldn't see it, of course. The rest of the players circled around and cheered until it was their turn.

One day Creed Gilmer and Tim Bates, who were defensive players and good friends, kind of got together. While Creed was on defense, Tim would very subtly signal which way the ball was going. He was cheating for the defense, or at least for Creed. And Creed did pretty well in the drill.

But when Creed went out and Tim was on defense, Creed didn't reciprocate, for whatever reason. So Bates had a lot tougher time of it and got pretty mad at Creed. I think they can finally laugh about it now.

I considered some other schools when I was being recruited out of Vigor High School in Prichard. But I flew up to Alabama and met Coach Charley Bradshaw, who was a very smooth recruiter. And Coach Dude Hennessey also helped recruit me. Then I met with Coach Bryant, and that confirmed my decision to go to Alabama. It turned out to be a great decision for me.

Playing at Alabama has given me a reference point. Part of it is that people remember you, even that far back, which is nice. But the personal reference point is the hard work, commitment, and dedication it took to play for Coach Bryant and Alabama. Each of us has a period in his or her life that has a profound effect or results in a huge change. For me that period was my time as a player at Alabama. It has served as the reference point for the rest of my life.

After my Alabama playing career I was signed as a free agent by the New York Jets. I was there from 1966 through 1973. That meant I got to play in the Super Bowl with Joe Namath when we won the World Championship against Baltimore in Miami. That was a case of being in the right place at the right time. So I got a Super Bowl ring to go with my 1964 and 1965 national championship rings.

And after my playing career, I got to come back to Alabama and work under Coach Bryant coaching linebackers in the mid-'70s. Coach Bryant was really interesting on the sidelines. If it was a really tough game, he was very calm. But if we were playing a game we were supposed to be able to win without much trouble, he would be a bear over there.

I left Alabama after the 1977 season, just before Alabama would win two more national championships, to go to Ole Miss. We weren't very successful, so I got out of college coaching and moved to Mobile, where I'm the director of the Catholic Youth Organization.

*Paul Crane was an All-America center and linebacker for Alabama in 1965 and was named Outstanding Lineman in the South that year. He was captain of the 1965 team. He played on teams that went 28–4–1 and won two national championships, then won a Super Bowl playing for the New York Jets.*

*chapter 2*

# GREAT MOMENTS *in* ALABAMA FOOTBALL

THE 116 SEASONS OF ALABAMA FOOTBALL (there were no teams in 1898, 1918, or 1943 due to wars) have produced plenty of historic days, big games, and memorable moments for those who follow and cherish the Crimson Tide. The following is a timeline of those events that made Alabama football what it is today.

### NOVEMBER 11, 1892
Led by captain William G. Little and coach E.B. Beaumont, Alabama plays its first football game, beating Birmingham High School 56–0. The next day, the Cadets, as they were then known, lose to the Birmingham Athletic Club 5–4, a team they would beat 14–0 a month later.

### FEBRUARY 22, 1893
Alabama meets Auburn in football for the first time, before roughly 4,000 fans at Birmingham's Lakeview Park. Auburn wins 32–22, giving Alabama a 2–2 record for its first season of football competition.

### NOVEMBER 28, 1901
Alabama and Tennessee face off for the first time in football, playing to a 6–6 tie in Birmingham. Foreshadowing the contentious

nature of the rivalry, the game was called due to darkness after fans rushed the field to argue with a referee's decision.

## NOVEMBER 16, 1907
Alabama and Auburn play to a 6–6 tie in Birmingham. The two teams would not play again for more than 40 years due to a dispute over several issues, including who would pay referees and how much players would be compensated for travel.

## FALL 1912
George Hutcherson "Mike" Denny becomes president of the University of Alabama. As school president until 1936, Denny would oversee and champion the rise of Crimson Tide football for nearly a quarter century. Denny Field (later Denny Stadium and eventually Bryant-Denny Stadium) and Denny Chimes are among the campus landmarks named in his honor.

## SEPTEMBER 11, 1913
Paul William Bryant is born near Moro Bottom, Arkansas. Bryant would earn the nickname he carried the rest of his life at age 13, when he wrestled a bear at the Lyric Theater in nearby Fordyce. The bear's owner skipped town without paying Bryant the $2 he was owed.

## SPRING 1919
After not fielding a team in 1918 due to World War I, Alabama hires its first successful coach the following season. Xen C. Scott, a former sportswriter from Ohio, went 29–9–3 in four seasons with the Crimson Tide. Scott was forced to retire following the 1922 season and died of oral cancer at age 41 in 1924.

### NOVEMBER 4, 1922
Alabama beats Penn 9–7 at Franklin Field in Philadelphia, its first major victory outside the South. The Crimson Tide had beaten Case College (Scott's former school) 40–0 in Cleveland, Ohio, in 1920, but Penn was at the time considered a national power, having won six national championships in college football's early days.

### SEPTEMBER 29, 1923
Wallace Wade coaches his first game at Alabama, a 12–0 victory over Union College in Tuscaloosa. Wade would coach the Crimson Tide for eight seasons, winning 61 games, four Southern Conference championships, and national championships in 1925, 1926, and 1930.

### JANUARY 1, 1926
Alabama defeats Washington 20–19 in the Rose Bowl in Pasadena, California, the first of its record 33 bowl victories. Trailing 12–0 at halftime, the Crimson Tide scored three touchdowns in the third quarter to secure the victory. The win also resulted in the first of Alabama's 13 national championships.

### JANUARY 1, 1927
Back in Pasadena for the second straight year, Alabama ties national powerhouse Stanford 7–7 to complete a 9–0–1 season. The Crimson Tide also trailed late in this one, getting Jimmy Johnson's one-yard touchdown run and Herschel Caldwell's extra point to tie the game with less than four minutes to play. Soon after, Alabama was voted national champion once again.

## 1930–1931

Following a third national championship secured by a 24–0 victory over Washington in the Rose Bowl, Wade departs Alabama following a dispute with Denny. He would go on to coach for nearly 20 years at Duke, which renamed its stadium in his honor in 1967. Denny hired as Wade's replacement Frank Thomas, a former Notre Dame star.

## FALL 1931

Bryant enrolls at Alabama. He would go on to be a standout for the Crimson Tide, teaming with All-American (and future Green Bay Packers star) Don Hutson to give Alabama one of the best end tandems in the country. Bryant was also noted for his toughness, playing the 1935 Tennessee game with a broken leg.

## JANUARY 1, 1935

Alabama crushes Stanford 29–13 in the Rose Bowl to sew up its fourth national championship, and first under Thomas. Dixie Howell was the Crimson Tide's star on this day, rushing for a pair of touchdowns and throwing one to Hutson. He ended the day with 111 yards rushing and 160 passing, and punted for a 43.8-yard average.

## SEPTEMBER 30, 1944

Freshman Harry Gilmer makes his Alabama debut, running a kickoff back 95 yards for a touchdown in a 27–27 tie at LSU. Behind Gilmer and fellow stars such as Vaughn Mancha and Lowell Tew, the "War Babies" won the 1945 SEC title and beat Southern Cal 34–14 in the Rose Bowl, the Crimson Tide's last postseason appearance in Pasadena for 64 years.

## Crimson Tide in Their Own Words

# HARRY GILMER

### HALFBACK, 1944–1947

The best way to throw a pass is not a jump pass, and in my years of coaching I never taught the jump pass. It doesn't lend itself to today's ball. But it worked for me. I always felt that Coach Thomas didn't like for me to do it. Sometimes we'd have younger people around practice, and if they saw me throw a jump pass they would try to do it. Coach Thomas would tell them to stop, to do it the correct way. Ed Salem, the passer who followed me, jumped and threw one time, and Coach Thomas ran up to him, got in his face, and told him to stay on the ground and throw like he was supposed to.

I started throwing the jump pass when I played on the sand lots. At Woodlawn High School I kept doing it because I could start out on an end run and then turn it into a pass. If the receiver wasn't open, I kept running.

If you just think through the actions of a passer, you know if you drop back and set up in the pocket, you certainly aren't going to jump. You're going to be on the balls of your feet so you can bounce and stay ready to throw.

But if you throw on the run, you're usually running toward the sideline, and you're going to throw at a right angle to that. So you need to get your body and your hips turned downfield. You either have to stop running to do it or you jump. If you jump, you can turn your hips around. I just naturally did that.

Although I was the team's passer, I wasn't a quarterback. I was the left halfback in the single wing, or Notre Dame box, formation.

The closest thing to it today is the shotgun formation. Ideally, the left halfback was able to run, throw, or kick.

The jumping came about because I could throw the ball on the run. I didn't have to stop to turn my body. And maybe I was a little more accurate than most people. A lot of people back then would try to jump and throw. It's not the best way to pass, but it's the best way if you are throwing on the run.

I went to Alabama during unusual times, as World War II was winding down. Alabama didn't have a football team in 1943 because all the men were in the service. They recruited us to play in 1944, and we had four years of doing all the playing. I was a junior before we had people coming back out of the service to compete with us for those jobs.

I had played for a very strong Woodlawn team. We had a great coach in Malcolm Laney and never lost a game in my four years there. I wasn't good enough to be a starter until I was a senior. I had opportunities to go to several colleges, but Alabama was the closest and the one I knew the most about, so it was an easy decision to make. I really didn't know much about Alabama before I got there, but I have a great love for the school now. I have followed Alabama closely and been proud that the football program has continued to be successful over the years.

When I got to Alabama, it was the reverse situation of high school. There was no waiting. I was a starter as a freshman.

We were very successful during my four years at Alabama. We went to the Sugar Bowl my freshman year and the Rose Bowl my sophomore year. That was Alabama's last appearance in the Rose Bowl. We beat Southern Cal 34–14, and it wasn't that close. After that, the Rose Bowl shut out Alabama and the other southern schools.

Our third year, 1946, we lost our coach, Frank Thomas. His health broke down in the middle of the season, and we lost four

Harry Gilmer came to Alabama during World War II and was a four-year starter and All-America halfback who led the Tide to its last Rose Bowl victory until 2010.

games toward the end of the year. Red Drew took over in 1947, and we went back to the Sugar Bowl.

I probably gained some attention when we went to play Duke in the Sugar Bowl at the end of the 1944 season. That game meant a lot to me because we only threw eight passes, but we completed all eight of them. The last play of the game was a pass I threw to Ralph Jones. He was out long and the pass was a little short, so he was able to adjust and make the catch. But that also allowed the last Duke defender to get him. The guy who was covering him dove and slapped Ralph's foot and tripped him up. He was the only guy who could have caught him. Duke was a team of veterans, Navy trainees, and was heavily favored, and we lost by the slim margin of 29–26.

The great old-time sportswriter out of New York, Grantland Rice, was at that game, and he called my performance "better than Baugh," referring to the great Sammy Baugh of Washington Redskins fame. He shouldn't have written that, and I probably shouldn't repeat it, but it was an honor, particularly when you consider we passed only eight times.

Alabama prepared me for a life in football. After I played at Alabama, I went into pro ball and played nine years with the Redskins and Detroit. Then I went to Pittsburgh as an assistant with the Steelers for four years. I went with Norm Van Brocklin to a new franchise, the Minnesota Vikings, and coached defensive line for four years. I got the head job at Detroit, but didn't win enough games and was there only two years. I was quarterbacks coach with Jim Hart, the quarterback at St. Louis, for three years, then went to Atlanta and rejoined Van Brocklin. After five years in Atlanta, I went back to St. Louis for seven years, then scouted for St. Louis for 11 years. If you add it up, after Alabama, I played for nine years, coached for 27 years, and scouted for 11 more. I was a scout for the Cardinals when Gene Stallings was head coach.

Add that up, and it's 47 years in pro football.

I always enjoyed returning to Tuscaloosa to scout Alabama players. I have great respect for and loyalty to Alabama, and I am appreciative of the great record in football there.

I'm still in St. Louis because I have children, grandchildren, and now great-grandchildren here. You can tell where I coached by where we left our children—one in Detroit, one in Atlanta, and two in St. Louis.

*Harry Gilmer was All-America and SEC Player of the Year in 1945 and MVP of the 1946 Rose Bowl. He accounted for an Alabama record 52 touchdowns, ranks second all-time in interceptions, and first all-time in punt returns. In 1946 he led Alabama in rushing, passing, interceptions, punt returns, and kickoff returns. He was inducted into the College Football Hall of Fame in 1993.*

## NOVEMBER 30, 1946

Frank Thomas, suffering from heart disease and high blood pressure, coaches his final game at Alabama, a 24–7 victory over Mississippi State in Tuscaloosa. He retires following the season with a 115–24–7 record, four SEC championships, and two national titles, and dies May 10, 1954 at age 55.

## DECEMBER 4, 1948

Under orders from the state legislature, Alabama and Auburn finally resume their series at Legion Field in Birmingham. In what would eventually become known as the "Iron Bowl," Alabama wins 55–0 behind three touchdowns rushing, one touchdown passing, and seven extra points from Ed Salem.

## JANUARY 1, 1953

The period between 1946 and 1958 was a turbulent one for the Crimson Tide, but perhaps the high point comes at the conclusion of the 1952 season. Alabama throttles Syracuse 61–6 in the Orange Bowl, setting school postseason records for points and point differential that still stand. Bobby Luna and Tommy Lewis each scored two of Alabama's nine touchdowns in the game.

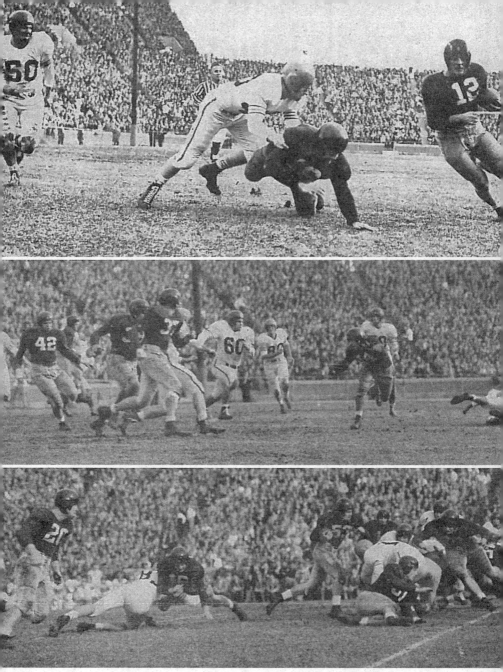

After nearly 40 years of dormancy, the Alabama-Auburn rivalry was renewed in 1948. The Crimson Tide won 55–0 that year, and the rivalry has gone on to be among the most heated in college football.

## JANUARY 1, 1958

Bryant, hired away from Texas A&M, begins his first day of work as Alabama's football coach and athletics director. He would win 232 games, 13 SEC championships, and six national championships with the Crimson Tide in the ensuing 25 years. He would also retire as college football's all-time-winningest coach, with 323 victories.

## DECEMBER 19, 1959

Alabama loses to Penn State 7–0 in the Liberty Bowl, the first of 24 consecutive bowl trips under Bryant. The game, played in frigid conditions in Philadelphia, also marked the first time the Crimson Tide played against an integrated team. Penn State scored the game's only touchdown in the second quarter, an 18-yard pass from Galen Hall to Roger Kochman.

## DECEMBER 2, 1961

Alabama clobbers Auburn 34–0 at Legion Field in Birmingham to secure an undefeated regular season. The Crimson Tide would go on to beat Arkansas 10–3 in the Sugar Bowl and win the first of six national championships under Bryant. In 11 games that season, Alabama outscored its opponent 297–25, including six shutouts.

## SEPTEMBER 22, 1962

Sophomore Joe Namath enjoys one of the greatest debuts in college football history, passing for 179 yards and three touchdowns in a 35–0 victory over Georgia in Tuscaloosa. Namath would go on to go 22–3 as a starter, leading Alabama to the 1964 national championship before embarking on a Hall of Fame career with the New York Jets.

## JANUARY 1, 1963

Alabama beats Oklahoma 17–0 in the Orange Bowl, completing a 10–1 season. The game is largely remembered for the performance of junior linebacker Lee Roy Jordan, who totaled an astounding 31 tackles for the Crimson Tide. The game also marked a passing of the torch from Oklahoma's Bud Wilkinson to Bryant as the greatest coach of his generation.

## JANUARY 1, 1964

Playing in place of the suspended Namath, sophomore Steve Sloan leads the Crimson Tide to a 12–7 victory over Ole Miss in the Sugar Bowl. Kicker Tim Davis provided all of Alabama's points with four field goals, as Bryant played it extra-conservative with the young Sloan under center and the game played in a rare New Orleans snowstorm.

---

## *Crimson Tide in Their Own Words*

# STEVE SLOAN
### QUARTERBACK, 1963–1965

Playing football at Alabama in the mid-'60s was sort of like being in the brotherhood of coal miners. You didn't know if you were going to get out of that mine or not. It was a tough process. But the winning made it fun.

Both at the time and ever since, I felt honored to be a part of the team and to play for Coach Bryant and the assistant coaches. They were all so dedicated, and I was fortunate to be a part of it.

I grew up in Cleveland, Tennessee, not far from Knoxville, and I was a Tennessee fan. I also liked Georgia Tech and Vanderbilt.

Alabama never entered my mind until the recruiting process started. Coach Clem Gryska, Coach Howard Schnellenberger, and Coach Gene Stallings seemed to be there all the time. They just did a better job of recruiting than anyone else. And, of course, Alabama was doing well. I always felt fortunate to get a scholarship to play football at Alabama.

Steve Sloan (14) was MVP of the 1966 Orange Bowl, passing for two touchdowns and leading Alabama to a 39–28 victory over the Nebraska Cornhuskers as the Crimson Tide won another national championship.

I'm not sure how much of a factor it was, but we were a T formation team in high school, and Tennessee was still running the single wing. I had played defense all through high school and thought I could play defense at Tennessee. But I was sold on quarterback and Alabama.

When I got to Alabama in the fall of 1962, we had about 65 freshmen, and it seemed to me that a lot of them were quarterbacks. Mal Moore was a senior; Joe Namath was a sophomore and the starter; and they had Jack Hurlbut, who was kind of like me, a guy who could play offense and defense.

I played on the freshman team in 1962, and then in 1963 played nothing but defense until the Sugar Bowl game at the end of the season. I only started a couple of games on defense, but I played on kicking teams. And then near the end of the season, Joe was suspended for the rest of the season. Only Joe and Coach Bryant know why. I think Jack played all or most of the Miami game. We went to Biloxi to practice for the Sugar Bowl, and at some point Coach Bryant decided I would start at quarterback. He may have thought Jack would be better on defense than I was. In any event, that's a heck of a time and place to get your first start at quarterback. I think I got a little older that week.

It snowed in New Orleans, which is unusual, and we played Ole Miss, a team we rarely played in the regular season in those days. We did play them my senior year in that 17–16 win. They had a very good team, but our defense played well, Tim Davis kicked four field goals, and we won the Sugar Bowl 12–7.

I remember one play in particular. I was running a down-the-line option and went the wrong way. I made a nice pitch, but the only one there was the referee, and he didn't catch it. I was able to recover the ball, but Coach Bryant wasn't very happy about that play.

It was good to win the game, although I didn't have much to do with it. But I did get some experience. The hard thing was we called our own plays, and because I had worked so little on offense, that was difficult.

Joe was back in 1964, but he got hurt in the North Carolina State game, which was early in the season. I was starting in the secondary, but I was the back-up quarterback. I had broken a finger in practice and hadn't gotten much work on offense. But I played the rest of the game at quarterback, and we won 21–0. Roman Gabriel was quarterback for North Carolina State. One funny thing that happened was I guess the coaches forgot I was playing in the secondary, and they left me in, playing both ways until halftime, when they got that changed.

After the game, in the dressing room, Coach Bryant came over to me and said, "How do you think you played?" in a way I thought he didn't think I'd played very well. I said, "We won the game." It was the first time I remember seeing him laugh.

I started the rest of the games, except Florida. Joe came in and got us wins against Georgia Tech and Auburn, and we were 10–0 and national champions. We both had bad knees when we played in the Orange Bowl and lost to Texas.

It was an enjoyable year playing offense and defense, especially since we got all those wins.

Coach Bryant had a way of making things work out. I don't know how he did it, but I'm convinced he was able to make things come around to the way we needed. We started out slow on offense in 1965, but we were good on defense. And by the time we got to about mid-season, we were a good offense and a good football team. In our last three games, we scored 30 or more points against LSU, South Carolina, and Auburn, which was a lot of points in those days. And so we made it to the Orange Bowl against Nebraska.

They were waiting until after the bowl games to choose the national champion, and we were ranked about fourth. But a couple of teams in front of us lost that afternoon in bowl games, and that night we were playing Nebraska for the championship.

The quarterbacks called the plays then, but Coach Bryant told me to open the game with a tackle-eligible pass to Jerry Duncan. That was a lot of fun. Jerry had been a running back and he was fast, and the tackle-eligible, which was later banned, was like getting the ball to a halfback on a screen. We won the game 39–28 and another national championship.

Back then we had so many good players that the quarterback may have looked better than he was. Nobody dropped a pass and nobody got to the quarterback.

I played with the Atlanta Falcons for a couple of years but had a bad shoulder. I came back to Alabama with the intention of going to graduate school. I was in the library, and someone told me Coach Bryant was looking for me. Ken Meyer was leaving to take the San Francisco 49ers head coaching job, and so I was hired to work with quarterbacks.

The quarterbacks were closer to Coach Bryant than any other segment of the team. As a player, you don't know everything that goes on behind the scenes. As a coach, it was a different perspective.

When I was a junior or senior at Alabama, I took a management course that focused on four basic principles: organization, leadership, planning, and control. I had a great teacher in that course, and I realized that those four principles were utilized by Coach Bryant. I'm not sure he would have known of those four principles, or that he was aware he employed them. His organizational skills were extraordinary, which I appreciated more when I became an assistant coach. I don't know where he got that. And his planning skills were great. And he was an all-time motivator.

I certainly admired what he did. Even though we might have different thoughts about some things, I regard him as an extraordinary man.

I know that everyone who had the opportunity to be exposed to Coach Bryant has thought about ways in which he affected their careers, and that may be more frequent for those of us who remained in athletics. He had a stronger personality than I have. He was a little tougher than I can be. But his planning and organization and all those things have really helped me out in my career in athletics. People like Coach Bryant don't come along very often. He's in a class with people like General Patton—forceful, charismatic. I always think of him fondly.

I think the driving force for him was that he had grown up poor and he never wanted to be poor again. He was exceptional in a lot of ways.

In 1987 I had the privilege to return to Alabama as athletics director when Ray Perkins, who had been coach and athletics director, left to go to Tampa Bay. In the interview I was asked who I would hire as head coach. Bobby Bowden had let it be known he would take the job. Whoever was interviewing me told me Coach Bowden was too old. They asked me about Bill Curry, who was a good friend. I didn't think the Georgia Tech thing would pose the problem it did.

It was a tough situation to come into. I really didn't have any choice on a lot of the issues. We were going to have to go to Auburn, and they were going to come to Tuscaloosa eventually. I think Ray had said we would never go to Auburn to play. And Coach Bryant never would have. It was a tough issue, but there was no other way to do it. We couldn't terminate the game. It was a really complex issue. I thought I did the right thing. I got hundreds and hundreds of letters, and only one supported me.

And there were some other problems that proved sticky.

Because I've always been in athletics, I've missed a lot of the reunions and things with my former teammates, but we still keep up with one another. I keep up with Alabama, and not just football. I follow all the teams. I got to be good friends with Sarah and David Patterson, and I follow gymnastics, and really everything. It's interesting to me that so many people still remember me as an Alabama football player.

*Steve Sloan was All-America, Academic All-America, led the nation in passing efficiency (153.8), and was MVP of the Orange Bowl as a Crimson Tide senior in 1965. He was the athletics director at Tennessee-Chattanooga before retiring in 2006.*

---

## OCTOBER 10, 1964

Joe Namath, having been reinstated to the team during the off-season, suffers a serious knee injury during a 21–0 victory over North Carolina State. He split time with Sloan the rest of the regular season, then replaced him during the early stages of the January 1 Orange Bowl against Texas. Namath passed for 255 yards and two touchdowns, but was stopped just short of the goal line on the game's final play in a 21–17 Alabama loss. The Crimson Tide was still awarded the first of two consecutive national championships.

## OCTOBER 15, 1966

Vying for its third straight national championship, Alabama beats Tennessee 11–10 in Knoxville when the Volunteers' Gary Wright misses a last-second field goal. Led by quarterback Kenny "Snake" Stabler, Alabama would finish the season 11–0 with a 34–7 victory over Nebraska in the Sugar Bowl. However, Alabama would be denied a third straight national championship, ending up third in the national polls behind Notre Dame and Michigan State.

## DECEMBER 10, 1968

Pat Trammell, the star quarterback on Alabama's 1961 national championship team, dies following a battle with testicular cancer. Trammell, perhaps Bryant's favorite player, had passed on a professional football career to become a doctor. The "A" Club Charitable Foundation was established in Trammell's honor and eventually led to the Paul W. Bryant Scholarship, which allows any child or grandchild of a former Bryant player to attend the university tuition-free.

## OCTOBER 4, 1969

Alabama beats Ole Miss 33–32 at Legion Field in Birmingham in what was one of the greatest passing shootouts in college football history. The Rebels' Archie Manning sets an SEC record with 539 yards of total offense (436 passing, 103 rushing) and accounts for five touchdowns, but the Crimson Tide's Scott Hunter—who passed for 300 yards himself—has the last laugh when he hits George Ranager for the winning touchdown with 3:42 to play.

## SEPTEMBER 10, 1971

After three subpar seasons, Alabama opens the year with a 17–10 victory over Southern Cal in the Los Angeles Memorial Coliseum. The game features two notable debuts: the powerful wishbone offense the Crimson Tide would ride to nine SEC championships and three national titles in the next 11 years, and defensive end John Mitchell and halfback Wilbur Jackson, Alabama's first black varsity players.

## *Crimson Tide in Their Own Words*

# WILBUR JACKSON

### HALFBACK, 1971–1973

It seems to surprise everyone that no one ever mentioned to me when I was being recruited that I would be the first black football player to sign with Alabama. If it ever came up, I don't remember it. I remember a few years ago talking to Chuck Strickland, who was captain with me on our 1973 team, and telling him that it had been tough on me, so tough that I thought about quitting. He laughed and said, "We all thought about quitting because it was so tough."

I felt as though I was treated just like everyone else, and I also felt that is how it should have been. I didn't want anything given to me because I was black, but I didn't want anything taken away from me, either. As far as I could tell, I was treated no differently than any other player. It was a tough experience on the field, but it was tough on everyone. But when I had success, it meant everyone on the team had success. And when someone else had success, so did I.

I guess the closest thing anyone ever said about me being first was during a recruiting trip to Tuscaloosa. I came up for three games, and each time there were 75 to 80 guys on the sideline. After the game, we'd go to the dressing room. On one of those trips, Coach Bryant had all the prospects at his house. He pulled me aside, took me into a separate room, and told me if I would come to Alabama, he'd make me the best wide receiver in the nation. Alabama wasn't running the wishbone yet, and I was recruited as a wide receiver.

He said if I ever had any problems to go see him—no one else—and he'd make sure everything was taken care of. I guess that might have been about me being black.

When we were growing up, we had two channels on television, and on Sunday afternoons we watched the Alabama and Auburn highlights. So I was watching *The Bear Bryant Show* each week, and I knew he was very well known nationally, as well as in the state, of course. So when he told me things were going to be fine, I believed they were going to be fine.

I played at an all-black high school, T. A. Smith, in Ozark until my senior year. Dexter Wood and Ellis Beck from Carroll High in Ozark had signed with Alabama in 1969, and I signed in 1970. We hadn't played together in high school, but it helped me that they were here. And we had guys from Dothan and Troy and Elba. They were all white, but we were all from the same area and had a good connection.

I didn't have a car, but if I needed to go somewhere, I could always catch a ride with a teammate or even borrow a car. And when I see one of my old teammates now, even if it has been years since we've seen each other, it is like we were just together.

When I played pro football, I found out I had a lot of other teammates, too.

I never thought about playing professionally until my junior year when I got a letter from the Dallas Cowboys. But my goal was to play football for Alabama and to get an education. As it turned out, I did get that professional football opportunity. One thing I learned is that it was a lot easier to play pro ball than it was to play at Alabama. The Alabama practices were a lot tougher than the games. And we were winning. I wondered sometimes what the practices would be like if we were losing. But, of course, it paid off.

Wilbur Jackson (80) was recruited as a receiver but became an outstanding running back in Alabama's wishbone offense. This 80-yard touchdown run broke Tennessee's back as the Tide scored three fourth-quarter TDs en route to a 42–21 win in 1973.

The other thing was the camaraderie of former Alabama players, Coach Bryant players. When we'd finish a game, guys on other teams like Lee Roy Jordan and Kenny Stabler, who had played before me at Alabama, would make it a point to come and talk to me after the game. And later I'd talk to guys who came after me, Barry Krauss and E.J. Junior and Curtis McGriff, who was from the same area I was, but I didn't know him until we were both in the NFL.

What we talked about was what was going on in Tuscaloosa. We had all played for Coach Bryant and we were tough. We all have our own story to tell, but ask anyone who played for Coach Bryant and ask about poise and pride and you'll get the same answer. We have a common bond based on what we had gone through and what the university and Coach Bryant had meant to us.

And I'm sure the guys playing now have that Crimson Tide bond.

I was recruited by Coach Dye. Because the guys at T.A. Smith were going to move over to Carroll the next year, my senior year, we went through spring practice at Carroll in 1969. Coach Dye had come down to check on Ellis and Dexter, I believe, and the coach at Carroll, Tom McClendon, showed Coach Dye a jamboree film of me. Coach McClendon brought Coach Dye over to T.A. Smith to meet me. He checked on my transcript.

The next year we opened the season against Montgomery Lee, and Coach Dye was there. He was also looking at some Lee guys, Paul Spivey and John Rogers, who both signed with Alabama. He talked to me after the game.

Coach Dye had the recruiting area, but Joe Kelley, who was from Ozark, was a graduate assistant, and he came down a lot, too.

All our teams at Alabama were good, but the 1973 team my senior year was really good. We lost to Notre Dame in the Sugar Bowl 24–23, which was a shame. Notre Dame made the plays to win and you have to credit them, but we were probably the best team in the country. We didn't lose many games, and I certainly remember the big wins over Auburn and Tennessee and Georgia.

After I finished playing pro ball, I came back to Ozark, where I have owned a commercial janitorial service for the past 20 years. And even in that I think about Coach Bryant's lessons. His pre-game speech might change a little, but it was always the same in talking about pride and poise and confidence. He said to have a plan for everything. He said, "If you get behind, are you going to fight back, or are you going to fold your tent?" Those things have stuck with me about always doing my best.

*Wilbur Jackson was an All-SEC halfback in 1973 and was captain of the national championship team as a senior. He is the Alabama career leader in yards per rush, 7.2 yards per carry with 1,529 yards on 212 rushes. He was one of four backs to rush for more than 100 yards in the same game for one team, an NCAA record. He played professional football in San Francisco and Washington. The 1983 Super Bowl was his final game.*

## OCTOBER 21, 1972

Alabama beats Tennessee 17–10 in Knoxville, despite trailing 10–3 with less than three minutes remaining. Jackson scored from two yards out to tie the game, and then defensive end Mike DuBose forced a fumble by Tennessee's Condredge Holloway to get the ball back. Moments later, Terry Davis raced into the end zone from 22 yards away for the winning touchdown.

## DECEMBER 2, 1972

In perhaps the most gut-wrenching loss in Alabama history, the Crimson Tide blow a 16–7 lead late in the fourth thanks to breakdowns in the kicking game. In what would come to be known as "Punt, 'Bama, Punt," Auburn's Bill Newton blocks two straight punts, and David Langner runs both in for touchdowns to hand the Tigers a 17–16 victory. It would be Alabama's only SEC loss between 1970 and 1976 and its last loss to Auburn until 1982.

## OCTOBER 27, 1973

One of the most dominant offenses in Crimson Tide history enjoys its biggest day against Virginia Tech in Tuscaloosa. In a 77–6 victory, the Crimson Tide roll up school records for total offense (833), average yards per play (11.9), and rushing yards (748). Four Alabama players rush for 100 or more yards in the game, part of an 11–0 regular season that also featured blowout wins over California (66–0) and Auburn (35–0).

## DECEMBER 31, 1973

After nearly three-quarters of a century as college football's dominant programs, Alabama and Notre Dame finally meet on the football field in the Sugar Bowl at New Orleans' Tulane Stadium. The game does not disappoint, with the Fighting Irish scoring a 24–23 victory thanks to a late 35-yard pass from Tom Clements to Robin Weber that helped kill the clock. Despite the bitter end to the season, Alabama had already been awarded the UPI national championship.

## NOVEMBER 29, 1975

Alabama pounds Auburn 28–0 at Legion Field, sewing up its fifth consecutive SEC title. No other team in SEC history had won more than four straight conference championships. The Crimson Tide went 11–1 and beat Penn State 13–6 in the Sugar Bowl (its only loss of the year to Missouri in the season opener), its third consecutive one-loss finish.

## JANUARY 2, 1978

Third-ranked Alabama beats Ohio State 35–6 to finish 11–1 and looks in prime position to win the national championship after both top-ranked Texas and No. 2 Oklahoma lost their bowl games. But fifth-ranked Notre Dame, which had beaten Texas 38–10 in the Cotton Bowl behind quarterback Joe Montana, vaults over the Crimson Tide to finish first in the final rankings.

## JANUARY 1, 1979

In perhaps the most famous play (or series of plays) in Alabama history, the second-ranked Crimson Tide stops top-ranked Penn State with a goal-line stand late in the fourth quarter to seal a 14–7 victory and its first national championship in five years. Alabama would go on to win the national title again the following year, going 12–0 and beating Arkansas 24–9 in the Sugar Bowl.

## NOVEMBER 1, 1980

Alabama sees its 28-game winning streak and bid for a third straight national title fall by the wayside in a 6–3 loss against Mississippi State in Jackson. Dana Moore kicks two field goals for the Bulldogs, and Tide quarterback Don Jacobs fumbles inside the 10 in the final seconds to secure the loss. It would be the last time a Bryant team would be ranked No. 1 in the country.

## NOVEMBER 28, 1981

Bryant becomes college football's all-time-winningest coach, as the Crimson Tide beats Auburn 28–17 in Birmingham for career victory No. 315. Walter Lewis hits Jesse Bendross for a 38-yard touchdown to give Alabama the lead for good in the fourth quarter. The game also clinches the last of Bryant's 14 SEC titles, which the Crimson Tide shared that year with unbeaten Georgia.

## DECEMBER 29, 1982

Two weeks after announcing his retirement, Bryant coaches his final game against Illinois in the Liberty Bowl in Memphis. Behind three interceptions from Jeremiah Castille, the Crimson Tide beats the Illini 21–15. Bryant's players carry him off the field. Less than a month later, on January 26, 1983, he died following a heart attack.

## DECEMBER 1, 1984

Alabama gets a little payback for the heartbreak of 1972, beating Auburn 17–15 at Legion Field to knock the Tigers out of the Sugar Bowl. The Crimson Tide went 5–6 that season, its first losing record since 1957, but is able to end the season on a positive note thanks largely to a Rory Turner's fourth-quarter, fourth-down stop of Auburn's Brent Fullwood inside the 5-yard line.

## NOVEMBER 30, 1985

The Iron Bowl is a classic for the second straight year, as Alabama's Van Tiffin kicks a 52-yard field goal in the final seconds to give the Crimson Tide a 25–23 victory. The game was one of the most hotly contested in the history of the series, with four lead changes in the fourth quarter and a pair of electric rushing performances by Alabama's Gene Jelks and Auburn's Bo Jackson.

---

## *Crimson Tide in Their Own Words*

# VAN TIFFIN

### PLACE-KICKER, 1983–1986

Every kicker would say that the situation that came to me was a dream come true, because a kicker always dreams of making the winning field goal in the last second of a big game. But when you're standing on the sideline and see the possibility of it coming down to you, you have second thoughts about it. And that was the situation in 1985 against Auburn.

As our final drive started with us trailing 23–22 and almost no time remaining, I didn't see us getting into field-goal range, at least not after Mike Shula got sacked on first down. But two plays later, we were up toward midfield. I was still a little in denial that we would get into field-goal range, but the guys on the sideline with me were yelling encouragement, that it was going to come

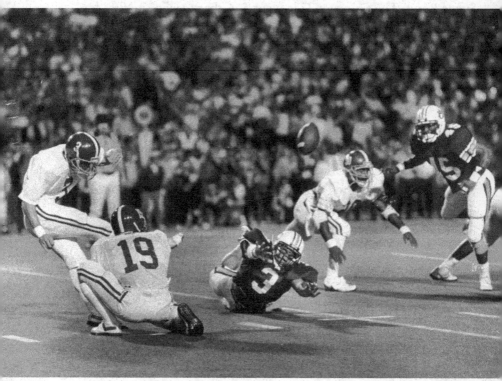

Van Tiffin kicked one of the most famous field goals in Alabama history, a 52-yarder as time ran out to beat Auburn in 1985. He never missed an extra point.

down to me. And when Greg Richardson got out of bounds at the 35-yard line, the opportunity was there.

Auburn didn't call a timeout, so everything was just rush, rush, rush. And that's the way I wanted it. I didn't want time to think about it. I never enjoyed having to wait through a timeout, even though by then I had gotten used to that and handled it better. But I'm glad Auburn didn't call a timeout, because I don't know how I would have handled it in that pressure situation.

Kicking is a lot like hitting a golf ball or a baseball. When you don't feel anything, you know you've hit it good. And that's the way it was. I can just remember getting back and kicking it, not feeling it, and looking up and there it was going right down the middle. I thought, *This can't be true. This can't be real.* Also, I could just feel Kevin Porter, the Auburn end, coming from the left side, and I knew it was going to be close. When I got out there on the field it was, "Line set. Snap." I was expecting more of a delay in snapping the ball, so I was just a little bit late getting to the ball. Kevin Porter was offside, so he was actually a little early. Had he not been offside, he might have blocked it.

It was like it happened yesterday. That's all people remember me for, and that's okay. At least they don't remember me for missing that field goal. That would really be bad.

It was particularly meaningful for me since I had grown up an Alabama fan. I was about nine or 10 when I went to my first Alabama-Auburn game, and in the '70s my parents started buying season tickets. After the high school game on Friday night, we'd leave and go to the Alabama game. I was at the 1979 Sugar Bowl game against Penn State. So I was a fan.

But I almost didn't go to Alabama. Alabama wasn't going to give a kicker a scholarship, and I was close to going to Southern Miss. But about two weeks before signing day, Coach Perkins called and said, "We want you to come to Alabama." That was all I needed to hear. And he said if I won the starting job, he'd put me on scholarship.

I won the kicking job as a freshman. My birthday was late compared to everyone else in my recruiting class. I think Cornelius Bennett and I were the youngest players on the team. Coach Perkins called me in on September 6, my 18th birthday, and told me I would be the kicker when we opened the season against Georgia Tech. Of course, he didn't know it was my birthday. The next January, Coach Perkins called me in and gave me a scholarship. That was an exciting day for me and my family.

Perkins was intimidating to me. I would cringe every time he walked by, hoping he wouldn't say anything to me. He'd come up and stare right through you. He was a good man and always had good intentions with players. We all had such respect for him. I would do anything for him. I have talked to him some the past few years. If I talk to him even now, I start getting butterflies and on edge.

He was a high-class individual and expected high class out of players. He wouldn't tolerate anything the way it shouldn't be. I respected him and didn't realize that's what I had for him. I believe if he'd stayed at Alabama, he'd have won a national championship. In his and my last year, he was 10–3 and really strong, but you couldn't blame him for leaving for a better offer. I think he was a great coach.

I know kickers are sometimes considered strange, but I didn't think of myself that way. I got along well with my teammates. Coach Perkins always made kickers do everything everyone else did, except for the full contact. We did all the running and the off-season program everyone else did.

I really never got a big kick that had a bearing on the game until 1984 against Penn State. We won that game 6–0. In the fourth quarter, the score was 0–0, and I tried a 53-yarder and made it. I don't know if Alabama still has the record for consecutive extra point kicks, but I know we set the record. We reached 199 before we had a miss. It started with Peter Kim, who made his last 50 or so. Paul Trodd kicked one when Peter got hurt. I had 135 in a row when I was at Alabama. And then Philip Doyle finished it out. We went five or six seasons without missing one. I missed the first extra point I ever tried in high school, then never missed another one. But when we were breaking the NCAA record, I just barely made it. The pressure nearly got to me. It takes good holding, good snapping, good blocking, and good luck for a streak like that.

The longest field goal I had was 57 yards against Texas A&M. I made two or three that day. The 57-yarder was just before half-time, and we had a nice wind helping. You always wanted to be really positive with Coach Perkins. In the third quarter, we had that same wind against us and were facing a 51-yard field-goal situation. He looked at me and said, "Can you make it?" Well, I wasn't going to tell him no, but as I was walking out there I was thinking, *No way*. So I was a little surprised when I made it.

During my freshman year, Malcolm Simmons and Paul Fields held for me. Larry Abney held for me my sophomore, junior, and senior years. Darren Whitlock was the snapper, and he didn't do anything else but snap. He was a good one. When he snapped, eight of 10 times the laces were turned up perfectly. All Larry did was hold. Anytime I wanted to snap and hold, they were ready. That's so important for a kicker. When I walked out there, I knew the snap and hold were going to be there. It was almost an unfair advantage.

I got to play a little professional football with Miami, but when I got cut the next year, I went back to Alabama to finish my degree work. I'm in the family business, Tiffin Motor Homes, in Red Bay, and we go to games as part of the big RV community. It's a good way to stay familiar with our products and our customers. Dr. Gary White, who was assistant athletics director under Coach Perkins, helped me get a summer kicking camp started in 1987, and it's still going. That's a nice change of pace for a few days.

Playing at Alabama was a dream come true. I really enjoy seeing my old teammates at games. And I can see how football helps you all your life. You have to be able to focus, and you have to give full effort. That's every day in football.

> *Van Tiffin was an All-American in 1986 and was selected to the Team of the Century. He holds the NCAA record for best extra-point percentage for a career (135 of 135, 100 percent). He hit one of the most famous field goals in Crimson Tide history, a 52-yarder as time expired to beat Auburn 25–23 in 1985, and also kicked the winning field goal against Auburn in 1984. He had a school record 14 points by kicking (three field goals, five extra points) against Mississippi State (since broken).*

---

## OCTOBER 28, 1989

In perhaps the high point of the Bill Curry era, Alabama beats Penn State in State College. With memories of the 1979 Sugar Bowl's goal-line stand no doubt fresh in his mind, Penn State's Joe Paterno elects to go for a game-winning field goal in the closing seconds rather than run the ball with All-American Blair Thomas. Alabama defensive end Thomas Rayam blocks Ray Tarasi's kick, and the Crimson Tide wins 17–16.

## FALL 1990

Gene Stallings' career as Alabama coach begins inauspiciously with consecutive losses to Southern Miss, Florida, and Georgia, but he turns things around with a pair of late-season victories. First, the Crimson Tide beats Tennessee 9–6 on Philip Doyle's last-second field goal, and then a 16–7 win over Auburn snaps a four-game losing streak in the Iron Bowl.

## JANUARY 1, 1993

In a stunning upset, Alabama rips past top-ranked Miami 34–13 in the Sugar Bowl to win its first national championship in the post-Bryant era and 12th overall. Defense is the story of the day for the Crimson Tide, which intercepts Heisman Trophy–winning quarterback Gino Torretta three times. George Teague is Alabama's big star, with an interception returned for a touchdown and a memorable strip and recovery from Miami's Lamar Thomas.

## JANUARY 1, 1997

Stallings goes out a winner, with Alabama beating Michigan 17–14 in the Outback Bowl to give him 70 victories in seven years as Crimson Tide head coach. Alabama gets Shaun Alexander's 46-yard touchdown run and Dwayne Rudd's 88-yard interception return to cap off a 10-win season, its fourth in five years under Stallings, who also won SEC West titles in 1992 and 1994.

## FALL 1999

Alabama turns a rare double play, beating Florida twice in the same season on the way to the SEC championship. First up was a 40–39 overtime victory in Gainesville on October 2, a game in which Florida missed its overtime extra-point attempt to hand Alabama the win. Then came a 34–7 demolition in the SEC Championship Game, which featured an electric performance from all-purpose star Freddie Milons. Alabama went 10–3 that season, falling to Michigan in the Orange Bowl.

## NOVEMBER 16, 2002

An Alabama team ineligible for postseason play due to NCAA sanctions demolishes LSU 31–0 in Baton Rouge, scoring a dominant victory over future head coach Nick Saban in the process. Shaud Williams and Santonio Beard each eclipse the 100-yard rushing mark as the Crimson Tide rolls up 477 yards of offense and hand LSU its worst shutout loss in 52 years.

## OCTOBER 22, 2005

One of the most memorable moments in the history of the Alabama-Tennessee series comes in this low-scoring affair in Tuscaloosa. With the score tied 3–3 and time winding down, Crimson Tide safety Roman Harper pops the ball loose from Volunteers fullback Cory Anderson near the end zone to force a touchback. Minutes later, Jamie Christensen drills a 34-yard field goal to give Alabama a 6–3 win.

## JANUARY 3, 2007

Nick Saban is hired as Alabama football coach, landing at the Tuscaloosa County Airport to a throng of cheering fans. After a 7–6 debut season, he quickly turned the Crimson Tide around, going 36–5 over the next three seasons. The Crimson Tide played in three consecutive January bowl games during that time, and won the 2009 national championship.

## FEBRUARY 6, 2008

Alabama lands what is universally regarded as the top recruiting class in the country, a star-studded group that features the likes of Julio Jones, Mark Ingram, Marcell Dareus, Dont'a Hightower, and Mark Barron. Ingram would go on to win the Heisman Trophy as a sophomore in 2009, while he, Jones, Dareus, and James Carpenter would all be first-round NFL Draft picks in 2011.

## NOVEMBER 29, 2008

Alabama finally beats Auburn in Tuscaloosa, and does so in dominating fashion with a 36–0 whitewashing of the archrival Tigers. The Crimson Tide snaps a six-game losing streak in the series, dating back to 2001. Ingram and fellow running back Glen Coffee combine for 208 yards and three touchdowns as Alabama completes a 12–0 regular season.

## OCTOBER 24, 2009

Every championship team needs to get lucky once in a while, and the Crimson Tide certainly did in its annual showdown with Tennessee. Alabama held just a 12–3 lead and was trying to run the clock out when Ingram fumbled with 3:29 left. Tennessee answered with a touchdown, then got the ball back and drove within field-goal range. But Alabama's Terrence "Mount" Cody blocked the kick to preserve both the win and the Crimson Tide's perfect season.

## DECEMBER 12, 2009

Mark Ingram becomes the first Heisman Trophy winner in Crimson Tide history, delivering a tearful and impassioned speech before members of the Downtown Athletic Club in New York. Ingram finished his historic season with 1,658 rushing yards and 17 touchdowns, adding in another 334 yards and three touchdowns receiving. Prior to Ingram, no Alabama player had finished higher than third in the Heisman voting.

Mark Ingram (22) slips by two Texas defenders in Alabama's 37–21 victory in the BCS Championship Game on January 7, 2010, at the Rose Bowl. *Photo courtesy of Getty Images*

## JANUARY 7, 2010

Alabama rolls past Texas 37–21 to win the BCS National Championship game at Pasadena's Rose Bowl, the site of the Crimson Tide's first four national title victories. The Crimson Tide got 100-yard rushing games from both Ingram and Trent Richardson and knocked star Texas quarterback Colt McCoy out of the game with a shoulder injury in the first quarter. Dareus delivered not only the hit on McCoy, but also returned an interception for a touchdown in the second quarter to spark the victory.

*chapter 3*

# THE MANY SIDES OF PAUL W. "BEAR" BRYANT

NO MAN IS MORE SYNONYMOUS with one college football program than Paul W. "Bear" Bryant is with Alabama. Through three seasons as a player, four as an assistant coach, and 25 as head coach, Bryant was part of 284 Crimson Tide victories, 16 Southeastern Conference championships, and seven national titles. Here is Bryant's story, as told by the men who played with and for him.

## BRYANT THE PLAYER

Born September 11, 1913, in Moro Bottom, Arkansas, Paul William Bryant grew up on what he always referred to as a "truck farm." After picking up his nickname for wrestling a carnival bear at age 13, he played football at nearby Fordyce High School and was good enough to draw the attention of Hank Crisp, lead recruiter for coach Frank Thomas at Alabama. Bryant had been captivated by Crimson Tide football ever since listening to the 1926 Rose Bowl over the radio and left home for Tuscaloosa in the fall of 1931.

After taking some remedial high school courses to get his academics in order, Bryant joined Thomas' Crimson Tide varsity team as an end in 1933. He was, by most accounts, a good but not great player, one who got by on hard work and toughness as much as athletic ability.

Though he was known as "the Other End" (to All-American Don Hutson), Paul "Bear" Bryant was regarded as a talented—and tough—player in his days at Alabama.

"We had some great players in guys like Dixie Howell, Bear Bryant, Don Hutson, Tom Hupke, B'Ho Kirkland, Bill Lee," remembered Howard Chappell, a senior on the 1933 Alabama team. "Bryant couldn't catch too well, but he was the best on defense."

Led by Howell and Hutson, Alabama went 10–0 and beat Stanford in the Rose Bowl in 1934, earning the national championship. Bryant started at end across from Hutson, one of the great players of early 20th century college football and later a Hall of Famer with the NFL's Green Bay Packers.

Hutson was gone by 1935, Bryant's senior year. It was then that his toughness became truly legendary. "I thought I was going to start the Tennessee game in Knoxville in 1935," fellow end Ben McLeod remembered nearly 70 years later. "Bryant had a broken leg. But they took him out of the cast and started him. He didn't play long, maybe a quarter, but he played well. He caught at least two passes, which he lateraled to Riley Smith. I think one went for a touchdown and the other one set up a touchdown, and we beat Tennessee pretty handily, 25–0. It was really hot that day, and after the first quarter, I went in for Bryant and went the rest of the game. That was the only game I ever played where I about gave out. That Bryant was about as tough as they come."

Bryant made the transition into coaching the following year, serving three years on Thomas' staff before spending two seasons at Vanderbilt. Following a stint in the U.S. Navy during World War II, he coached one season at Maryland, eight at Kentucky, and four at Texas A&M, posting a 91–39–8 record as a head coach.

It was during the late fall of 1957 that "Mama called," and Bryant returned to Alabama as head coach. He inherited a team that had won a total of just eight games in four straight losing seasons, but he quickly set about remaking the Crimson Tide in his own image.

## BRYANT THE RECRUITER

Bryant was still a relatively young man of 46 when he became head coach at Alabama and hit the recruiting trail hard in those early days. He dismissed or ran off many of the players he inherited from coach J.B. "Ears" Whitworth and began to formulate a plan to bring top talent to Tuscaloosa.

He put together a young and energetic staff, hiring as assistant coaches several men who had coached or played for him at Texas A&M, including Phil Cutchin, Gene Stallings, and Bobby Drake Keith. In 1960 he brought in former Kentucky player Larry "Dude" Hennessey and a former Alabama halfback who was working as a high school coach, Clem Gryska.

"We both coached one day before hitting the road as recruiters for two and one-half years," Gryska said. "Coach Bryant wanted it done the right way. A lot of recruiters would go in, see the football coach, and then talk to the prospect. Coach Bryant told us to go in and first see the principal, then the coach, then the teacher, and finally the prospect. We always did it the right way."

Bryant rounded up much of the top talent in the state of Alabama in those early years, landing such future stars as Billy Neighbors, Pat Trammell, Bill Battle, Richard Williamson, Charley Pell, Tommy Brooker, and Lee Roy Jordan. All played major roles on the Crimson Tide's 1961 national championship team, the first under Bryant, whose recruiting pitch to those in-state standouts was a simple one.

"[Assistant coach] Pat James came to see me," said Brooker, who grew up 60 miles south of Tuscaloosa in Demopolis. "He was coming in with Coach Bryant. He asked me if I was good enough to whip Auburn. I told him that was why I was going to Alabama."

Bryant also expanded his recruiting scope outside Alabama's borders, and even dipped into the junior-college circuit. One of his early defensive stars was Darwin Holt, an undersized linebacker from Texas who had originally signed with Bryant at Texas A&M.

The man who was perhaps Bryant's most-celebrated recruit had signed on the winter before Alabama won the 1961 national championship. He used assistant coach Howard Schnellenberger's connections in Western Pennsylvania—along with his friendship with Maryland coach Tom Nugent—to land future superstar quarterback Joe Namath, though Bryant might have ultimately signed the Beaver Falls, Pennsylvania, standout because he played it clean.

"There were deals out there," Namath said. "The first coach who ever came to my house to recruit me took me outside after he had talked to me and my family. He told me if I would sign with him that I would have a vehicle and a certain amount of money each month. I've forgotten now if it was $100 a week or $300 a month or exactly what it was, but I know at the time it was an astronomical amount. But my brother Frank said, 'What kind of people do you want to be with? If they're cheating now, they will cheat you later. Or they will have you becoming a cheater.'"

With Pat Trammell and later Namath under center, the Crimson Tide won a combined 21 games in 1961 and 1962, and began to attract the attention of players all over the South. He occasionally found a diamond in the rough, such as Petal, Mississippi, end Ray Perkins or Sparta, North Carolina, offensive lineman Jerry Duncan.

"I wasn't really a very good football player, although I was probably a decent athlete," Duncan said. "I played at a very small program with 25 or 30 guys on the team in the smallest county in the state. And I found out later that Coach Gryska was sent up to sign me without even talking to my coaches or looking at film. I never did know what Coach Bryant had heard about me."

With four SEC titles and three national titles by the 1970s, Bryant's program had begun to sell itself. There was little need for much of a recruiting push to bring in such standouts as Johnny Musso, Wilbur Jackson, Richard Todd, Tony Nathan, Jeff Rutledge, and Ozzie Newsome.

"There were a lot of factors in my choosing Alabama, but unquestionably the No. 1 factor was Coach Bryant," Newsome said. "It begins and ends with him. I told a story many years ago about other schools recruiting me and telling me that their coach had played for Coach Bryant or had coached under Coach Bryant. And I thought, *I could go to the branch, or I could go to the trunk.*"

The Crimson Tide's national reputation also helped land several out-of-state stars, such as linebacker Barry Krauss of Pompano Beach, Florida. Krauss was being recruited by all his in-state schools but was sold on Alabama after his official visit. Just in case he had second thoughts, Bryant made a special trip to Krauss' home to close the deal.

"I had gone to our football banquet," Krauss said. "And when I came home and opened the door, there was Coach Bryant. He had flown down, and my family knew he would be there, but I didn't. He had my scholarship, and I signed right then. Coach Bryant was not the kind of man you said no to."

Bryant's weekly TV highlight program *The Bear Bryant Show* also played a major role in recruiting. Among those who got their first exposure to Crimson Tide football through the Sunday afternoon program were future All-Americans Don McNeal and Jeremiah Castille.

Bryant slowed down somewhat as a recruiter in his later years, but he still knew how to put on the full-court press for a key prospect. One of those was quarterback Walter Lewis, a Brewton native who was also being heavily recruited by Auburn. Lewis recalled:

> When Coach Bryant first approached me about signing with the Crimson Tide, I turned him down. When it came time for recruiting, I thought Alabama was "slow playing" me, kind of keeping me as a prospect in case something better didn't work out.
>
> Alabama sent four assistant coaches to see me—Bobby Marks, Sylvester Croom, Bryant Pool, and Perry Willis. When they were leaving, Perry Willis told me it cost $45 a minute to make a call from the airplane, but that he was going to call me on the way back, and that if I'd commit they'd turn the plane around and come back. But I didn't commit.
>
> I was in school, and it was getting late in the recruiting season, and my father came to the school. He said Coach Bryant had called from [Cotton Bowl] practice, and they had only three scholarships left. They wanted me, but they had to know something. I called Coach Bryant and committed.

## BRYANT THE TASKMASTER

Above all, Bryant's reputation as a young head coach was that of one who would work his players to their physical and psychological limits. It was a reputation he had come by honestly at both Kentucky and Texas A&M, where he conducted the famed "Junction Boys" training camp before the 1954 season.

Having turned the Aggies from a one-win team to Southwest Conference champions in just three years, Bryant used many of the same tactics he'd employed in College Station to strip down and rebuild the Crimson Tide. His first spring at Alabama was extraordinarily intense.

"It started in January with what was known as the gym program," lineman Fred Sington Jr. remembered. "That was so tough that we thought it was a relief that we would finally get onto the football field for spring practice. We were wrong. There was no relief. My father had told me when Coach Bryant was hired that I didn't know what tough was, but that I'd know when Coach Bryant got there. There was nothing he could have told me that would have prepared me for the ordeal. You really didn't know if you were going to survive. When we had a 40-year reunion of the 1958 class in 1998, we found a pre-spring roster with 362 names. That was before 25 days of spring practice. When we reported in the fall, we had 42 left."

Bryant actually set the tone of hard work in the first meeting with his players upon taking the Alabama job. He told the team that if they did as he instructed, they would win a national championship by the end of their careers (and those 1958 freshmen did so as seniors four years later). "I figured it out soon enough," Brooker remembered. "I learned it on the practice field, in the drills. You'd find out that when you thought you had given all you could give, that somehow you could reach down and find a little more. And that was every day as we tried to survive."

Bryant could be toughest on those players with the most talent, particularly the quarterbacks. Though Bryant considered him not only the greatest athlete he ever coached but also one of his favorite players, his relationship with Namath was often contentious, as Namath tells it:

> At Alabama, the quarterback got to see Coach Bryant more than players at the other positions. One of the things I enjoyed was the walk the quarterbacks made with him the morning of every game. We'd walk down the street and talk about the

game plan. On one of the first walks we made, he said, "Joe, you got the plan?"

I said, "Yeah, I think so."

"You *think* so?" he said. "You *think* so? Boy, it's time to *know*."

That was the last time I made that mistake.

By the 1970s, a new generation of college football player—and a new generation of college student in general—had arrived at Alabama and other universities. While Bryant relaxed his rules somewhat on hairstyles and off-the-field clothing in later years, he still insisted that his players always show class, something that to this day remains a watchword of the Crimson Tide program.

"At the time, I didn't always agree with everything Coach Bryant did, but he was probably right, and I respected the man," All-America split end Wayne Wheeler said. "I felt like he was doing what he felt was best for us. I think Coach Bryant was like a father. He expected things of us that our own families would expect, and I think that carries over into life after football—in what's important to you, how you look at things morally, and everything else. I think as you get older, you realize it more and more. It's kind of funny because I was a kid when I signed with Alabama, and I didn't start to realize I had been learning life lessons at Alabama until probably 10 years later."

Alabama racially integrated its football team in 1971, when defensive end John Mitchell and halfback Wilbur Jackson took the field as the Crimson Tide's first African American players. Just two or three years later, nearly a dozen black players dotted the Alabama roster, including stars such as fullback Calvin Culliver, linebacker Woodrow Lowe, center Sylvester Croom, and cornerback Mike Washington.

"In our first meeting with him as freshmen when there were only a few black players on the team, he told us that he didn't care who we were, he didn't care who our momma and daddy were, and he didn't care what color we were," Washington said. "He said we were going to get an education and we were going to play football—in that order. And he stuck to his promise. If you did what you were supposed to do in the classroom and on the football field, everything was fine. And if you didn't do the right thing, you found out about it."

The program remained regimented, and Bryant would not hesitate to discipline even star players who ran afoul of the rules. Namath was suspended for part of the 1963 season, and quarterback Richard Todd remembered that Bryant actually sent the names of those players who missed curfew before the 1975 Sugar Bowl to the players' hometown papers.

"You think about him being a disciplinarian, and he was," Todd said. "What he did was not cripple the team, which wouldn't have been fair to the innocent players, but he made us accept responsibility for what we had done. That was a typical move for Coach Bryant. He treated everyone fairly. There was no favoritism for any reason."

Above all, Bryant respected those players who took responsibility for their actions. Linebacker Barry Krauss learned that early in his Alabama career:

> My sophomore year I wasn't happy about my place on the depth chart. And we had a quarterback who wasn't happy because they were moving him to defensive back. One night after a game, we went out and we missed curfew. It so happened that this was a night that Coach Bryant made room checks himself. I knew we were dead.

Paul Bryant is considered the greatest college football coach of all time, and those who played for him consider him to have been much more than just their coach.

I didn't wait for him to call me. I went to see him. And I cried and apologized and begged for mercy. The quarterback didn't do anything. Coach Bryant kicked him out of the dorm and took his scholarship. He gave me a second chance. I kept my scholarship and learned a big lesson.

---

## Crimson Tide in Their Own Words

# JOHN MITCHELL
### DEFENSIVE END, 1971–1972

Growing up in Mobile, I knew all about Alabama and the great football stars like Joe Namath and Lee Roy Jordan. I knew all about the great wins and the national championships. I watched Alabama when they were on television and listened to the games on radio and watched *The Bear Bryant Show* on Sundays. Any kid would have wanted to go there.

But I couldn't go to Alabama. Alabama was not recruiting African American players when I finished high school at Williamson in 1969. And if they had been, I probably would not have been the one they would have taken because I was kind of a skinny kid.

I did have a chance to go to Alabama. I was part of the science fair team at our school, five little African American kids. And we won our local and state competitions and went to South Carolina for a competition and won there. And all five of us had academic scholarship offers to Alabama and to Auburn. And none of us accepted. Two went to Tuskegee and two to Alabama State.

I wanted to play football, so I went to Eastern Arizona Junior College, where I got bigger and better. And I had my choice of a lot of schools when I finished after the 1970 season. I finally decided on Southern Cal. I made a recruiting visit there, and my hosts were Sam Cunningham and Charles Young. I met O.J. Simpson. And I really liked it. Coach John McKay had a great program, and I was excited about playing there.

Alabama didn't cross my mind. I didn't know Alabama had signed Wilbur Jackson in 1970. I thought Alabama was still all-white. I graduated in December and was back in Mobile when I got a call from Judge Ferrill McRae, an Alabama alumnus in Mobile. Alabama was interested in me. It seems that Coach McKay had told Coach Bryant they were going to sign an Alabama boy who was playing at Eastern Arizona. Coach Bryant got on the phone to Coach Gryska and told him to recruit me. They never even saw a film of me. Coach Gryska and Coach Riley recruited me strictly on the basis that, if Southern Cal wanted me, I must be good enough.

I also realized my family had never seen me play in Arizona and would probably never see me play if I went to Southern Cal. But by my going to Alabama, they could drive up to Birmingham or Tuscaloosa and see me play. I really thought about that later when, after the first home game, I walked out of the dressing room and saw my parents waiting for me. It was one of the biggest moments in my life, and I know they were so happy to be able to see their son play for Alabama.

It's ironic that my first Alabama game was at Southern Cal. As it turned out, I played in the game before Wilbur did, so I became the first black player to play football for Alabama. I never felt like anything except a part of the team. I had to work my way up the depth chart to get a chance to be a starter. Coach Bryant got on me the same way he would any other player. And I was certainly aware that Alabama had been good before I got there, and I knew that Alabama would be good in the future. Whether John Mitchell played and whether John Mitchell was the first black player was not a major effect on Alabama football.

Southern Cal had beaten Alabama badly the year before, and for us to go to Los Angeles and beat them was very, very big. I can still remember when we recovered a fumble late in the game to clinch the victory. That was about as happy as I had ever been.

Lynn Swann was a great player on that Southern Cal team and a great player for the Pittsburgh Steelers. We live in the same neighborhood and see each other. I never let him forget that game.

Richard Williamson was my position coach. His father died that week, so he didn't go to Los Angeles with us, and I didn't know if he would be there. He was a great coach, and I really relied on him. I had come from a junior college where we had three or four coaches total. At Alabama every position had its own coach. About 15 minutes before we were to go out, Coach Williamson stuck his head in the dressing room. That says a lot about him and how much he cared for his players. I still see him because he's coaching at Carolina and I'm coaching at Pittsburgh, and we play each other.

I got to Alabama in the summer before all the players checked in, and they put me in a room in Bryant Hall. Later my roommate, Bobby Stanford, showed up. Bobby was white and from Georgia, and we became and remain the best of friends. His parents would come up, and if they brought him something, they brought me something. His father is gone now, but his mother, Frances, is still the same wonderful woman who kissed her son good-bye and then kissed me good-bye when they left.

Every player has memories of his favorite game. Mine has to be the 1972 game in Knoxville. We were not playing well, and Tennessee had a 10–0 lead at halftime. Luckily, we had played well on defense or it would have been worse. But we scratched out a

John Mitchell could have gone to Alabama on an academic scholarship, but 'Bama was not signing African American football players when he finished high school. He went to junior college, then played and coached for Alabama.

field goal, and our defense kept playing well. Finally, we broke through for a touchdown and tied the game with a minute or two to play. A few plays later, Mike DuBose knocked the ball loose, and I recovered it. Terry Davis ran it in, and we won 17–10.

One thing that makes that game so memorable is the halftime. Coach Bryant never ranted and raved at halftime. When he came in, we had long faces and he just said, "Get those frowns off." Then he let the coaches teach us. And before we went back out, he said, "You're Alabama. They have to beat you." No one beat us very often.

I had graduated in December after the 1972 season. I was in Mobile and called Coach Bryant to see if my scholarship would extend to going to graduate school because my parents couldn't afford it. He said he wouldn't talk to me about it on the phone. So I drove up on a Wednesday to talk to him. I hoped he would give me some little graduate assistant position and pay for my school. Instead he said he was offering me a full-time job on his staff and asked if I would take it. I said, "Yes, sir." And he said, "Well, then, get to work."

I got a room in the dorm and had to wash the clothes I had worn every night because I hadn't brought any more clothes. That weekend I went back to Mobile for my clothes. Every day I look at my 1973 national championship ring that I got while coaching.

Back in the mid-'90s, we started a little reunion of players who were on the 1971 and 1972 teams. It started with Bobby Stanford, Jimmy Rosser, Ed Hines, Johnny Musso, Jack White, and me in Jacksonville, Florida. Now we meet every other year in Gulf Shores and have about 50 guys show up.

I don't know if any of them have a greater appreciation for Alabama than I do. I was a little African American kid who knew nothing and who was nurtured by and learned from Coach Bryant. He gave me my opportunity. Any success I have had I owe to him. There is no way I could ever repay The University of Alabama.

*John Mitchell started all 24 games in his Alabama career as the Tide compiled a 21–3 record and won two SEC titles. He was a two-time All-SEC player and All-American in 1972 and captain of the 1972 team. He is assistant head coach for the Pittsburgh Steelers.*

## BRYANT THE MOTIVATOR

In his early days at Alabama, Bryant motivated his players mostly through intimidation. An imposing man at 6'3" and nearly 200 pounds, many Crimson Tide players were simply afraid of him even if he never raised his voice.

"I remember we played a freshman game against Tulane on a Saturday night in Denny Stadium when the varsity had played in Knoxville that afternoon," quarterback Mal Moore remembered. "We had lost to Tennessee 14–7. I don't remember how we were doing in the freshman game, but I remember we were in the dressing room at halftime, and [freshman team coach Sam] Bailey was about to put something up on the blackboard. Just then the door slammed open, and there stood Coach Bryant in a big topcoat. We hadn't expected to see him.

"One of the guys sitting there clapped his hands and said, 'Let's go, guys, let's go!' Coach Bryant said, 'I don't want to hear that phony stuff.' Then he said he had seen all the bad football he could stand in one day. And he said, 'Come Monday, if you don't love it, you'll never make it.' And about 12 or 13 guys quit, including two who had started the Tennessee game."

Bryant could be just as intimidating during a game, with not even star players escaping his wrath. Namath learned that lesson the hard way, when he was benched for poor play against Vanderbilt in 1962.

"I was having a bad game and got taken out of the game in the first quarter," Namath said. "I knew I was messing up, and that was the reason I was pulled. I went over to the sideline by the bench, took off my helmet, and threw it on the ground. I sat down on the bench with my head in my hands. Coach Bryant came over and sat down beside me and put his arm around my shoulder. Then he put his hand on my neck and started squeezing.

And it was hard, like one of my big brothers squeezing me. It told me what he thought of that kind of behavior, and how fast he'd kick my ass back to Beaver Falls, Pennsylvania, if I ever displayed that kind of selfish attitude again. I looked Coach Bryant right in the eye and told him I wasn't upset with him or the coaches. I was only upset with myself."

Bryant's early teams won several games against teams with superior talent, including a comeback victory over Georgia Tech in 1960. Lineman Jack Rutledge said Bryant had an uncanny ability to make his players believe they were better than they were.

"We were down 15–0 at halftime," Rutledge said. "That's when Coach Bryant came into the dressing room and we all expected to get chewed out, and he said, 'We've got 'em right where we want 'em.'

"In the second half he benched Bobby Skelton as his quarterback, told him he would 'never play another down.' Pat Trammell came in and did good, taking us to a score. But we had a play where someone jumped [offside], and when he did, a Georgia Tech man ran right past me and hit Trammell—a cheap shot that hurt him. That's when Coach Bryant called [for] Skelton and told him he was going to give him one more chance. Digger O'Dell kicked a field goal, and we won 16–15."

By the 1970s, Bryant's reputation as a hard-nosed coach was such that players often lived in fear, sometimes to comedic levels. Defensive end John Croyle admitted years later to having a flash of dread upon suffering a serious knee injury his freshman year.

"Maybe it was because I had just seen the movie *They Shoot Horses, Don't They?* that I had a little moment of panic," Croyle said. "I had been working at wide receiver in practice my freshman year. I was running a drill and planted my foot. My knee started to separate about the time Robin Parkhouse hit it. When everything was over, my leg was just swinging. Every ligament but one was torn. Coach Bryant came over and looked at it and said, 'What a waste.' I thought they were going to shoot me."

Croyle soon realized Bryant was trying to motivate him to work hard and return to the field.

"After that injury, I went to work," Croyle said. "And I kept working and working. And then one day I knew I was going to make it back. [Trainer Jim Goostree] was watching me work out. He said, 'It looks like you know what you're doing.' That's when I knew I would make it.

"As bad as the injury in 1970 may have seemed at the time, it taught me how to work. And that has helped me as I have carried on with children. It made me learn to persevere. And the rewards were getting back up and having a chance to play, and having Coach Bryant say, 'Good job.' That's a rush."

Alabama's teams of the 1970s won eight Southeastern Conference championships, three national titles, and never lost more than three games in one season. The Crimson Tide was so talented that it could often play poorly and still win.

On the rare occasions Alabama found itself trailing at halftime, Bryant's locker room speeches were legendary. But not for the reasons you might think.

"Coach Bryant never ranted and raved at halftime," defensive end John Mitchell said. "When he came in, we had long faces, and he just said, 'Get those frowns off.' Then he let the coaches teach us. And before we went back out he said, 'You're Alabama. They have to beat you.' No one beat us very often."

During the heyday of the 1970s, the Alabama players often used competing with each other as motivation. One such player was defensive tackle Marty Lyons, who worked his way up to second-team behind All-American Bob Baumhower in 1976.

Lyons played in every game that season, which is why he was shocked to find he did not receive a letter after the season. He went to Bryant's office seeking an explanation.

"I sat in that famous sofa where I nearly sank to the floor and looked up at him smoking his Chesterfield and looking down at me over those half glasses," Lyons said. "I told him I thought I had played enough to letter. He said, 'Marty, I'm not sure that letter means enough to you.' Well, I thought I had an answer for anything he'd say, but I didn't have an answer for that.

"In looking back, I think he was right. That letter didn't mean enough to me then. But after that meeting, I was inspired to be an All-American. Coach Bryant knew how to treat men."

Like many coaches, Bryant had a special place in his heart for overachievers, players who did not have outstanding physical gifts but worked their way into prominent roles on the Alabama team. Undersized players such as Darwin Holt, Jerry Duncan, and wide receiver Joey Jones were particularly dear to Bryant.

"My freshman year was rough. I was about sixth-string," Jones said. "And Coach Bryant made some remarks in the newspaper that I was too small a target for the quarterback.

"But my sophomore year a bunch of receivers got hurt, and he pretty much had to start me. As luck would have it, I scored a touchdown and had a pretty good game. The next week we played Kentucky, and I had another good game and also started returning punts. The following Monday, Coach Bryant told me not to dress out. He said I had been in a couple of physical games and was beaten up. I wasn't hurt, but it was his way of telling me I had finally made it. He winked at me and told me to sit out practice. My confidence meter was sky high after that."

## Crimson Tide in Their Own Words
# MARTY LYONS
### DEFENSIVE TACKLE, 1975–1978

Winning 10 or 11 games a year will give you confidence. Playing in the national championship game provides an opportunity to exhibit it. Alabama football teams had come up just short of national championships in my freshman season in 1975 and in my junior year in 1977. I was captain of the 1978 team, the last time I would have the opportunity. The Crimson Tide, undefeated and ranked second in the nation, met coach Joe Paterno's undefeated and No. 1–ranked Penn State in the Sugar Bowl.

The game was a classic and turned on one of the defining moments in college football history. Alabama had a 14–7 lead late in the fourth quarter when Penn State drove to a first down inside the 'Bama 10-yard line. Three more plays left the Nittany Lions a yard short of the goal line.

As captains, Penn State quarterback Chuck Fusina and I were standing at the spot of the ball just outside the Alabama end zone. We had met on *The Bob Hope Show* when we were presented as All-Americans a few weeks earlier. After examining the spot of the ball, Fusina said, "Marty, what do you think we ought to do?"

I said, "Chuck, you've got about a yard to go. You'd better pass."

Penn State didn't pass. And the run up the middle was stopped cold, preserving the score and leading to Alabama winning the national championship.

No one prepared like we did. Coach [Ken] Donahue met with the linebackers and defensive linemen every night after we started

Marty Lyons (93) and Barry Krauss celebrated being No. 1 after a goal-line stand against Penn State in the 1979 Sugar Bowl gave 'Bama the national championship.

bowl practice. We watched Penn State film. Then Coach Donahue would show us a Penn State formation. He'd have the linebackers call the defense, then test the defensive linemen on what our responsibilities were. We knew everything they were going to do if they stuck to their tendencies. And most teams do stay with their tendencies. When we got in our huddle, we knew what to expect. Everyone did his job. Barry [Krauss] made the play, but it was David Hannah who took the blocker's legs out. It was Alabama at its best. And no player could ask to end his career better than to go out as national champion.

I was the 14th player taken in the following year's NFL Draft, selected in the first round by the New York Jets, and I was fortunate enough to have a very successful professional career, playing from 1979 to 1990. But the best thing ever said about me was that I was an even bigger success outside football in the best possible way.

It is commonplace for college players on bowl trips to make a trip to visit sick children in a hospital in the bowl city. I had that experience, but I didn't let it end there. I continued to visit children in hospitals when I went to the Jets. And in 1982 a teammate, Kenny Schroy, and I made a commitment to do more. The result was The Marty Lyons Foundation, which continues to grant wishes to children with terminal or life-threatening illnesses.

One of the things that Coach Bryant stressed was how important it was to make a difference. He was the reason I started the foundation. He told us about the opportunities we had. I knew when I was on those hospital wards watching those children pulling IV poles that they weren't going to have the opportunities I had.

The Marty Lyons Foundation has sponsored more than three thousand kids. It has a budget of between $750,000 and $1 million a year. It has two paid employees, but hundreds of volunteers.

I love success stories. In 1985 we had a little girl with leukemia. The doctors said if she was fortunate enough to survive that she would never have children. At the foundation's annual "Celebration of Life" reunion, the young woman was one of 1,300 who returned. And she had her two children with her.

It tells us that what we're doing makes a difference years later.

But every story does not have a happy ending. As much as we try to help the kids, a lot of them don't make it. But they've touched our lives in such a way that when we do lose them, they've given us the strength to keep going.

You can help support The Marty Lyons Foundation, 326 W. 48th St., New York, NY 10036. We also appreciate "in kind" donations, such as airplane tickets. And if you can't help financially, give us your thoughts and prayers. Maybe it will save a life.

The New York Jets have been supportive. And so have my former Alabama teammates, like Tony Nathan and Barry Krauss, as well as hundreds of other professional athletes, such as baseball's David Cone.

And I get a boost from [former Tide teammate] Rich Wingo. I have great respect for Rich for what he has done with his life. His pro career was cut short, but his life is an inspiration, a real role model. And when a child passes away—one of those valleys in the peaks and valleys—I can call Rich, and after talking to him a while, know that everything is going to be all right.

I went to Alabama because of the tradition and because of Coach Bryant. At the first Alabama game I went to as a prospect, Alabama won big, and it seemed about 100 Alabama guys played. The first time Coach Bryant met me, he shook my hand and told me, "I want you to come to The University of Alabama. I can't promise you anything, but if you're good enough, you'll get a chance."

I frequently thought Alabama was trying to get rid of me. In my freshmen year, the graduate assistant coaches working with me were Mike DuBose and Wayne Hall, and they did everything they could to find out if I was mentally and physically tough enough to make it. During my first year, I got to play a little at defensive end behind Leroy Cook. In my second year, I got moved inside, to tackle. I went from working under Dude Hennessey to playing for Ken Donahue. Although you don't realize it until later, anyone who had the opportunity to play for Coach Donahue came out of it a better player and, more important, a better person. We were the last ones off the field every day. I always enjoyed running, and it was a good thing. He stressed the fundamentals, which is probably why I was able to go into the National Football League and play at 245 pounds.

Most Alabama football players say the only thing they are promised in the recruiting process is the opportunity, that everything else is up to them. I was given one other promise, that I would have a chance to play baseball beginning in the spring of my sophomore season.

During my sophomore year, I played in every game behind Bob Baumhower. Then when the lettermen were announced, I didn't get a letter. I knew I had played more than some guys who got letters. So I went to see Coach Bryant.

I sat in that famous sofa where I nearly sank to the floor and looked up at him smoking his Chesterfield and looking down at me over those half glasses. I told him I thought I had played enough to letter. He said, "Marty, I'm not sure that letter means enough to you." Well, I thought I had an answer for anything he'd say, but I didn't have an answer for that.

Then I said I had one more thing. I wanted to ask him about playing baseball. He told me he had promised me that I could do that. Then he asked if he could give me some advice. That advice was, "Be good at one thing before you try to be good at two things." That was the end of my baseball career.

In looking back, I think he was right. That letter didn't mean enough to me then. But after that meeting, I was inspired to be an All-American. Coach Bryant knew how to treat men.

I have nothing but fond memories of my days at Alabama.

It starts with the players. There was a closeness that is difficult to describe. We practiced hard, we played hard, and we did things together off the field. And there was accountability. When we were in a big game, we knew we could trust one another.

When I went to the NFL, Richard Todd was with the Jets and kind of took me under his wing to shield me a little from the hazing rookies get. And we had guys all around the league, particularly in the East with Barry [Krauss] going to Indianapolis and Tony [Nathan] going to Miami. And Miami had Bob Baumhower and would later get Dwight [Stephenson] and Don McNeal. I couldn't have gone to a better place at a better time unless it was when Joe Namath—another former Alabama player—led the Jets to the Super Bowl championship.

And, of course, we had Coach Bryant. He was bigger than life. He was bigger than the government. Every year before the start of the season after I went to the Jets, I'd get a telegram from Coach Bryant wishing me good luck and the Jets good luck and reminding me to show my class.

And the Alabama fans could not have been more gracious to a guy from Florida who came to play there. When I was inducted into the Alabama Sports Hall of Fame, it was one of the biggest moments of my life.

I have a lot of sadness that I have to deal with, with our children. But I have never been sadder than the day I learned of Coach

Bryant's death. I cried like a baby. I had lost my coach and a man who had allowed me to become his friend. There is no man who could have had my greater respect and who could have been more influential other than my own father.

> *Marty Lyons was All-America in 1978 and defensive captain of Alabama's national championship team. He was All-SEC in 1977 and 1978 and was selected to Alabama's Team of the Century and to the Team of the Decade for the '70s. He was elected to the College Football Hall of Fame in May 2011.*

## BRYANT THE TACTICIAN

Though he had won more games than any coach in college football history by the time he retired, Bryant was not particularly noted for being an innovator, either offensively or defensively. More often, he took what other coaches had introduced to the game and perfected it.

The most notable example of this was the installation of the wishbone offense. After three disappointing seasons, Bryant consulted during the winter of 1970–1971 with Texas coach Darrell Royal, whose longtime assistant, Emory Bullard, had invented the offense some years earlier. The Crimson Tide installed the wishbone in total secrecy the following fall, unveiling it in a nationally televised, season-opening game at Southern Cal. Alabama would run some variation of the offense for Bryant's final 12 seasons, winning 124 games, nine SEC championships, and three national titles from 1971 to 1982.

"The wishbone offense fit Coach Bryant perfectly because he was such a strong believer in winning games with good defense and a sound kicking game," longtime assistant Mal Moore said.

"And the wishbone fit that philosophy. He told us we were going to open the 1971 season against Southern Cal with the wishbone, and we were going to close the season against Auburn with the wishbone. There would be no changing our minds.

"It was a total team effort. The wishbone is a team-oriented, ball-control offense. Everyone gets hit, everyone is involved in blocking. It takes 11 people. You're not counting on one player having a great game. It fit Coach Bryant at that time in our history."

The wishbone utilized smaller, quicker offensive linemen, something Bryant had always recruited. It also left at least two defenders unblocked on each play, which meant the Crimson Tide could put many of its best athletes on defense. Above all, it got the entire offensive unit involved in the game. The wishbone called for mass substitutions at several positions, even quarterback.

"Coach Bryant believed in playing men if they had earned it," said Steadman Shealy, who quarterbacked Alabama to a national title in 1979. "I probably played about 10 snaps a game as a sophomore and about 25 snaps a game as a junior, backing up Jeff [Rutledge]. And why not play the backup quarterbacks? Everyone needs to play. I'm convinced that when the backup gets a chance, he gives about 110 percent effort. I think it's ridiculous the way teams play just one quarterback."

Though the wishbone was primarily (and perhaps secondarily as well) a running offense, Bryant was not afraid to call for the big pass play when it was needed. Alabama and Tennessee both entered the 1973 game at Birmingham's Legion Field undefeated, but Bryant decided to try and establish his team's dominance on the first play of the game.

"Coach Bryant set the play up," split end Wayne Wheeler remembered. "We had opened every game that year with a dive play out of the wishbone. Gary Rutledge was our quarterback, and before the game, Coach Bryant told him and me that we were going to throw it on the first play of the game. I was wide open, and we had an 80-yard touchdown to start the game."

As he showed with the wishbone, Bryant had never been afraid to rely on the unconventional if it helped the Crimson Tide win games. With All-Americans such as Namath, Steve Sloan, and Ken Stabler under center in the 1960s, Alabama's offenses were often considered pass-happy for their day.

Bryant often utilized trick plays, as well. One of his favorites was the tackle-eligible pass, which briefly made Jerry Duncan a star when he caught a fourth-down pass against Ole Miss in 1965 and later hauled in several during the Crimson Tide's Orange Bowl win over Nebraska for the national championship.

"In those days, you could line up so that the tackle was an eligible pass receiver," Duncan said. "In fact, they would change the rule later because of the success we had. We ran three or four tackle-eligible plays, including one on the first play of the game, and we used three or four onside kicks. By the time we got to the fourth quarter, our offense had kept their defense on the field so long they were exhausted. We won 39–28."

Of course, Bryant was at heart a defensive coach. The numbers, as relayed by Darwin Holt, tell the story better than any anecdotes could. "I did a little research on Coach Bryant," Holt said. "He was head coach in 425 games. He won 323 of them and tied 17 others. And in those 425 games, the opponent scored seven points or fewer in 235 games. His teams had 93 shutouts. Goose eggs, he called them."

## Crimson Tide in Their Own Words

# KEN STABLER

### QUARTERBACK, 1965–1967

From the day you first pull on that crimson jersey to the end of your life, you reap the reward of playing football for Alabama. That reward is in being remembered. It may be for something specific, or it may be just for being a former Crimson Tide player.

It still amazes me the number of people who will tell me about seeing the run in the mud. The details of the rain and wind, umbrellas turned inside out, clothes ruined, and yet they stayed to watch as we beat Auburn 7–3 in 1967. And I hear this virtually every day from some Alabama fan. I listen to the whole story because it is a thrill for them, and it is a great feeling for me that they remember. And we old Alabama players like to talk about Alabama football, too, particularly a win over Auburn.

A lot of people think the Alabama-Auburn game is the most emotional rivalry in college football, and it is gratifying to have been part of a play that will live forever because it was Alabama-Auburn and a game-winning play. I go through airports, and inevitably someone will yell, "Roll, Tide" or "Hey, Snake."

I have two daughters, and it's great for them to see where Dad fit into the mix in the legacy of Alabama football, to see people ask me for autographs or talk to me because I am a former Alabama player. They can look at the photographs or even the old films, but it is the people who make it real.

To have been an Alabama football player is, as Coach Bryant said, to be part of a family. And no matter your role, you were a productive part of that family.

And more than anything, Alabama football was Coach Bryant. I don't think I realized what he was doing for me until I was old enough to look back on it. In my case, I was young and dumb and wild, and when I became a disciplinary problem, Coach Bryant disciplined me. At the time I couldn't see it, but he was teaching me a life lesson. I was close to throwing everything away, and he saw something worth saving. He suspended me, then gave me the opportunity to get back. Don't think I got off light. I got the hell beat out of me at practice, but he didn't let me throw it away.

Coach Bryant had a knack for treating everyone fairly, and in a way that everyone thought was the same. You believed that he was as polite to the janitors cleaning up the stadium as he was to the president of the university, that he treated the fourth-team guard the same way he treated the All-American.

He was taking care of me. He saw I needed a kick in the pants. I was just about to throw away my college career, which led to a 15-year career in the NFL and to a lot of other good things in my life. Without Coach Bryant saving me, I guess I'd be a bartender somewhere.

He gave me two opportunities. The first was when he offered me a scholarship to the university. The second was when he saved me from myself with his discipline. He prepped me for the next level, the next level of football with his teaching of fundamentals and understanding, and the next level of life with lessons that seem to come back to me all the time.

The greatest disappointment was an excellent season. We were two-time defending national champions going into the 1966 season, and that year we went 11–0 and outscored our opponents 267–37 in the regular season. We had six shutouts. And then we beat Nebraska 34–7 in the Sugar Bowl. Yet we finished third in the nation.

Ken Stabler (12) was a masterful QB as a runner or passer in leading the Crimson Tide to a 34–7 victory over Nebraska in the Sugar Bowl for an undefeated 1966 season. After a fine pro career, Stabler joined the Alabama football radio broadcast team.

I had watched as a kid as Pat Trammell won a national championship, then watched Joe Namath and Steve Sloan win national championships, and I thought 1966 was my turn. We made a pretty good run, but we didn't get there. It was disappointing, but I believe we did all we could do.

I was around a lot of winning football. In high school under Coach Ivan Jones at Foley, we went 29–1 in my three years. Then at Alabama we were 28–3–2. And then I went to Oakland, where I played for John Madden, who was like a big brother. We made it to the championship game five times, then finally beat Pittsburgh to get to Super Bowl XI, where we beat Minnesota 32–14. And then I finished my career in New Orleans for Bum Phillips, who was like a grandfather. I always played for someone I respected and wanted to please.

I wasn't highly recruited out of high school. Dee Powell recruited me for Alabama, and Lee Hayley recruited me for Auburn, and I think I got some letters from Mississippi State and Tulane. I was a typical small-town athlete, playing football until it was time to play basketball and then playing basketball until it was time to play baseball and on and on.

My father was a huge Alabama fan. He would really get excited on Saturdays as we got ready to listen to Alabama games when Pat Trammell and Billy Richardson were playing in the early '60s. Being around him and listening to Alabama football on the radio sold me pretty early.

I did consider going straight to pro baseball. I threw hard and had a good overhand curve and good control. A Yankees scout offered me $50,000 and a college education. I had to take a pretty hard look at that. In 1964 in Foley, $50,000 was a lot of money, and it could have been a help to my family. My father was a hard-working mechanic for automobile dealerships, and we were probably lower-middle class. But we had the essentials and didn't absolutely have to have the money. My parents left it up to me and were genuinely supportive. They wanted me to be happy.

I loved baseball. But I also had a love of football and of Alabama.

Coach Bryant came to my house and had dinner with us and told me he wanted me to come to Alabama and play football. Alabama was winning; I wanted to follow in the footsteps of Trammell and Namath; I wanted to play for Coach Bryant; I wanted to win a national championship; and I wanted to be a part of the Alabama football lore that my father loved.

Looking back, I made the right decision to be a part of the Alabama family. And I always thought I would have a chance later to make some money as an athlete.

I love my relationship with the football program now, being able to participate as a member of the radio broadcasting team. It is a thrill to be close to the program where I played.

*Ken Stabler was an All-American, SEC Player of the Year in 1967, and MVP of the Sugar Bowl as he completed 12 of 17 passes for 218 yards and one touchdown, and rushed for 40 more yards and another touchdown. In 1992 he and Joe Namath were selected as quarterbacks on Alabama's Team of the Century.*

## BRYANT THE MENTOR

College football is ultimately a form of teaching, and Bryant wasn't just training his players to win games during their time in Tuscaloosa or in a potential future pro football career. He was teaching them to succeed in life, whatever their chosen profession.

Of course, many of Bryant's former players went on to coach. Some of them, like Gene Stallings, Danny Ford, Howard Schnellenberger, Charley Pell, Jackie Sherrill, and Mike Riley, went on to enjoy extraordinary success as college head coaches.

Stallings coached against Bryant only once, in the 1968 Cotton Bowl. His Texas A&M team pulled off a stunning upset of the Crimson Tide, winning 20–16. "When the game ended, I went to midfield to meet Coach Bryant and shake hands," Stallings said. "He stooped down and picked me up. I was in complete shock. He was saying congratulations. Alabama had the better team, and I'm sure he was disappointed in the way his team played, but he was happy for me. I think the majority of those who played for Coach

Bryant and worked for him all felt that he had a way of making us feel special. And I think he believed we were special. I loved him and appreciated that, cherished every one of his compliments."

Just as numerous are the former Alabama players who became lifelong assistants. Many of them got their start on Bryant's own Crimson Tide staff. "I had graduated in December after the 1972 season," John Mitchell remembered. "I was in Mobile and called Coach Bryant to see if my scholarship would extend to going to graduate school because my parents couldn't afford it. He said he wouldn't talk to me about it on the phone. So I drove up on a Wednesday to talk to him. I hoped he would give me some little graduate assistant position and pay for my school. Instead he said he was offering me a full-time job on his staff."

Bryant kept tabs on his former players who moved on to pro football, often sending good luck letters or telegrams at various times in their careers. All-America linebacker Woodrow Lowe remembers receiving one before each of his first seven seasons with the NFL's San Diego Chargers (Bryant died before Lowe's eighth season of 1983).

He would contact NFL coaches and advise them to draft a player he was particularly fond of. But just as important was the guidance Bryant gave those players when they were still in Tuscaloosa.

Quarterback Ken Stabler was an All-American for the Crimson Tide in 1966 but was just as noted for his wild off-field lifestyle. Stabler said he didn't realize until years later what Bryant had done for him. "At the time I couldn't see it, but he was teaching me a life lesson," Stabler said. "I was close to throwing everything away, and he saw something worth saving. He suspended me, and then gave me the opportunity to get back. Don't think I got off light. I got the hell beat out of me at practice, but he didn't let me throw it away. He was taking care of me. He saw I needed a kick in the pants. I was just about to throw away my college career, which led to a 15-year career in the NFL and to a lot of other good things in my life. Without Coach Bryant saving me, I guess I'd be a bartender somewhere."

Bryant was legendary for assisting his former players in their post-football lives, whether financially or with a well-timed phone call or letter or recommendation to a potential employer. He also donated generously with his time and money when former players were starting their own businesses or charitable organizations, as he did when John Croyle started the Big Oak Ranch, a foster home for abused children near Gadsden, Alabama. Croyle recalled:

> After my Alabama career was over, I told Coach Bryant I wanted to play pro football so I could earn the money to have the ranch. He knew I wasn't good enough to play pro football. But he told me not to do it unless I wanted to be married to it. He told me to follow my dream.
>
> Six days before he died, I went to see Coach Bryant. He wanted to know if a guy had sent me $1,000. I said he had. The man had asked Coach Bryant to sign a sweatshirt, and said if coach would do it he would send $1,000 to the Big Oak Ranch. That check was the last $1,000 we needed to build the Paul Bryant Home.
>
> I wanted to be someone in football. But I know if you are a great football player, but a loser inside, you haven't done anything. Coach Bryant was one who molded football players into men. I wasn't a football legend, but I wouldn't trade places with anyone I know. Being a legend might have been fun, but I would rather have helped a 10-year-old boy who had no other chance.

I have never been depressed and never had a second thought or second guess about what I do. And Coach Bryant saw that for me before I did.

---

## *Crimson Tide in Their Own Words*
# JOHN CROYLE
### DEFENSIVE END, 1971–1973

Maybe it was because I had just seen the movie *They Shoot Horses, Don't They?* that I had a little moment of panic. I had been working at wide receiver in practice my freshman year. I was running a drill and planted my foot. My knee started to separate about the time Robin Parkhouse hit it. When everything was over, my leg was just swinging. Every ligament but one was torn. Coach Bryant came over and looked at it and said, "What a waste." I thought they were going to shoot me.

Most people would say that was a bad time. But when I remember the good things about playing football at Alabama, I also remember the bad parts as being good. After that injury, I went to work. And I kept working and working. And then one day I knew I was going to make it back. Coach Goostree [trainer Jim Goostree] was watching me work out. He said, "It looks like you know what you're doing." That's when I knew I would make it. And I was lucky to play on football teams that won a lot of games. We just lost one regular season game and we were 32–4 and won a national championship.

As bad as the injury in 1970 may have seemed at the time, it taught me how to work. And that has helped me as I have carried on with children, including my biological children. It made me learn to persevere. And the rewards were getting back up and having a chance to play, and having Coach Bryant say, "Good job." That's a rush.

I know I'm only known now as Brodie's father. But I took positive experiences out of my Alabama playing career. And with Brodie having been injured, I have seen how he has learned to work. One day when he's grown, he'll know he has to get up and go to work.

Before every ball game, Coach Bryant would look at us and say, "In this game there will be four or five plays that will determine the outcome. You never know when they are coming. It's up to you if you'll be a winner or the goat on those plays." And that's the way it is in life. There are four or five plays in your life. One of mine was God using Coach Bryant to mold me into a man and making me a part of his family.

I knew for a long time I wanted to play for Alabama and Coach Bryant. When I was a sophomore in high school and on the basketball team for Coach John Bostick at Gadsden, we went to the state tournament in Tuscaloosa. At that age I was already about 6'4" and 195. A family friend, Dr. John Duncan, told me he wanted to introduce me to someone, and took me to the athletics offices. There was Coach Bryant. He said, "Hey, son," and that was the beginning of my devotion and commitment to him and to the university. I was immediately aware of his charisma, his mystique, and it only grew with the passing of time.

Three of my high school football coaches—Gerald Stephens, Clark Boler, and Ingram Culwell—had played for Coach Bryant, which helped sell me, too. And I was recruited by Dude Hennessey.

But it was Coach Bryant. He had "it." Alabama had a couple of down years in 1969 and 1970. Coach Bryant admitted later he had some distractions in that time. But we could just tell that

John Croyle was an outstanding defensive end who had to overcome severe injuries. His son, Brodie, was an Alabama quarterback, and his daughter, Reagan, was an Alabama basketball player and homecoming queen. John is best known now for his work with abused children.

things were about to get better. Think about the coaches—Ken Donahue, Dude Hennessey, Pat Dye, and Bill Oliver on defense; Mal Moore, John David Crow, Richard Williamson, Jack Rutledge, and Jimmy Sharpe on offense. Coach Bryant talked about surrounding yourself with winners, and he did.

He also had a gift. Not motivating people, although he was good at that, but finding motivated people and directing them. The great ones—Namath, Stabler—were strong characters, and it took a strong character to lead them.

In our first meeting he told us, "Don't tell me how good you are. Just go with me and win championships." And in September 1971 we went to Los Angeles and beat No. 1–ranked Southern Cal. Everyone knows we surprised them with the wishbone, but it was coaching and those intangibles you can't measure that made it possible.

We feared Coach Bryant. But I think you sometimes fear a person before you respect him. And he certainly had everyone's respect. He had an ability to get average guys to believe they could beat anyone in the country. I was just average, but he'd say things to me that would convince me I could run through a wall.

And he genuinely cared about each of us as a person. I had talked to him about what I wanted to do with my life, having a ranch for kids. He said, "When I left Arkansas, I tried to forget everything I knew about farming. I can't help you." But, of course, he did help.

I was 19 when I came up with the idea for a farm or ranch or something to help the children that no one else will help. I had worked at a summer camp in Mississippi. I met a boy whose mother was a prostitute in New Orleans and he handled her business. I taught the boy how to become a Christian. And he did. And he came back and told me; and I realized I had been given a gift to help kids who are hurting—to be a father figure, to guide them.

One year the Skywriters came to Tuscaloosa, and I was one of the ones being interviewed by these writers from all over the South. Someone asked me what I wanted to do, and I told them—build a home for kids. I remember Clyde Bolton of *The Birmingham News* was very skeptical. Now he's one of our staunchest supporters.

After my Alabama career was over, I told Coach Bryant I wanted to play pro football so I could earn the money to have the ranch. He knew I wasn't good enough to play pro football. But he told me not to do it unless I wanted to be married to it. He told me to follow my dream.

You don't really know how you are going to do something sometimes. I had gone with Woodrow Lowe on a speaking engagement. When we got back, my father said he wanted me to see something. It was 140 acres for sale for $45,000. Dr. William Buck, an oral surgeon in Birmingham, gave me $15,000, and John Hannah took his signing bonus and gave me $30,000. Our first house was the John Hannah Home. We would not be where we are without John Hannah.

Originally, the only plan was for a boys ranch. Then we met a 12-year-old girl whose mother had held her down while her father raped her. We wanted to keep her, but we had to send her home. She was murdered.

Now we have the girls ranch. And we were given a school that is midway between the boys ranch and the girls ranch. We operate without state or federal funds, and we are debt-free. We have more than 100 children who call the Big Oak Ranch their home. In 31 years we have had more than 1,500 children. A number have gone to college. These are people who just needed a chance. Our first child is now more than 50 years old.

When I was 24, I went to Coach Bryant and asked for three things: I wanted him to write a letter of endorsement; I wanted him to serve on our advisory board; and I wanted to build a Paul Bryant Home that was going to cost $70,000. He said okay to one and two, and "let's see" to number three.

Six days before he died, I went to see Coach Bryant. He wanted to know if a guy had sent me $1,000. I said he had. The man had asked Coach Bryant to sign a sweatshirt, and said if coach would do it he would send $1,000 to the Big Oak Ranch. That check was the last $1,000 we needed to build the Paul Bryant Home.

There is not a day that goes by that I don't use something I got from him. In business, or dealing with a boy who is being cantankerous, or hugging a little girl who just needs a chance. In your life you are going to impress, impact, or inspire. He was master of all three and best at the last. And that's the one that lasts. That's the one that lasts when you are gone. That's anywhere—on a football field, in business, or in a children's home.

I wanted to be someone in football. But I know if you are a great football player, but a loser inside, you haven't done anything. Coach Bryant was one who molded football players into men. I wasn't a football legend, but I wouldn't trade places with anyone I know. Being a legend might have been fun, but I would rather have helped a 10-year-old boy who had no other chance.

I have never been depressed and never had a second thought or second guess about what I do. And Coach Bryant saw that for me before I did.

When I was at Alabama, we all lived together in Bryant Hall, and I think that made us a family. And I see and talk to my former teammates often. I know the guys today have more freedom, but I think there was something to be said for living in the dorm and building team unity.

I can't tell you how many of those men I played with have helped us in our efforts to save children. And if you want to help, you can do so by contacting Big Oak Ranch, P.O. Box 507, Springville, AL 35146.

*John Croyle was winner of the "Jerry Duncan I Like to Practice Award" in 1972 and went on to earn second-team All-SEC the following season at defensive end.*

## BRYANT THE LEGEND

Roger Shultz, an All-SEC center at Alabama in 1990, never got to play for Bryant, he was too young. But as a child growing up in Birmingham in the 1970s, he was in awe of the man who had become a statewide and national legend by that time.

"In 1980 I was in the sixth grade, but some of us were going to get to go with the high school team to Legion Field and sell Cokes for the Alabama-Auburn game," Shultz remembered. "That would mean we could get into the game. We didn't have seats, so we stood around the fence. We got to see Coach Bryant in person."

Bryant won his last SEC championship in 1981, though he admitted the team lost a couple of games it might have won in earlier years. That was even truer the following year, when the Crimson Tide lost three straight games to end the regular season, including a particularly galling last-second defeat to Auburn.

Rumors of Bryant's imminent retirement had been circulating for years, but they became especially pronounced that fall. Bryant made it official in mid-December: the season-ending Liberty Bowl against Illinois would be his last game as a college football coach.

"When [longtime sports information director] Charley Thornton left to go to Texas A&M, I got the opportunity to work as host of the Bear Bryant television show each Sunday," Shealy said. "I may have been the first person to know he was going to retire. He said after the Southern Mississippi game that he wasn't on top of it, that he was allowing his assistants to make decisions he didn't agree with, that he thought maybe it was time to hang it up."

Alabama rallied to win that final game 21–15, sending Bryant out with a record 323 victories. By that time, one-time star end Ray Perkins, who was coaching the NFL's New York Giants, was already in place as Bryant's successor. Perkins remembered:

He called my office. "Raymond," he said—he was the only one who ever called me Raymond—"Raymond, are you interested in this thing down here?"

I said, "Coach Bryant, I would walk to Tuscaloosa for it."

He said, "Well, I didn't think you would be interested. I thought you were making so much money up here you wouldn't be interested."

I assured him I was interested.

That afternoon I got a call from Joab Thomas, the president of the university. He invited me down for an interview in Birmingham. The rest is history.

Bryant then set about his retirement, though it didn't last long. He died January 26, 1983, just 28 days after coaching his final

Paul Bryant was not the only great coach in Alabama football history, but his mark on Crimson Tide football and college football has never been equaled.

game. The news of Bryant's death reverberated across the state and in the hearts and minds of those he had coached and mentored through the years.

"I was sitting at my desk in the [Dallas] Cowboys' offices when Linda Knowles [Bryant's secretary] called me to tell me Coach Bryant had died," Stallings said. "Over the years, I've realized how many people know where they were when they heard the news, like when President Kennedy died. I was stunned. I couldn't believe it. I thought he would live forever. I was sort of in a fog for a while after I got the news, and obviously the people of Alabama felt the same way. Things just sort of came to a standstill."

Bryant's legacy has only grown in the nearly 30 years since his death, even as many of those who played and coached under him approach and enter old age. Steve Sloan, an All-America quarterback for the Crimson Tide in 1965 and later a college football coach and athletics director, said thoughts of Bryant will be with him for the remainder of his life:

> I know that everyone who had the opportunity to be exposed to Coach Bryant has thought about ways in which he affected their careers, and that may be more frequent for those of us who remained in athletics. He had a stronger personality than I have. He was a little tougher than I can be. But his planning and organization and all those things have really helped me out in my career in athletics. People like Coach Bryant don't come along very often. He's in a class with people like General Patton—forceful, charismatic. I always think of him fondly.
>
> I think the driving force for him was that he had grown up poor and he never wanted to be poor again. He was exceptional in a lot of ways.

*chapter 4*

# ALABAMA'S OTHER GREAT COACHES

EVERYONE WHO HAS EVER COACHED or will coach football at Alabama lives in the shadow of Paul Bryant, but "the Bear" is far from the only great coach in Crimson Tide history. Here's a look at some of the other men, both head coaches and assistants, who helped shape Alabama football over the years.

## WALLACE WADE, HEAD COACH 1923–1930

Hired away from Vanderbilt when Xen Scott was forced to resign due to illness, Wallace Wade went 61–13–3 and won three national championships during eight years with the Crimson Tide. He took Alabama to its first bowl game, the 1926 Rose Bowl, where the Crimson Tide beat Washington 20–19 to secure its first national title.

Wade also led the Crimson Tide to four Southern Conference championships and recruited and coached such stars as Pooley Hubert, Johnny Mack Brown, Hoyt "Wu" Winslett, and Fred Sington. He left Alabama in 1931, following a dispute with university president George Denny, and went on to coach 20 years at Duke.

Nearly all of the men who played for or coached with Wade at Alabama have long since died, but former Crimson Tide halfback Howard Chappell shared the following thoughts in 2005:

Wallace Wade won three national championships in eight seasons as head coach at Alabama, then left for Duke, where the Blue Devils' football stadium is named in his honor.

I went to Tuscaloosa during the 1929 season and told Coach Wade that I wanted to come to Alabama to play football. He said, "You're mighty small." And I said, "Yes, but I'm mighty fast." And he said he liked that because we were going to be playing against teams with fast guys. And he gave me a scholarship beginning in the fall of 1930.

Freshmen couldn't play in those days. So I practiced all year but couldn't play in games. And when the team went to the Rose Bowl at the end of the 1930 season, Coach Wade told me that he was sorry, but that since I wasn't eligible to play, I wasn't eligible to make the trip. And I had practiced all year against those great players. I particularly remember kickoff practice after we had finished practice. I'd return three or four of them and be worn out.

Even though I never got to play in a game for Coach Wade, I learned a lot from him. He was a wonderful coach. He was as good as Bryant, and as tough—tough as nails. He meant for you to do what he said to do.

Wallace Wade was inducted into the College Football Hall of Fame in 1955, and Duke's football stadium was renamed in his honor in 1967. He died in 1986 at age 94.

## Frank Thomas

Many would say that Frank Thomas is Alabama's second-greatest football coach after Bryant. He posted 115 victories, four SEC championships, and two national titles in 15 seasons with the Crimson Tide.

Thomas recruited and coached several of Alabama's all-time legends, including Bryant, Dixie Howell, Don Hutson, and Harry Gilmer. A Notre Dame graduate and protégé of the legendary Knute Rockne, Thomas won 81 percent of his games before being forced to resign due to health reasons following the 1946 season.

"Coach Thomas was one in a million," said Ben McLeod, a Crimson Tide end in the 1930s. "I think he was a great football coach because he had an uncanny knack of anticipating what the opposition was going to do. He never hollered or bullied his teams into producing their best but had a quiet and firm control on his players. When he wanted something done, it was done."

Said longtime Alabama assistant Clem Gryska, "I was fortunate to play for Coach Thomas for two years before he became too ill to coach. Years later when I was working for Coach Bryant, who had played for Coach Thomas, I could see where Coach Bryant had learned a lot of lessons from Coach Thomas. That was particularly true in organization and attention to detail. Under

Frank Thomas, shown here with All-Americans Harry Gilmer (52) and Vaughn Mancha (41), won a pair of national titles at Alabama, in 1934 and 1941.

both, you ran a play correctly. And that meant doing it over and over and over until every detail was perfect. Any mistake and the whistle meant, 'Do it again.'"

Thomas was inducted into the College Football Hall of Fame in 1951, and Alabama's baseball facility—Sewell-Thomas

Stadium—is conamed for him and Baseball Hall of Famer Joe Sewell (an Alabama graduate). Thomas died in 1954 at age 55 following a lengthy battle with heart trouble.

---

*Crimson Tide in Their Own Words*

# CECIL "HOOTIE" INGRAM

## CORNERBACK AND QUARTERBACK, 1952–1954

There was never any doubt in my mind that I was going to play football for Alabama, and the reason for that is Coach Frank Thomas, even though I never got to play for him. I grew up in Tuscaloosa, and Coach Thomas' son, Hugh, was one of my closest friends growing up. Even though he was not my neighbor, I thought of Coach Thomas the way you would think of a next door neighbor.

That he would be instrumental in me signing with Alabama is understandable.

But not many people know that Coach Thomas is probably the reason that Willie Mays signed with the New York Giants. I was at the Thomas house one evening eating sandwiches when the doorbell rang. It was an old Notre Dame classmate of Coach Thomas. The guy was a scout for the New York Giants baseball team. He said he was headed to Florida to look at some players and just stopped by to say hello.

Coach Thomas was a great baseball fan. He told this scout that we were getting ready to go see the best baseball player in the world. I can remember the guy saying he knew what a poor-mouther Tommy was, and I guess that's what convinced him to go see this player.

The Birmingham Black Barons were playing at Alberta Park, and Willie Mays played for them. I guess he had a typical game. I remember he had a triple and that he threw a guy out at home.

After the game, the scout said, "I don't know if he's the best in the world, but he's among them." The scout also said that the one thing they'd have to teach Mays is how to catch a ball, that he couldn't use that basket catch. The scout didn't go to Florida, and he did sign Willie Mays. And, of course, Willie Mays continued to use that basket catch and is in the Hall of Fame.

I also remember Coach Thomas came back from spring training one year and said he had seen a skinny kid trying to make the Braves. He said he had the best wrists he had ever seen, and, of course, he was talking about Hank Aaron.

Coach Thomas had become too ill to coach after the 1946 season, and I played for Coach Drew. But Coach Thomas stayed active and interested in Alabama football. He didn't want to just sit around and die. He had people who would drive him to practice. He'd sit in his car and watch baseball games from behind the right-field fence and park just beyond the corner of the end zone to watch football games. He died in May 1954, prior to my senior season.

After I got to Alabama, I would go on Thursday nights to his house and visit with him, spending an hour or two with him. He wanted to know what we were doing in practice, how we planned to stop Georgia Tech, or whatever. He enjoyed talking football strategy. Even when he was dying, he wanted to stay in there with football, to keep up.

The last year he coached, he was unable to move, and so they built him a little house on wheels with glass all around. He had a chair and a microphone and speaker, and that's how he coached practice.

Cecil "Hootie" Ingram was a record-setting cornerback in the '50s and returned to Alabama as athletics director to hire Gene Stallings as head coach in 1990.

One of my great thrills was in a game at Denny Stadium when he was parked down in the corner of the end zone with Mr. Hocutt and Mr. Pate. I was playing safety, and the opponent threw one of those throwback passes that if you intercept, there is no one in front of you. I picked it off, ran it back, and kept going on straight for his car—I could see how happy Coach Thomas was.

Alabama didn't have to recruit me. I had been practicing to be an Alabama player since I was in about the fourth grade. And I spent a lot of time on the Alabama practice fields watching as a kid.

I got letters from other schools, but I was never going anywhere else. One day during basketball season, Coach Crisp asked me when I was going to sign. I told him I didn't know I had an offer.

He told me to come by his office the next day, which I did. He then sent me to Coach Lew Bostick's office to sign the scholarship. Coach Bostick told me it was out on the table, to fill it out and sign it. And I did. Years later when I was working for the Southeastern Conference, I went back in the files and found my scholarship papers that I had filled out myself.

I was playing baseball my freshman year after spring practice, and Coach Crisp came by to see what I was going to do in the summer. He told me I needed to stay in shape "because it looks like we're going to have to play you next fall." It wasn't exactly a compliment.

I may have set a record in my first game as a sophomore. It was against Southern Miss in Montgomery. I fumbled three times, but I also recovered three fumbles. I only touched the ball three times—one punt return and two interceptions. It was raining, and the ball was slick, and on each of the times I had the ball, I fumbled when I got hit. But I was able to get all three of them back.

That 1952 team was good, the one that beat Syracuse 61–6 in the Orange Bowl. One of our biggest wins was against Maryland, which had won the national championship the year before. Our pregames were usually the same. Coach Drew would say the same thing every game, and when he finished he'd say, "Coach Hank, you got anything to say?" And Coach Crisp would say, "Nah." But this time was different. He gave us a Knute Rockne–type speech, telling us we couldn't compete with Maryland, but to just go out and do the best we could and not get hurt. We beat them 27–7. The thing that stands out to me was that we were leading 14–7 late in the game, and Maryland had fourth down from their 10 with five or six minutes to play. And they went for it. I intercepted the ball at about the 40. If I had just knocked it down, we would have had the ball at their 10. But I intercepted it and ran it back for a touchdown. One of the writers wrote that I must have had more confidence in myself than I did in our offense.

I went into the Army after my Alabama career, but I wanted to coach. I was at Brookwood High School when Coach Bryant came back. Jerry Claiborne came out to one of our practices to look at our kids. Usually those coaches would just stay a few minutes, but Jerry stayed the whole practice. When it was over, he said, "You're running our stuff," meaning the schemes Coach Bryant was putting in at Alabama. I said, "No, you're running our stuff." And I took him in and showed him the playbooks that I had from Coach Thomas—who had been Bryant's coach.

I couldn't help but notice over the years the number of things that Coach Bryant had taken from Coach Thomas. I think Coach Bryant would have been great no matter where he had been, but he obviously had taken so many things from Coach Thomas, like bragging on his players even when they lost, taking the blame for things that went wrong, and poor-mouthing after a win.

I had a career in coaching and then in administration. I went from the SEC office to being athletics director at Florida State, and then was fortunate enough to return to my hometown as athletics director at Alabama in 1989. At the end of that year I had to hire a football coach, and we had to get someone stable, someone who was fundamentally sound. Coach Sam Bailey had told me before that not just anyone could coach at Alabama. He said that at a lot of places a guy could get through the season and then have a hobby, fishing or playing golf. But that at Alabama being the head football coach was an everyday deal, that he had to have a thick skin and be able to bow his neck and get through the tough times.

I had known Gene Stallings when he was an assistant at Alabama and when he was at Texas A&M, and I knew he had done a great job for Coach Bryant and Coach Landry. I knew he could take the heat and do the job, and that's why I chose him. I think Dr. Sayers may have been skeptical, but he wasn't after he met Gene. And I don't think we could have gotten anyone who could have done a better job. And we got along great, maybe because we were both pretty ornery, two hard-headed people working together.

> *Cecil "Hootie" Ingram was All-SEC as he set Alabama records with*
> *10 interceptions for 163 yards in returns and two touchdowns in*
> *1952. The 10 interceptions was best in the nation that year.*

---

## GENE STALLINGS

A survivor of Bryant's infamous 1954 "Junction Boys" training camp as a player at Texas A&M, Gene Stallings was considered something of a coaching retread when Alabama hired him in 1990. Following a seven-year tenure as a Crimson Tide assistant under Bryant (where he was noted for being the lone staffer who pushed to suspend star quarterback Joe Namath following a 1963 arrest), Stallings had had limited success in head-coaching stops at his alma mater and the NFL's St. Louis/Phoenix Cardinals.

Stallings posted a 7–5 record in his first year at Alabama (though the Crimson Tide did beat Tennessee and Auburn), and then things took off in 1991. The Crimson Tide went 11–1 that year, then won the SEC and national championships with a 13–0 record in 1992, and posted two more 10-win seasons before Stallings stepped down following the 1996 season with a record of 70–16–1 and four SEC West Division titles.

"I knew he could take the heat and do the job, and that's why I chose him," said Hootie Ingram, the athletics director who hired Stallings. "I think [university president Roger] Sayers may have been skeptical, but he wasn't after he met Gene. And I don't

Gene Stallings never expected to be 'Bama's head coach after he was passed over for the job in 1983 following Paul Bryant's retirement, but he was hired seven years later.

think we could have gotten anyone who could have done a better job. And we got along great, maybe because we were both pretty ornery, two hard-headed people working together."

Said Eric Curry, an All-America defensive end in 1992, "Coach Stallings was a great believer in post-practice conditioning. One day before we ran, Derrick Oden, one of our captains, had the courage to say, 'Coach, if you don't run us after practice today and just let us off every now and then, we promise you we'll win the national championship.' He promised that everyone would give it his all in practice. I can't remember if Coach Stallings ran us after that practice—I think he did—but from time to time he would reward a good spring practice by giving us a day off from running. I loved Coach Stallings. He was a player's coach. As best I can tell, he was the next best thing to Paul 'Bear' Bryant."

Now retired and living in his native Texas, Stallings was inducted into the College Football Hall of Fame in 2010. His son, John Mark, who was born with Down Syndrome and was a fixture around the Alabama program during his father's coaching days, died in 2008.

## NICK SABAN

Alabama football was at a crossroads in 2007, having had four head coaches since Stallings retired 11 years earlier. The Crimson Tide needed a proven winner, and athletics director Mal Moore pulled off a coaching coup when he hired Nick Saban away from the NFL's Miami Dolphins.

Saban, the son of a coach who played defensive back at Kent State, spent more than two decades as a college and NFL assistant before head-coaching jobs at Toledo, Michigan State, and LSU. He won two SEC championships and the 2003 national title in five seasons at LSU before departing for the NFL.

Saban immediately began rebuilding the Alabama program from the ground up, and the Crimson Tide suffered through a 7–6 record in his debut season. But Alabama has been among college football's elite ever since, posting a 36–5 record the last three years, highlighted by the 2009 national championship.

Noted as tireless in recruiting and near-obsessive in preparation, Saban can come off as somewhat gruff to those who don't know him well. But Greg McElroy, the quarterback on that national title team two years ago, said that Saban is the ultimate player's coach:

> Coach Saban is not at all what people take him to be. He is very serious, very driven, but he has a soft spot for all his players. He wants his players to be successful in every area, including football, but not exclusively football.
>
> Coach Saban has a very high intellect. From a football standpoint, he does a great job of scripting defenses, devising defenses that are well-disguised. His defenses make life very difficult for a quarterback. Even though he is a defensive coach, he is hands-on about everything we do as a team.
>
> I didn't spend a lot of one-on-one time with Coach Saban insofar as watching film, for instance. That's something I prefer to do by myself. And I spent a lot of time with [offensive coordinator Jim] McElwain. But that said, Coach Saban and I had a great relationship on and off the field.
>
> Coach Saban is a coach you want to win for. You want to go out and do your best job, put on a good show. I wouldn't say that you play the game to win for your coach. You play the game for the fun of it. But you want to execute and you want to win. You want the coach to feel good and you want to feel good about yourself on Monday when you begin to prepare for the next game.

Saban has posted a 43–11 record with the Crimson Tide through 2010, and is the first modern-era college football coach to win national championships at two schools. Now in his late fifties, he has said Alabama will be his last coaching stop.

Nick Saban, who took over as head coach in 2007, hoists the BCS trophy after the Crimson Tide won the BCS National Championship Game 37–21 over the Texas Longhorns at the Rose Bowl on January 7, 2010. *Photo courtesy of Getty Images*

## GREAT ASSISTANTS

Bryant once said that the key to success in coaching is to surround yourself with winners. Through the years, Alabama head coaches have taken that philosophy to heart. Here are some of the Crimson Tide's all-time great assistant coaches.

## Hank Crisp

Perhaps best known as the assistant coach who recruited Paul "Bear" Bryant to Alabama, Hank Crisp served a total of 30 years on the staffs of five Crimson Tide head coaches: Xen Scott, Wallace Wade, Frank Thomas, Red Drew, and Ears Whitworth. Known as "Hustlin' Hank," he also served for several years as the Crimson Tide's basketball coach and athletics director.

"Anything I accomplished in football I owe to Coach Crisp," former Alabama lineman Harry Lee said. "He took an interest in me and was an excellent coach."

Crisp died in 1970 at age 73 and was soon after inducted into the Alabama Sports Hall of Fame. The Crimson Tide's indoor football practice and tennis facility is named in his honor.

## Ken Donahue

Perhaps the greatest of all Alabama assistant coaches, Ken Donahue led Crimson Tide defenses that 10 times led the SEC in scoring defense and seven times in total defense. A former star lineman at Tennessee, Donahue coached at Alabama for 21 years, serving on five national championship staffs under Bryant.

"Coach Donahue was something," nose guard Gus White said. "After I got there, I thought I must have gotten a track scholarship. We'd practice and then everyone would be gone except the defensive linemen. He kept us out there running. Looking back, I would thank him every day if he was here. It was that conditioning that made the difference in a lot of games. He said that fatigue would make a coward of you, and he wasn't going to let that happen to us. He prepared us mentally and physically."

Donahue stayed on with coach Ray Perkins for two years following Bryant's retirement, but retired himself following the 1984 season. He died in 2001 at age 76 but in 2009 won the American Football Coaches Association Outstanding Achievement Award.

---

## *Crimson Tide in Their Own Words*

# RAY PERKINS

### SPLIT END, 1964–1966

I can give you a short answer as to why I chose Alabama to play football and go to college. Alabama was the only school that offered me a scholarship. Dude Hennessey recruited me for Alabama. He came to a game on Friday night, and following the game he offered me a scholarship.

Alabama was the only school that recruited me. Alabama was the only school that invited me for a visit. I went to Alabama when they played North Carolina State in 1961. Roman Gabriel was North Carolina State's quarterback. I had a great visit. I got to meet Coach Bryant and talk with him for a little while. They made me feel like I was wanted.

It worked out great that Alabama would be the only school that recruited me because Alabama was the only school I was interested in. I had wanted to go to Alabama since I was a sophomore in high school.

One of those odd things is that I had a cousin who was a good friend of a nephew of Coach Bryant. All he could talk about was Coach Bryant and winning. And he told me if I went to Alabama to play for Coach Bryant, that I could play for anyone—that if I went to Alabama, I would win. Winning was a big thing to me when I was young. I wanted to win.

Ray Perkins (88) was an outstanding receiver for quarterbacks like Joe Namath (12) in the mid-'60s at Alabama. In 1983 he replaced Coach Bryant as Alabama's head coach, where he mentored players like quarterback Mike Shula (11).

I grew up in Petal, Mississippi. Across the river, in Hattiesburg, was a guy named Andy Anderson who was a big fan of Coach Bryant and Alabama. I met him when I was a sophomore in high school, and he gave me an Alabama press guide. I read through it, all the tidbits about Alabama and Coach Bryant and the players, and got it in my mind I wanted to go to Alabama.

One good bit of information I got from Coach Bryant's nephew through my cousin was that we did win at Alabama. The five years I was there were five of the greatest years of my life. And what made it that way was the football success—the winning.

We won two national championships and three SEC championships during the years I played in 1964, 1965, and 1966. Our record was 30–2–1.

The players from that era still have a great bond. We meet somewhere every year to go hunting or do something, 20 or 30 of us. I enjoy that little reunion because my time as an Alabama player was a great time, a very memorable time.

After I left Alabama, I played for the Baltimore Colts and Coach Don Shula from 1967 through 1971. I spent one year coaching receivers at Mississippi State, then went back to the NFL. I coached receivers at New England (1974–1977), was offensive coordinator at San Diego in 1978, then was with the New York Giants from 1979 to 1982.

Being head coach at Alabama was a dream come true. I had thought about that job for a long time before I got it. Every year Coach Bryant came to the National Football Foundation Hall of Fame banquet in New York, and he would always call me and ask me to sit with him at his table. He did that in 1982. He had already announced that he was retiring at the end of the season, and it had already been announced that his last game would be the Liberty Bowl.

The next morning he called my office. "Raymond," he said. He was the only one who ever called me Raymond. "Raymond, are you interested in this thing down here?"

I said, "Coach Bryant, I would walk to Tuscaloosa for it."

He said, "Well, I didn't think you would be interested. I thought you were making so much money up here you wouldn't be interested."

I assured him I was interested.

That afternoon I got a call from Joab Thomas, the president of the university. He invited me down for an interview in Birmingham. The rest is history.

The most meaningful thing about my time as a player at Alabama were the people I played with, the coaches I played for, and of course, Coach Bryant. I love the memory of Coach Bryant because he meant a lot to me as a coach and later as a friend.

The most meaningful thing about my time as coach was the players. And I still hear from a lot of them and keep up with a lot of them. That is rewarding.

Having my quarterback, Mike Shula, back at Alabama as head coach means a lot to me.

So the most meaningful thing is the people I met and played with and had associations with—and still do. I made a lot of great friends with those two experiences.

One of the things I'm asked most about is whether I wish I had turned down the Tampa Bay opportunity after the 1986 season and perhaps stayed at Alabama for a 15- or 20-year career. I can't say I have never thought about that, but it has been very little. I don't dwell on it. In the coaching business you make decisions based on the information you have and try to do what is best. And just as I don't think about making the decision to go to Tampa Bay, I've never dwelled on the question of whether I should have stayed in New York and not taken the Alabama job. There's no use in playing that game.

I did go to Tampa Bay for four years and then I thought I was retired from football. But in 1992 Charley Thornton, who had been sports information director at Alabama when I played, called from Arkansas State, where he was athletics director. That was not a great job, but I went back into football. I stayed just one year at Arkansas State, then went back to the NFL as offensive coordinator at New England, then offensive coordinator at Oakland, and finally spent a couple of years at Cleveland before retiring from football for good.

*Ray Perkins was an All-American in 1966 and was captain of Alabama's undefeated team. He set an Alabama bowl record with nine receptions in the 1966 Orange Bowl as Alabama defeated Nebraska 39–28 to win the national championship. He had an Alabama bowl record 178 yards in the 1967 Sugar Bowl. He played in two Super Bowls. He was Alabama head coach from 1983 to 1986 and in the NFL was head coach of the New York Giants and Tampa Bay Buccaneers.*

## Pat Dye

Pat Dye was so well-respected during his nine years at Alabama that many people thought he would one day succeed Bryant as head coach. The former Georgia All-American was a standout recruiter for the Crimson Tide from 1965 to 1973, signing such standouts as Wilbur Jackson and Gus White.

"Midway through my senior year [of high school], I blew out a knee when I got clipped," White said. "I had surgery and was in a cast from my toes to my hip. I thought football might be over. Just about everybody dropped me except Coach Dye. He continued to call and check on me. He said he had made a commitment to me and if I wanted to play football for Alabama, I would have a scholarship."

Dye coached at East Carolina and Wyoming before landing the Auburn job in 1981. He won 99 games in 12 years with the Tigers and was inducted into the College Football Hall of Fame in 2005.

## Clem Gryska

A halfback at Alabama in the late 1940s, Clem Gryska was one of the top recruiters on Paul "Bear" Bryant's staffs from 1960 to 1976. He was instrumental in signing John Mitchell, the first black star player in Crimson Tide history.

"It seems that Coach [John] McKay had told Coach Bryant they were going to sign an Alabama boy who was playing at Eastern Arizona," Mitchell said. "Coach Bryant got on the phone to Coach Gryska and told him to recruit me. They never even saw a film of me. [Alabama] recruited me strictly on the basis that, if Southern Cal wanted me, I must be good enough."

Gryska served for many years as the unofficial tour guide at the Paul W. Bryant Museum, retiring in 2010 after 50 years of being employed by his alma mater.

## Mal Moore

Alabama has won 13 national championships, and Mal Moore has been directly involved in more than half of them. He was a backup quarterback on the Crimson Tide's 1961 title team, then won six more rings as an assistant coach under Paul Bryant in 1964, 1965, 1973, 1978, and 1979, and under Gene Stallings in 1992. Moore was quarterbacks coach and unofficial offensive coordinator under both Bryant and Stallings, and was instrumental in the Crimson Tide's mastery of the wishbone offense in the 1970s.

"After my playing career, I stayed around as a graduate assistant while I was in law school," former Alabama quarterback Steadman Shealy said. "By then I had a lot of confidence in knowing the offense, and it was then that I recognized what a great wishbone innovator Coach Moore was."

Moore has been Alabama's athletics director since 1999, contributing to an eighth national championship when he hired Nick Saban as coach in 2007. The Crimson Tide's football building was renamed in his honor in 2006.

## Crimson Tide in Their Own Words
# STEADMAN SHEALY
### QUARTERBACK, 1977–1979

There were probably a lot of reasons for me to not go to Alabama to play football. When I signed in 1975, Alabama had Jeff Rutledge and Jack O'Rear and five other quarterbacks. I was one of about five guys who signed that year who had been high school quarterbacks, although I was the only one of the freshmen who worked at quarterback.

I wasn't going to a place to turn it around. Alabama had a record of 54–6 in the five years before I got there. Alabama wasn't even recruiting me as hard as Auburn or Mississippi State or Georgia Tech.

I was sitting in our living room in Dothan with Doug Barfield, who was Auburn's head coach. Vince Dooley of Georgia was out front of the house in his car waiting for Coach Barfield to leave so he could talk to me. The phone rang, and my mother came in and said, "It's Coach Bryant."

I went to the phone, and he asked, "What jersey have you always wanted to wear?"

"Crimson," I answered.

"Then what's the problem?" he said.

To be honest, I didn't think Alabama was all that hot to sign me. My sister was a "Bear Girl," and all the Shealys had graduated from Alabama, and I had always been an Alabama fan. Paul Crane was the first coach to recruit me for Alabama, then Bill Oliver. Years later, after I had finished playing and was helping Mal Moore with the quarterbacks while I was in law school, Dee

Powell and Bobby Marks would dig Coach Moore about when they were recruiting me. Coach Moore had said, "We'll take him, but we'll never win any championships with him."

And so Alabama took me over Charley Trotman, and Auburn took Charley Trotman over me.

Arriving at Alabama was unreal. I can remember being interviewed and being asked, "What's it like being in a long line of great quarterbacks?" And then he started naming them: Bart Starr, Pat Trammell, and on and on through Namath, Sloan, Stabler and the rest. And that's when it started sinking in: what an opportunity! Quarterback at Alabama is a long, rich tradition. And I felt God had led me to go there.

I had to prove myself to Coach Moore, and it took a while. During my freshman year, I quarterbacked the junior varsity team. In 1977 I went in for the first time in the second game of the year at Nebraska. That was the game where Jeff Rutledge threw five interceptions, and we lost 31–24, the only game we lost that year. It was not an auspicious debut. On the first play, I fell down for about a five-yard loss.

I was probably going to be redshirted in 1977, but Jack O'Rear tore up his knee, and I got to play eight or 10 plays in every game. Even after the loss to Nebraska, we kept fighting back. We went to Los Angeles and upset Southern Cal, which was ranked No. 1. I got to play a lot in that game.

The thing I remember most about that trip came before the game. Jeff, Keith Pugh, and I got together before games to pray. I'd pray for things like for God to keep us safe and help us play our best, that sort of thing. And then Keith prayed and said that he knew that game wasn't that important in the great scheme of things. I had never thought about that.

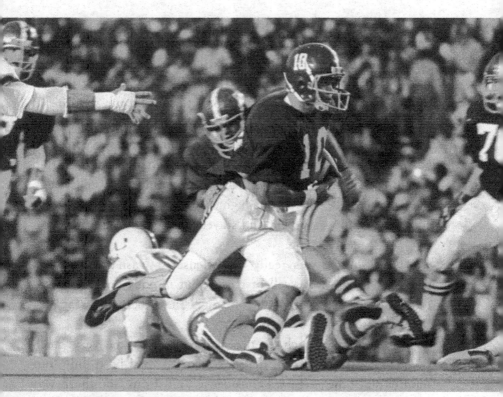

Steadman Shealy (10) was Alabama's leading rusher (791 yards) and passer (717) when he quarterbacked 'Bama to a 12–0 season and the 1979 national championship.

Our lives revolved around football. It was basically 16 hours a day. All I did six days a week was football, watch film, eat, study, and sleep. That was the commitment you have to have at Alabama.

When we went to the Sugar Bowl to play Ohio State, we thought if Notre Dame could beat Texas, which was No. 1, we could win the national championship. All that happened, except Notre Dame went from fifth to first, and we finished second.

Coach Bryant showed a lot of faith in me in that Sugar Bowl game. The game was on the line, and he put me in at quarterback. Our second unit went on two 80-yard drives.

I had torn up my knee the next spring, and Dr. E.C. Brock had opened me up for full surgery. Not only that, I got an infection and lost about 30 pounds. I was probably going to be redshirted that year, but I worked all summer with our trainers, Jim Goostree and Sang Lyda. I was having trouble getting my knee bent. They told me if I could get a 125-degree bend that I would have a chance to play. I wanted to play. So the night before I was going to be measured, I tied my knee bent and stayed up all night with it tied at over a 125-degree bend.

The wishbone was really my offense. It wasn't really Jeff's offense. He was an excellent passer. But nobody could run and move like I could, although that might have been in great part because of fear.

I don't think Coach Moore wanted to play me very much because I was coming off the knee injury. It had been only four months since the surgery. I consider it a gift from God that I was able to play. In the first game against Nebraska, Coach Bryant put me in, and I ran for nine yards. Coach Bryant realized how I had worked all summer to be able to play, and he had faith in me. That's one of the reasons that I love and adore him to this day.

Coach Bryant believed in playing men if they had earned it. I probably played about 10 snaps a game as a sophomore and about 25 snaps a game as a junior, backing up Jeff. And why not play the back-up quarterbacks? Everyone needs to play. I'm convinced that when the back-up gets a chance, he gives about 110 percent effort. I think it's ridiculous the way teams play just one quarterback.

We lost to Southern Cal in 1978, but came back and got back to No. 2, and this time we got to play No. 1 Penn State in the Sugar

Bowl. And that win gave us the national championship. We had been 11–1 my sophomore year and 11–1 my junior year. I made up my mind as a senior we were going to be 12–0. On offense we had nine seniors, and our juniors were Major Ogilvie and Billy Jackson. And some of our guys were fifth-year seniors. And we had smart guys, like Mike Brock on the offensive line, who could call the checks. And, of course, we had another great defense.

The toughest game we had was at LSU. It rained, and they had the grass on the field about six inches deep, so it was almost impossible to run. The whole game was played on their end of the field, but we only got a field goal and won 3–0. I was hospitalized after that game. I couldn't run, so I was a sitting duck, and they beat me up pretty good.

We were ranked No. 1 and playing Auburn, and they were not very good. But our offense had fumbled, and we'd been benched. We got the ball back on the 18-yard line and we were behind. On the first play, I bounced the pitchout to Major, but he got it. And eventually we drove it on down, and I scored the winning touchdown and conversion. We were 11–0 and going back to the Sugar Bowl to play Arkansas.

Coach Moore came up with the double wing offense to run the wishbone in the Sugar Bowl, and we won pretty easily to win the national championship again. A few years later, I got to talk to Coach Lou Holtz, who had been at Arkansas, and he talked about that scheme.

The national championship is the standard Coach Bryant set for us. We won two and should have won three.

I wasn't allowed to throw much until my senior year. Until then, I'd run the veer, and Jeff was in on the passing plays. But in 1979 I had to pass because they'd put everyone on the line to stop the run. Keith Pugh and I had a great relationship. We'd stay after practice and work on our own to make sure we knew exactly what we were doing. We'd throw an out-cut, and he always had one-on-one coverage, so we had great success. It really hurt our offense when he missed a few games.

After my playing career, I stayed around as a graduate assistant while I was in law school. I also had some scholarships from the National Football Foundation and as an NCAA Top Five scholar. By then I had a lot of confidence in knowing the offense, and it was then that I recognized what a great wishbone innovator Coach Moore was.

I spent a lot of time with Coach Bryant, and he would ask me about things as a guy who had been the quarterback. When Charley Thornton left to go to Texas A&M, I got the opportunity to work as host of *The Bear Bryant Show* each Sunday. I may have been the first person to know he was going to retire. He said after the Southern Mississippi game that he wasn't on top of it, that he was allowing his assistants to make decisions he didn't agree with, that he thought maybe it was time to hang it up.

When Ray Perkins came in the next year, he asked me to stay and help with the quarterbacks. It wasn't anything like what I had done with Coach Bryant. I enjoyed working with Dave Rader and a young quarterback named Mike Shula.

And then I was out of law school and into the real world. And I realized that that is what Coach Bryant had prepared me for. He taught me to be competitive and to work hard; that every day was not going to be a bed of roses, and when the down times came, you had to work harder. He was the best teacher I ever had.

*Steadman Shealy is a partner in the law firm of Shealy, Crum, Pike in Dothan and Tuscaloosa. He was All-SEC and Academic All-America as a senior.*

## Bill Oliver

A standout player at Alabama in the early 1960s and an assistant coach for a total of 15 years, Bill Oliver is best known for designing the defensive game plan for one of the Crimson Tide's most famous victories. It was Oliver who came up with the idea of placing all 11 defenders on or near the line of scrimmage in the 1993 Sugar Bowl, a strategy that resulted in a 34–13 victory for the Crimson Tide.

"Coach Bill Oliver was my position coach, and he was the man for a secondary player," 1979 All-American Don McNeal said. "He taught me everything. I was successful at Alabama and in professional football because of the techniques he taught."

Oliver was also a head coach at Tennessee-Chattanooga and interim coach at Auburn following the departure of Terry Bowden midway through the 1998 season. He remains so well-respected in coaching circles that he has been used as a consultant by such men as Steve Spurrier and Nick Saban.

## Howard Schnellenberger

An All-America tight end under Paul Bryant at Kentucky and an assistant at Alabama for five seasons in the early 1960s, Howard Schnellenberger was responsible for perhaps the greatest recruiting coup in Crimson Tide history. It was he whom Bryant dispatched in the spring of 1961 to recruit a talented quarterback named Joe Namath.

"My mother liked Coach Schnellenberger tremendously, especially when she found out he was at Kentucky when my brother Frank was at Kentucky," Namath said. "She went upstairs and packed a suitcase—a small suitcase—and came back down and said, 'All right, Joey. Take him, Coach.'"

Schnellenberger went on to win a national championship at Miami in 1983 and later coached at Louisville and Oklahoma. Now in his late seventies, he remains in the game as football coach and athletics director at Florida Atlantic University.

**Homer Smith**

One of the more celebrated offensive minds in college football history, Homer Smith had two stints at Alabama: under Bill Curry in 1988–1989 and under Gene Stallings in 1994–1995. He was noted for mentoring quarterbacks, including David Smith (no relation) and SEC Players of the Year Gary Hollingsworth and Jay Barker.

"Coach Smith expected nothing less than perfection," David Smith said. "He was the best quarterback coach a man could have. He knew all our strengths and weaknesses and how to use us to Alabama's best advantage."

Smith also served as offensive coordinator on four Rose Bowl teams at UCLA and was head coach at Davidson, Army, and Pacific. He died April 10, 2011, at age 79.

## GREATEST STAFF EVER?

Is it any wonder Alabama won the national championship in 1973? The coaching staff was certainly loaded with big names.

Six members of Bryant's staff that year went on to become college head coaches. Danny Ford would win a national championship at Clemson in 1981, while Pat Dye won four SEC titles during his time at Auburn.

Curley Hallman had some good teams at Southern Miss before moving on to LSU, while Bill Oliver coached four years at Tennessee-Chattanooga before returning to Alabama as defensive coordinator under Gene Stallings. Bud Moore was Big 8 Coach of the Year at Kansas in 1975, while Jimmy Sharpe had a four-year run at Virginia Tech in the late 1970s.

John Mitchell, now assistant head coach for the NFL's Pittsburgh Steelers, spent his first year in coaching as an Alabama staffer that year. And when you factor in Alabama "lifers" such as Ken Donahue, Clem Gryska, Dude Hennessey, Bobby Marks, Mal Moore, Jack Rutledge, and trainer Jim Goostree, the 1973 Crimson Tide coaching staff might just have been college football's greatest ever.

*chapter 5*
# ALL-TIME GREATS: ALABAMA'S HALL OF FAMERS

YOU CAN FIELD ALMOST A FULL TEAM with the Alabama players who have been enshrined in the College Football Hall of Fame. From Don Hutson in the first class to Woodrow Lowe in 2009, here are the 17 former Crimson Tide players (excluding coaches) who have received college football's ultimate honor.

## DON HUTSON (INDUCTED 1951)

Entering the Hall of Fame alongside such legends as Amos Alonzo Stagg, Sammy Baugh, Red Grange, Jim Thorpe, and Bronko Nagurski, Don Hutson was perhaps the first great receiver in college football history. Before going on to star for the NFL's Green Bay Packers, Hutson was an All-American for the Crimson Tide. He started three years at end, with fellow Arkansan Paul "Bear" Bryant on the other side. Called by coach Frank Thomas "the best player I ever saw," Hutson helped Alabama to an undefeated record and the national championship as a senior in 1934. He had a game-winning touchdown run against Tennessee and caught six passes for 159 yards and two touchdowns in the Crimson Tide's 29–13 victory over Stanford in the Rose Bowl. Following his

Don Hutson, widely regarded as football's first great receiver, was an All-American at Alabama in 1934 before going on to a celebrated professional career with the Green Bay Packers.

Alabama career, Hutson was an eight-time All-Pro with the Packers and retired as the league's all-time leader with 488 receptions, 7,991 yards, and 99 touchdowns. The touchdown total remains eighth all-time and stood until it was broken by Steve Largent in 1989. He was named to the college football's all-time team in 1989, Alabama's Team of the Century in 1992, and the NFL's 75th anniversary team in 1994. In addition to the College Football Hall of Fame, Hutson is also a member of the Pro Football Hall of Fame and Alabama Sports Hall of Fame. He died June 26, 1997, at age 84.

## FRED SINGTON SR. (INDUCTED 1955)

Perhaps the first Alabama football player to achieve national fame, Fred Sington was a two-time All-American for the Crimson Tide in 1929 and 1930. Massive for his time at 6'2" and 210 pounds, the Birmingham native was called the "greatest lineman in the country" by legendary Notre Dame coach Knute Rockne. Sington helped Wallace Wade's team win the Rose Bowl and the national championship as a senior, leading an Alabama defense that allowed just 13 points in 10 games. After the Crimson Tide beat Washington State 24–0 in the Rose Bowl, big band leader Rudy Vallee wrote a song about Sington, a nationwide hit called "Football Freddie." Sington did not play professional football, instead opting for baseball, seeing action for six seasons as an outfielder with the Washington Senators and Brooklyn Dodgers. Also a member of the Alabama Sports Hall of Fame, Sington was chosen for college football's centennial Southeast Area team in 1969 and for Alabama's Team of the Century in 1992. He served in the Navy during World War II and was later an SEC football official. Two of his sons, Fred Jr. and Dave, played for coach Paul "Bear" Bryant in the late 1950s. "I know that I was always very proud of what my father had done," Fred Jr. said. "I think it set a bar for me, and I tried to reach his heights, which may have helped me get a little better in some ways." Fred Sington Sr. died on August 20, 1998, at age 88.

## *Crimson Tide in Their Own Words*
# FRED SINGTON JR.
### TACKLE, 1958–1959

I have heard Mike Shula say that he knows something about having to follow a name, and I can certainly identify with that. I think when you are the son of someone who has made a name for himself and follow into that field, in the back of your mind there is always a bit of that pressure or responsibility. Most people say, "I just tried to do the best I could." And you do have to be your own self and do what you can.

I know that I was always very proud of what my father had done. I think it set a bar for me, and I tried to reach his heights, which may have helped me get a little better in some ways. But I was also able to recognize that certain ones come along just so often. I tried to do the best I could and come as close as I could.

My father was a tackle for Coach Wallace Wade from 1928 to 1930, playing on the undefeated and Rose Bowl champion team of 1930. Notre Dame coach Knute Rockne called him the finest lineman in the nation. He was also a Phi Beta Kappa student. He played professional baseball for the Washington Senators. He was inducted into the National Football Foundation Hall of Fame in 1955. He was known as Mr. Birmingham for his civic contributions.

And my father certainly loved The University of Alabama and Alabama football.

I had an unusual playing career at Alabama. I went to Alabama in 1953, recruited by Red Drew and Coach Crisp. I think everyone always assumed I would go to Alabama, but when I was finishing up at Ramsay High School in Birmingham, I was recruited by

Fred Sington Jr. (left) had a big name to live up to when he played for Alabama in the '50s, as his father (right) had been one of the Crimson Tide's all-time greatest players.

Florida and almost committed there on my visit. But, of course, a visit to Alabama changed that.

I was injured at Alabama and had to have a disk cut out of my spine, and that kept me off the field in 1954. I played for Coach Whitworth in 1955, then went into the Army, where I played service ball in 1956. I came back as a student coach under Whitworth in 1957. Then I played on Coach Bryant's first two teams, in 1958 and 1959. So my career spanned from 1953 to 1959, seven years. I don't think you could do that today.

My brother Dave, who is younger than I am, had come to the university in 1955, and he was a captain with Bobby Smith on Coach Bryant's first team in 1958.

In 1957 Dr. Frank Rose, who was president of the university, got on a plane in Birmingham and flew to Atlanta. My father was already in Atlanta. They got on another plane there under assumed names. That's something else you couldn't do today. Dr. Rose sat in the front of the plane and Dad sat in the back. In case one or the other was spotted, they didn't want to be seen flying together to Houston. (Actually, my father was spotted. I had dated the stewardess, and she said, "Aren't you Fred Sington's father?") Dr. Rose and Dad were part of a small group that was going down to get Coach Bryant to leave Texas A&M and return to Alabama, which they did.

Obviously, that was a wonderful thing for the university and for Alabama football. But I'm not sure I would have agreed with it in the spring of 1958, Coach Bryant's first spring practice. In fact, it started in January with what was known as the gym program. That was so tough that we thought it was a relief that we would finally get onto the football field for spring practice. We were wrong. There was no relief.

My father had told me when Coach Bryant was hired that I didn't know what tough was, but that I'd know when Coach Bryant got there. There was nothing he could have told me that would have prepared me for the ordeal. You really didn't know if you were going to survive. When we had a 40-year reunion of the 1958 class in 1998, we went back to the rosters. We found a pre-spring roster with 362 names. That was before 25 days of spring practice. When we reported in the fall, we had 42 left. You couldn't get away today with what they did to us, but Alabama football was in desperate shape, and the coaches did what they had to do.

Intensity had increased a thousand-fold. Under Coach Drew we had very large squads, and some worked hard, but there was a lot of standing around. There was no intensity under Coach Whitworth. But under Coach Bryant, it was there from the time you got to the dressing room until the time you left, and then some.

I think he changed everything. I believe that we could sense that things were not only going to be different and a lot tougher, but that they were also going to be better, that he would bring the program back. Even with all the pressure, we thought that was going to happen, that we were going to be winners.

I can't remember why Coach Bryant missed a practice in the preseason of 1958, but he wasn't there on a day when we scrimmaged the first recruiting class, Pat Trammell and that bunch. The freshmen beat the varsity, and we were scared to death of what was going to happen to us when Coach Bryant got back and heard about it. But he could surprise you. He said, "Well, we'll just throw that one out and start over." Talk about relief! We thought we'd be running until the first game.

In 1958 I was a tackle on offense and a linebacker on defense. But in the Georgia game I was lined up as a fullback, sort of like in the wishbone that Alabama would run later, except I was very close to the quarterback. I'd either get the tackle or the linebacker and we'd either go off tackle or pitch it. And we upset Georgia 12–0. In 1959 I was strictly a place-kicker.

There is nothing like having played football for The University of Alabama. I loved it, and many, many other people love it. And it's a good feeling to be a part of the greatest tradition in college football.

To have played for Coach Bryant helped prepare me for life. He instilled in us that when things are going bad, when things are tough, you stand tough and you come out of it. You can overcome obstacles.

And from my dad, I learned a love for the university, and that you give something back to it, which I have tried to do. I am proud of the university and proud that I was a part of Alabama football.

I enjoy returning to Tuscaloosa for games and having time to visit with guys I played with, the ones who were upperclassmen when I started and the ones I finished with. I played with a lot of people.

*Fred Sington Jr. is assistant to the mayor in Gadsden. He is past president of the National Alumni Association and active in the "A" Club and Red Elephant Club.*

---

## DON WHITMIRE (INDUCTED 1956)

Though he would not become a consensus All-American until after transferring to the United States Naval Academy in 1943, Don Whitmire was an outstanding player for two seasons for the Crimson Tide. The Decatur, Alabama, native starred on Alabama's 1941 national championship team, earning Most Valuable Lineman honors in the Crimson Tide's 29–21 victory over Texas A&M in the Cotton Bowl. The 5'11", 215-pound Whitmire helped Alabama go 8–3 and win the Orange Bowl as a junior in 1942, then transferred to Navy to join the war effort. An All-American for the Midshipmen in 1944, Whitmire won the Rockne Trophy as the nation's top lineman that same season. He rose to the rank of rear admiral in the Navy and directed the 1975 evacuation of

Saigon at the end of the Vietnam War. Upon his induction into the College Football Hall of Fame, Whitmire said, "Football taught me the virtue of team play and enhanced my leadership qualities. These traits have been most valuable in my Navy career. Football taught me to take hard knocks and come up fighting." Whitmire died May 4, 1991, at age 68. He is buried in Arlington National Cemetery.

## JOHNNY MACK BROWN (INDUCTED 1957)

Though he would go on to become a legendary Hollywood movie cowboy who starred in more than 150 films, Johnny Mack Brown was one of the early stars of Alabama football before that. Known as "the Dothan Antelope," the fleet-footed half-back helped the Crimson Tide to the Southern Conference championship (its first conference title) as a junior in 1924. Along with All-America quarterback (and fellow Hall of Famer) Pooley Hubert, Brown led Alabama to its first national championship the following season. He scored the only touchdown of a 7–0 victory over Georgia Tech on a 55-yard punt return and caught two touchdown passes from Hubert in the Crimson Tide's 20–19 win over Washington in the Rose Bowl on January 1, 1926, to give Alabama its first national championship. During the team's time on the West Coast, Brown took a Hollywood screen test, a move that changed his life forever. Brown became a matinee idol with the title role in King Vidor's 1930 film *Billy the Kid* and went on to star alongside such luminaries as John Wayne, Clark Gable, Jean Harlow, and Joan Crawford before retiring from film in the early 1950s. He has the rare distinction of being both a member of the College Football Hall of Fame and the owner of a star on the Hollywood Walk of Fame. He died November 14, 1974, at age 70.

## POOLEY HUBERT (INDUCTED 1964)

Though teammate John Mack Brown ultimately became more famous, Allison "Pooley" Hubert was a bigger star than his teammate during their Alabama playing days. Wallace Wade called Hubert, the quarterback on the Crimson Tide's first national championship team in 1925, the greatest player he ever coached. Hubert, a World War I veteran, enrolled at Alabama at age 21 in the fall of 1922 and started for four years on both offense and defense. Playing bareheaded during a time when most players wore leather helmets, Hubert was a two-time All–Southern Conference selection and an All-American as a senior in 1925 (the second Alabama player so honored, after Bully VandeGraaff 10 years earlier). He moved from fullback to quarterback that season, throwing for a touchdown and running for another in a 20–19 victory over Washington in the January 1, 1926, Rose Bowl. Following his playing days, Hubert coached both football and basketball at Southern Mississippi and Virginia Military Institute before retiring to become a peach farmer. He died February 26, 1978, at age 76.

## DIXIE HOWELL (INDUCTED 1970)

One of the great Alabama stars of the pre–World War II era, Millard "Dixie" Howell was so famous across the South in his day that his name was mentioned in the classic novel *To Kill a Mockingbird*. Howell played quarterback and halfback for coach Frank Thomas, earning All–Southeastern Conference honors twice and All-America recognition as a senior in 1934. It was that season that he led Alabama to a 10–0 record and the national championship, joining with star end Don Hutson to form one of the top passing tandems in early college football history. Howell threw two touchdown passes to Hutson in a win over Clemson in 1934 and hit him for 54- and 59-yard scores along with two rushing touchdowns of his own in an MVP performance during a 29–13 victory over Washington State in the Rose Bowl. He also rushed for two touchdowns each in wins over Georgia and Vanderbilt that season, while his 89-yard punt against Tennessee in 1933 remains the school record. Also an outstanding baseball player, Howell seemed destined for a major league career before a severe beaning suffered in the minors caused him to lose vision in one eye. He played briefly for the NFL's Washington Redskins and later coached at Arizona State and Idaho. The Hartford, Alabama, native is also a member of the Alabama Sports Hall of Fame and the Rose Bowl Hall of Fame. He died March 2, 1971, at age 58, following a battle with cancer.

## JOHNNY CAIN (INDUCTED 1973)

Most famous for his powerful left leg as a punter, Johnny Cain was a three-time All–Southern Conference selection and the starting quarterback on Alabama's 1930 national championship team as a sophomore. He picked up his nickname "Hurri" when coach Wallace Wade called him on the field during a game with the admonition, "Hurry, Cain!" Frank Thomas, who replaced Wade as coach in 1931, moved Cain to fullback because he was afraid Cain was too modest to call his own number and instead content to hand the ball to teammates. The Montgomery native was an All-American as a punter in 1932, when Alabama finished 8–2. His most famous game that year came against Tennessee, when he punted 19 times for a 48-yard average in a 7–3 loss. Veteran *Birmingham News* sportswriter Zipp Newman wrote of Cain, "He could run, block, punt, and play defense, the best all-around back I ever saw." Cain went on to serve as both football coach and athletics director at Southwestern Louisiana in the late 1940s and early 1950s, and later became an athletics administrator at Ole Miss. He died August 18, 1977, at age 68.

## LEE ROY JORDAN (INDUCTED 1983)

Legendary Alabama coach Paul "Bear" Bryant was fond of saying, "If they stay inbounds, old Lee Roy will get them." He was speaking, of course, of Lee Roy Jordan, an All-America linebacker for the Crimson Tide in both 1961 and 1962. Jordan led Alabama to the national championship as a junior, when the Crimson Tide surrendered only 25 points in 11 games. He secured his legend, however, in the following season's Orange Bowl. In a 17–0 victory over Oklahoma, Jordan totaled an astounding 31 tackles, an Alabama record for any game, let alone a bowl. The Excel, Alabama, native started three seasons for the Crimson Tide, leading an Alabama defense that posted 12 shutouts and allowed just 3.9 points per game during that period. Jordan was a first-round pick of the Dallas Cowboys in 1963 and a five-time Pro Bowler in 14 NFL seasons. The Cowboys won eight division titles and played in three Super Bowls during Jordan's career, winning Super Bowl VI over the Miami Dolphins in 1972. Jordan retired following the 1976 season as the Cowboys' all-time leader in tackles and was inducted into the team's Ring of Honor in 1989. Now a successful businessman in Dallas, Jordan said of his playing days at Alabama and in the NFL, "I can't imagine anyone being any luckier than I was."

## RILEY SMITH (INDUCTED 1985)

A teammate of fellow Hall of Famers Paul "Bear" Bryant, Don Hutson, and Dixie Howell, Riley Smith is widely regarded as one of the best blockers in Alabama football history. Playing quarterback in coach Frank Thomas' Notre Dame box offense, Smith was the primary lead blocker for Howell, who was the team's top passer. A starter on the Crimson Tide's 1934 national championship team, he was an All-American the following year, when he led Alabama to a 6–2–1 record following the graduation of his more famous teammates. Known as "General," Smith played in three national all-star games following his senior season and captained his team in each one. He was the second player chosen in the first NFL Draft in 1936 (after Heisman Trophy winner Jay Berwanger), but played only three seasons with the Boston and Washington Redskins before an injury ended his career. He later coached at Washington & Lee University and was a lieutenant commander in the Navy during World War II. Later a successful real estate developer in the Mobile area, Smith died August 9, 1999, at age 88.

## VAUGHN MANCHA (INDUCTED 1990)

A merchant marine for several years following high school, Vaughn Mancha did not enroll at Alabama until he was 22 years old. A giant for his time at 238 pounds, Mancha started immediately as a freshman, joining the Crimson Tide the same year as fellow Hall of Famer Harry Gilmer. Mancha started every game for four years at Alabama, starring at both center and linebacker. He was a first-team All-American in 1945, when the Crimson Tide went 10–0 and beat Southern Cal 34–14 in the Rose Bowl. His college coach, Frank Thomas, said Mancha was "a brilliant defensive man, fine at diagnosing plays, a great defender against passes, and a sure tackler. On offense he is a fine blocker, and a good, accurate snapper. And he loves football." Mancha was selected in the first round of the 1948 NFL Draft and played one season with the Boston Yanks before a knee injury ended his playing career. He later became head football coach at Livingston State College (now the University of West Alabama) and served as an assistant coach at Florida State. After finishing his Ph.D. at Columbia University, Mancha returned to Florida State as athletics director, a position he served in until 1972. Mancha died January 27, 2011, at age 89.

---

## *Crimson Tide in Their Own Words*

# VAUGHN MANCHA

### CENTER, 1944–1947

I fell in love with The University of Alabama at an early age, when I was playing football at Ramsay High School in Birmingham. There were so many things I appreciated about the opportunity I had. I was a poor kid, but I was lucky enough to have the skills to play for Alabama, which meant I was going to get three meals a day and not have to sleep with my big brother anymore. And I was lucky enough to have a coach, Frank Thomas, who stressed education.

And everything about it I appreciate even more today. My career in athletics and education has been mostly at Florida State, but my heart has always been at Alabama.

When I was growing up, The University of Alabama was a favorite destination for a lot of Ramsay High School graduates. I used to go to Legion Field and watch Alabama play. I had such great admiration for guys like Dixie Howell and Don Hutson. And because I was a center, I really loved to watch Carey Cox. I tried to emulate him.

I've tried to apply the lessons I learned from Coach Thomas throughout my life as a player, coach, administrator, and professor. Coach Thomas wanted every player to earn his degree. If you needed aid after your playing days, he would make sure you got it. I actually finished the work for my undergraduate degree just before my final game at Alabama. Coach Red Drew was our coach that last year after Coach Thomas became so ill.

I signed a professional football contract with the Boston Yanks, who are now the Indianapolis Colts. I was a No. 1 draft choice and signed for $7,500 plus a $2,500 signing bonus. In those days that made you a rich man.

I tore up my knee and ended my playing career, but I was able to take advantage of the deal for academic aid at Alabama and went back to get my master's degree in 1950. I actually got a little beyond the master's degree, which would prove important.

That's how I got my first job in athletics. Livingston University needed a coach, but you also had to be a professor and be beyond the master's level.

I enjoyed my time at Livingston. I particularly remember a game when we were going to play Florida State in Selma. I thought Cliff Harper, who was the best high school official in Alabama, was going to call the game, but there was a mix-up and no one ever contacted him. So we were ready to play and didn't have an officiating crew. We pulled some people out of the stands to officiate. We beat Florida State, and I told them later that three of the officials had been my teammates at Alabama. And actually, one of them had been.

That may have led to me getting a coaching job at Florida State under Tom Nugent. I was defensive coordinator and also served as a professor for six years. I went to Columbia in 1957 and was defensive coordinator and a professor while working on my doctorate.

I went back to Florida State in 1959 as athletics director. I left athletics in 1971, but stayed on as a professor until I retired in 1990. One of the highlights of my career as athletics director was

Vaughn Mancha was an All-America center and Hall of Fame player who became athletics director at Florida State.

when we opened the season in Birmingham against Alabama. Alabama had won national championships in 1964 and 1965, and gone undefeated in 1966, giving up just 44 points all year. It was quite a night in Birmingham. The scoreboard went out, and when the game ended, it was a 37–37 tie.

One of my classmates at Alabama was Claude Kirk. Later, when I was athletics director at FSU, Claude Kirk was elected governor of Florida. We got a lot of things done here in those days.

My career in athletics has enabled me to know some great people. I loved going to the coaches' conventions and being able to visit with Coach Bryant and people like that. Tom Landry was on the Texas team that beat us in the Sugar Bowl in my last game at Alabama, and I enjoyed knowing him when he was coach of the Dallas Cowboys. And I coached some guys who did pretty well, like Lee Corso of ESPN, who was a great running back; and Burt Reynolds, who wasn't as good a player; and at Columbia I coached Brian Dennehey. He said he couldn't understand a redneck like me, but he understood a kick in the butt.

But my fondest memories are of my playing days at Alabama. I actually signed with Alabama in 1941, but because of World War II, I didn't get there until 1944. When I was six years old, we were playing bow and arrow, and I got an eye put out, but I still had to do something. I joined the Merchant Navy and was in the Pacific for a couple of years. And somehow I got out in time to get to the university for the 1944 season.

Those were wonderful times with wonderful people. We went to two Sugar Bowls and one Rose Bowl. The first one was one of the great games ever against a powerful Duke team in the Sugar Bowl, and we came within a shoestring tackle of winning that game.

After the 1945 season, we went to the Rose Bowl. We got up 27–0 on Southern Cal and won easily, 34–14, to finish undefeated. That was the last time Alabama went to the Rose Bowl. After that game, the Rose Bowl signed a contract with the Big Ten to be the visiting team.

One of the great things about playing then as opposed to now is the time factor. Today you get on a jet, go to the game, get back on a jet, and go home. I think it must have taken us about half a month to go to California and back for that Rose Bowl game. They took professors with to tutor us. The train would stop every few hundred miles for us to practice and to meet fans.

When we got to California, we got to go to Johnny Mack Brown's ranch. He had been a great player at Alabama and was a famous movie star. We met Errol Flynn on the set. He was making *Robin Hood*. He was about 6'5" and really built and wearing those tights. We thought he would have made a good addition to the team.

And over the years I kept up with my teammates. But now I look at a picture of that last Rose Bowl team and see so many who are no longer with us. My time as a player at Alabama was very special. I have a lot of great memories of the thrills we had.

I've been awfully fortunate to have honors come my way. When I was inducted into the National Football Foundation Hall of Fame, one of my students was Deion Sanders. He was impressed. He said, "I didn't know you were bad." I told him I had been 228 pounds with Deion speed.

You never know how Alabama football is going to help you. When I was at Columbia, I got pulled over for speeding. The policeman was from Alabama and recognized my name from my playing days and let me off with a warning.

I make trips to Alabama as often as I can. Unfortunately, some of them are for funerals of old friends. But my son graduated from the Alabama medical school and is a doctor in Montgomery. I wish I could have spent more time in Alabama following the Crimson Tide, but I was always tied up at another school. Now we're active in the Alabama Alumni Association in Tallahassee.

I've had a great life. I think working in athletics helped keep me young. And I owe it all to The University of Alabama.

*Vaughn Mancha started every game for four years at Alabama and was a consensus All-American in 1945. He is a member of the Alabama Sports Hall of Fame and was selected to the Alabama Team of the Century. He was inducted into the National Football Foundation Hall of Fame in 1990.*

---

## HARRY GILMER (INDUCTED 1993)

Perhaps the greatest all-around performer in Crimson Tide history, Harry Gilmer is the only Alabama player to finish in the top five in the Heisman Trophy balloting twice. Gilmer finished fifth as a sophomore in 1945 and again as a senior in 1947. A contributor all four years as a single-wing halfback, he led the Crimson Tide to 30 victories, including a 10–0 record and a Rose Bowl victory in 1945. Gilmer rushed for 1,621 yards and 19 scores in his career, while passing for an additional 2,863 yards and 30 scores. He was named SEC Player of the Year as a sophomore in 1945, when he rushed for 552 yards and eight touchdowns, including 216 yards and three scores on just six carries against Kentucky. Gilmer was All-SEC as both a junior and a senior, and ended his career with 52 total touchdowns, including two on kickoff returns, one on a punt return, and another on an interception. He was drafted No. 1 overall by the Washington Redskins in 1948 and played eight years in the NFL with the Redskins and Detroit Lions. He twice earned Pro Bowl honors and went on to coach the Lions for two seasons. Tommy Lewis, who played fullback at Alabama in the 1950s, once said, "I admired every step Harry Gilmer took."

## Ozzie Newsome (Inducted 1994)

With Don Hutson and John Hannah, Ozzie Newsome is one of three Alabama players inducted into both the College Football and Pro Football Halls of Fame. Though he played in the run-oriented wishbone offense, Newsome held many of the Crimson Tide's all-time receiving records for more than 30 years following his last game. He started all but the first game of his 1974 freshman season with the Crimson Tide, earning All-SEC honors twice and All-America recognition as a senior in 1977. The Crimson Tide lost just two conference games during Newsome's Alabama career (both in 1976), winning the SEC three times. Known as "the Wizard of Oz," Newsome caught 25 passes for 529 yards (an astounding 21.2-yard average) with six touchdowns 1976, and followed that up with even better numbers as a senior: 36 catches, 804 yards (a 22.3-yard average), along with four scores. A first-round pick of the Cleveland Browns in 1978, Newsome played 13 seasons as a tight end in the NFL, retiring in 1990 with 662 receptions, 7,980 yards and 47 touchdowns. Following his playing days, Newsome became player personnel director for the Baltimore Ravens, helping build the 2000 Super Bowl champions before becoming general manager in 2002.

---

*Crimson Tide in Their Own Words*

# OZZIE NEWSOME

## SPLIT END/TIGHT END, 1974–1977

By almost any standard, we had a very successful four-year period at Alabama. We won three Southeastern Conference championships; finished in the nation's top 10 all four years; finished second in the nation in both 1974 and 1977; won 11 games three of the four years; won three bowl games defeating Penn State, UCLA, and Ohio State; and went 42–6.

The biggest disappointment is that we did not win a national championship. We could have won it on the field in 1974, but we lost by two points to Notre Dame in the Orange Bowl. And I thought we had won it in 1977, but Notre Dame won it again that year. In 1977 we played our final game in the Sugar Bowl against Ohio State. We were third in the nation going into the bowl games. Both the No. 1 and No. 2 teams lost, and we handed it to Ohio State pretty good, 35–6. That was the Bear vs. Woody game, Coach Bryant vs. coach Hayes.

Ohio State was a good team, and that was an impressive victory. I had met Chris Ward, who was the starting offensive tackle for the Buckeyes, at the Heisman dinner in New York. He was a nice guy, and I developed a friendship with him.

After the game we had a van to go to Mobile for the Senior Bowl. Johnny Davis, Bob Cryder, a player from Ohio State, and I drove over together. While we were driving, we heard on the radio they had voted Notre Dame the national champion. It made that trip twice as long. We just couldn't believe it.

I believe that game may have propelled Alabama to two more national championships. 'Bama won it in 1978 and 1979. It could have been three in a row.

My parents didn't realize the significance of me signing with The University of Alabama, but after I started playing, it was brought home to them. Their recognition in the community escalated. They'd go to the cleaners or the grocery store, and people would want to talk to them because their son played football at Alabama.

There were a lot of factors in my choosing Alabama, but unquestionably the No. 1 factor was Coach Bryant. It begins and ends with him. I told a story many years ago about other schools recruiting me and telling me that their coach had played for Coach Bryant or had coached under Coach Bryant. And I thought, I could go to the branch, or I could go to the trunk.

There was also the winning tradition. Alabama was the dominant team in the SEC and one of the best teams in the nation. I enjoyed watching *The Bear Bryant Show* on Sundays, and also enjoyed the *Shug Jordan Show* on Auburn football.

When I made my recruiting visit, the atmosphere was all about team, which appealed to me. There were no huge egos, no individuals. It was about The University of Alabama and the Crimson Tide football team.

Everyone connected with the program in any way was doing whatever he could do to help us win. And I don't mean just the coaches and players and trainers and managers. I mean the cooks and the men who kept the dorm clean. Everyone.

Leon Douglas had signed two years earlier to play basketball. He was close to me, and his brother, John, was in my class at Colbert County in Leighton. I'm still close to them and so happy that

Ozzie Newsome (82) is in both the college and pro football halls of fame because of his outstanding pass-catching ability, as shown by this amazing grab against TCU.

Leon is back in Tuscaloosa as head basketball coach at Stillman College.

It was amazing the things that came up in recruiting. Thad Flanagan was my teammate at Colbert County, and he had signed with Alabama a year ahead of me. Coaches at other schools would try to give me a guilt complex, like it would be wrong of me to compete against Thad. And some people thought I should go to Auburn and be reunited with my old high school quarterback, Phil Gargis.

When I got to Alabama, it was even better than I had expected. There was a family atmosphere. Every player cared for the next player. And the students were very supportive of the football players. It was a good feeling.

Alabama had lost a great wide receiver in Wayne Wheeler. I knew that everyone was saying that Alabama didn't have a replacement for him. I don't remember what I thought about that at the time, but looking back I can certainly understand it. The 1974 season was just the second one that freshmen could play on the varsity, and Coach Bryant probably wasn't sure if he could count on me.

We opened that year against Maryland. Joe Dale Harris and I alternated, taking plays in and out. Joe Dale started the Maryland game, and I went in on the second play. The next week I started, and I started every game the rest of my career.

We went 11–1 my freshman year and 11–1 my sophomore year. The oddity is that we had a two-game losing streak because we lost the Orange Bowl to Notre Dame at the end of the 1974 season and we lost to Missouri to open the 1975 season. We had 10-game winning streaks in both seasons, not losing a game until the Orange Bowl in 1974 and not losing a game after Missouri in 1975.

I learned a lesson in that Missouri game. I was playing wide receiver and had my head down. The Missouri cornerback rolled up and came up under my chin with his forearm. He whacked me pretty good and busted my lip. I learned then to keep my head up and watch what was going on.

After your career has been over a few years, you can look back and see that you were a part of an historic time. But at the time a place in history was the last thing on your mind. It was just playing football. Every day was a matter of making sure you gave your best effort. We had so many good players that I was just concerned with maintaining my place on the depth chart. It was a matter of that day, that practice, maybe that period of practice.

I can also look back and see how my time at Alabama has been helpful to me. Coach Bryant stressed priorities, which is the team. We learned what initiative is. He encouraged us to be as good as we could be because we wanted to, not because of outside motivation. And we learned that when we win, there is enough for everyone. Everyone can share in the glory when you win.

I learned to let the game come to me. If the opponent wanted to double-cover me, we were going to be able to run the ball. And if they put people up there to stop the run, I was going to get a lot of passes thrown my way. I also learned that every man on the team had to pull his share, which for me meant becoming a blocker sometimes.

I played most of my Alabama career at split end, but also played tight end. My first day as a pro at Cleveland, I was a tight end. But I was flexed out, the first "hybrid" tight end in the NFL. They told me they were going to throw me a lot of balls, and I caught a few, so I was happy.

It's the nature of my job that I can't make it to Alabama games or reunions. But I still talk to Johnny Davis at least once a week.

I see John Mitchell a few times a year. I see Dwight Stephenson at the Hall of Fame events. I see Richard Todd when I go home to Florence, where he lives now. I know his son, Gator, is a heck of a golfer for the Tide now. And each summer we go to Gulf Shores, and I get with a lot of the old guys. And I am making a special trip to Tuscaloosa to see the new facilities Mal Moore has put together.

> *Ozzie Newsome was an All-America split end in 1977, named the Alabama Player of the Decade for the 1970s, selected to the All-Century Team, inducted into the College Football Hall of Fame in 1994, and the Pro Football Hall of Fame in 1999. He is general manager of the Baltimore Ravens.*

## JOHN HANNAH (INDUCTED 1999)

An All-American in both 1971 and 1972 and a Pro Football Hall of Famer, John Hannah is widely regarded as perhaps the greatest lineman in football history. He helped the Crimson Tide to back-to-back SEC titles as a junior and a senior, winning the Jacobs Blocking Trophy as a senior. Known as "Hog," Hannah started at tackle as a sophomore in 1970 before moving to guard as a junior. Hannah was also a member of one of Alabama football's great families, as his father (Herb) and two brothers (Charley and David) all played for the Crimson Tide. He was the fourth overall selection by the New England Patriots in 1973 and was a nine-time Pro Bowler and seven-time All-Pro. In his final season (1985), he helped the Patriots to their first Super Bowl. He was named to Alabama's Team of the Century and ESPN's All-Time College Football team.

## JOHNNY MUSSO (INDUCTED 2000)

The classic great player on a mediocre team his first two seasons, Johnny Musso helped Alabama return to national acclaim as a senior in 1971. He rushed for 1,088 yards and 16 touchdowns out of the wishbone that season, as Alabama went 11–1 and won the first of five consecutive SEC championships. Musso finished fourth in the Heisman Trophy balloting in 1971 and was also named SEC Player of the Year and a first-team All-American. Musso rushed for 10 touchdowns for a 6–5 Alabama team as a sophomore in 1969 and became the first Crimson Tide back to eclipse the 1,000-yard mark as a junior in 1970, when totaled 1,137 yards and eight scores for the 6–5–1 Crimson Tide. Known as "the Italian Stallion" long before the Sylvester Stallone film *Rocky* co-opted the nickname, Musso rushed for 221 yards on 42 carries against Auburn in 1970 and finished with a then–school record 2,741 career yards. Drafted by the Chicago Bears in 1972, Musso elected to play two years in the Canadian Football League first. He later played three injury-riddled years with the Bears before retiring to embark on a successful business career in Chicago. One of Musso's four sons, Brian, was a star wide receiver and kick returner for Northwestern in the mid-1990s.

---

## *Crimson Tide in Their Own Words*

# JOHNNY MUSSO
### RUNNING BACK, 1969–1971

When I was 11 years old, I knew what I wanted to do, and I was able to live a childhood dream. I never lost the wonder of it. The reality of playing for Alabama never left me. I couldn't believe I was lucky enough to be wearing that crimson jersey and playing for Coach Bryant. It never lost its magic. Every time I slipped on that jersey, it was a wonder.

I grew up in a state where there was a great appreciation for the football tradition of Alabama, and for Auburn, as well. My sister went to Auburn, and they won a national championship while she was there. I think maybe because she was at Auburn my brothers and I became Alabama fans just to irritate her. But it stuck.

Coach Jordan had quite a presence at Auburn, but Coach Bryant was larger than life. And there were Auburn players I admired, Tucker Frederickson and others.

I saw my first Alabama game when I was 11 years old. I snuck into Legion Field in Birmingham to see the 1961 Alabama-Auburn game. I saw Coach Bryant get off the team bus. And then I saw Lee Roy Jordan. He looked like granite, a face carved from stone. I was really taken with that.

And then I watched Alabama win the game. Alabama played great, clearing the last hurdle to the national championship. If I was ever conflicted about my favorite team, watching Alabama play that day solidified my loyalty to Alabama.

I had started playing football the year before, YMCA ball. I was pretty good at it, and having success probably helped me develop a love for football. As I played, I had a goal to one day wear that red jersey. I wanted to play at Legion Field and be a part of Alabama football tradition.

A lot was going on at college campuses in the late '60s. There was the Vietnam war, the long hair, the pot, and the rebellion. It was a crazy time, and that extended to dynamics in college football.

When you play at Alabama you are linked to the past, the present, and the future. You carry a torch that others carried quite well before you, and there is a great responsibility on your part as an Alabama football player to carry it and pass it to the next generation of players. That can be weighty.

After playing freshman ball in 1968, we were in an I formation offense that was primarily a passing offense in 1969 and 1970. In those two years, there were only a couple of exceptions that the other team did not have better talent. And you found out real quick that representing Alabama was a burden because teams that had been beaten by Alabama for decades would beat you as bad as they could. There was no mercy, no calling off the dogs. We would be in the fourth quarter and playing for no other reason than pride.

But then we had the experience of doing it right, winning them all, getting back-to-championship caliber, and carrying the banner when things were going well. I can say now that I probably gained from both experiences. And I think most Alabama players have handled the responsibilities well because they have a genuine love for Alabama football.

Football is a great place to learn, a great environment for the other disciplines, life lessons. They can be learned in other places, but I don't know any place better than the football field. There is the toughness demanded of a physical game. And it is the ultimate team sport. It has to be 11 or it doesn't work. In basketball you can have one guy carry the load. Certainly, there are positions on the football field that can have a greater impact, but nothing like where you put four off to the side and let one player go one-on-one. I believe there are lessons that are unique to football.

And I think Coach Bryant at the heart of things was a teacher. He wanted to impact young men, and I think he understood the greater worth of the game. His motivation was to win. That was

Johnny Musso (22), "the Italian Stallion," was Alabama's leading rusher from 1969 to 1971. In 1970 he rushed for 221 yards against Auburn. The next year the Crimson Tide switched to the wishbone, and he was the leading back on a team that went 11–1.

his highest motivation. But his second was to have a positive impact on players, and I think he did a good job of that.

He confirmed what my mother taught me. She was a tough lady who went through a lot of hard stuff. As much as I admire Coach Bryant and as much as he impacted my life, I think my mom taught me those lessons and he reinforced them. And he gave me the environment to test it.

In 1971, my senior year, Coach Bryant made the decision to switch to the wishbone. I think the team received that very positively because Terry Davis was our best quarterback. He was a really good athlete and a great competitor, but he wasn't a great passer. But the players were excited about a player who could make things happen, who could make quick decisions, who could do things on the run. Our imaginations were sparked by having an athlete like Terry who could run the option.

I think he was the best wishbone quarterback ever. As the wishbone was developed at Alabama, it got much, much more sophisticated. In that first year, it was a true read, triple option with just a few other plays.

It took players being unselfish. The best example was David Bailey, a marvelous wide receiver who is still in the Alabama record book. He didn't have blazing speed, but he could get open and had great hands. He could have become frustrated, but he didn't. He became a great blocker. He put every bit of effort into helping the team.

For me personally, it was a little harder to direct the ball into my hands than it had been in the I formation. I'm glad I got to play in both. There wasn't a lot of variety in the wishbone, and there was a lot of blocking. I think everyone stepped up to make it work. And, of course, it helped to have John Hannah and Buddy Brown at the guard positions and Jim Krapf at center.

And it was fun because we kept it stealth. When the Skywriters— a group of sportswriters from throughout the South who visited every SEC team during August practices—came through, we had to waste a day of practice to run our old stuff. But we thought we had an edge. The last practice we had in Tuscaloosa before leaving to go to Los Angeles to play Southern Cal was at night because we were going to play at night. And it was the last practice we'd have on the wishbone because when we got to Los Angeles we would again practice the 1970 offense.

While we were practicing, the students were having a pep rally on the quad. The practice field was surrounded by curtains, but the pep rally moved to our practice field, and Coach Bryant allowed the curtains to be opened and eventually opened the gates to let the students in to see their team. And they saw we were doing something new, and you could tell they were excited, that they had the same hope we did.

We went out to Los Angeles and scored the first three times we got the ball and then held on to win. It was a great game, a great moment, particularly after the way they had beaten us the year before, and it was great to be part of it. I think that gave us the confidence to go through the season undefeated.

The players certainly believed in Coach Bryant. I thought back to the 1965 season when Alabama went to the Orange Bowl with a conservative offense to play Nebraska. Steve Sloan threw the ball all over the field, and Alabama won the national championship. Coach Bryant showed he had something up his sleeve, and he showed us he still had it. He could make things happen. It gave us confidence that Coach Bryant was back fully engaged, and that set the tone for the year.

Our last game of the year was against Auburn. We were both undefeated. And I didn't know if I was going to get to play. My Auburn friends think we staged the injury, but it was real. In fact, it still hurts. I dislocated my toe against LSU and didn't play against Miami. It was the most painful injury I ever had; you couldn't put an ounce of weight on it.

There is no way I can adequately express my admiration—my love—for Coach Jim Goostree, our trainer, for the work he did in those three weeks between the time I was injured and the Auburn game. He did a lot of experimenting with different types of plastic molds and lambskin and light foam to make a light cast. It had to have support, but it also had to have flex, or I wouldn't be able to run. I had treatment three times a day. And for an hour each night he would come to the dorm and rub cortisone onto my foot. We didn't want to inject it because that can cause damage, but it could be absorbed through the skin. He went beyond his job, and I'll never forget it. He was determined to give me a chance to play.

I wore a 10½ shoe on one foot and a size 12 on the other to accommodate the light cast on my toe. It was a little awkward. I couldn't run on Thursday before the game. We went to Birmingham for a walkthrough Friday, and I didn't do anything. Then Saturday in pregame warm-ups it felt better.

I learned later there was some question about whether I would start. I always thought I would start, but I also thought after a play or two or three that I would be hurt.

I did start, and as I got more and more confident, the awkwardness of the big shoe and the pain seemed to be less of a problem. And it worked out great with us winning 31–7.

*Johnny Musso was an All-American in 1970 and 1971, and SEC Player of the Year in 1971. He was also an Academic All-American and National Scholar-Athlete. He was named to the Alabama Team of the Century and was inducted into the College Football Hall of Fame in 2000.*

---

## BILLY NEIGHBORS (INDUCTED 2003)

Having grown up just across the river from Tuscaloosa in Northport, Alabama, Billy Neighbors didn't have to travel far to become an All-American at Alabama. A member of Paul "Bear" Bryant's first recruiting class, Neighbors was one of just nine who remained four years later (out of the original 108). Neighbors' senior season was a glorious one, as the Crimson Tide went 11–0 and won the national championship. A two-way starter at both offensive and defensive tackle, Neighbors joined with All-America linebacker Lee Roy Jordan to lead an Alabama defense that allowed only 25 points in 11 games. Neighbors also won the Jacobs Trophy as the SEC's top blocker that season. Neighbors was part of Alabama teams that went 26–3–4 during his three varsity seasons and outscored Auburn by a combined 47–0. Drafted by both the NFL's Washington Redskins and AFL's Boston Patriots, Neighbors elected to sign with Boston and played eight professional seasons, earning All-Pro honors in 1964. His son, Wes, and grandson, Wesley, have both gone on to play at Alabama, making the Neighbors clan one of only a handful of three-generation families in Crimson Tide football history.

---

## *Crimson Tide in Their Own Words*
# BILLY NEIGHBORS
### OFFENSIVE/DEFENSIVE TACKLE, 1959–1961

Coach Bryant and I both got to the university prior to the 1958 season. I'm sure he had never heard of me until maybe when I signed. I had never heard of him until he got here. I didn't know anything about him. But it didn't take me long to figure out he was different.

I remember my freshman year hearing some of the other players talking about Junction [Texas A&M's training camp], about how he'd tried to kill all his players at Texas A&M.

I was from Tuscaloosa County and a lifelong Alabama fan. My father was a big fan. He had gone to the Rose Bowl to see Alabama play. And my brother Sidney was on the team under [Coach J.B.] Whitworth. Alabama was the only place I wanted to go. I never even considered any other school, never visited any other place.

The first conversation I had with Coach Bryant was when I went out to practice that August. He walked up to me and told me I needed to get out in the sun and lose some weight. He was unbelievably imposing.

I made it a point not to have too many more conversations with Coach Bryant. Other than practices and games, I only talked to him twice one-on-one when I was in school. I stayed out of his way. I didn't want to fool with him.

Even after I finished, I felt that way. After my senior year, I lacked six hours to graduate. I was playing pro ball and wasn't going to fool with it. But he made me graduate. We all graduated. He called me up and chewed me out. I never knew how he got my telephone number in Boston.

I came back in the spring of 1963 and earned my degree while working as a graduate assistant coach. I was a flunky coach. He'd send me off to speak to civic clubs and things like that.

When I was playing pro ball, I'd get letters from him, and he'd ask me to call him. I never did. It's hard now for people to believe he was that imposing. I stayed away from him for years. I probably didn't see him until after I had been gone at least seven years.

I think we had more than 100 freshmen in our class. About half left before the season ended. Only eight of the original group finished four years later. He worked us pretty hard that first fall. He took some of us out and practiced us with the varsity, even though we couldn't play as freshmen. The next spring he started getting us ready to play. As soon as football was over, we started workouts in the upper gym. We worked all year, really.

I think I may have been on a track scholarship. I guess in those days you could do that to get extra football players. I know in the spring when we had home track meets, they'd send me over to the track to put the shot. I'd come in third every time and earn one point. In those days, a track team just traveled with one shot-put guy, so I'd come in third behind our guy and their guy. I never went to a road meet. Then after I did the shot put, I'd head back to football practice.

On Sundays we'd watch his television show, and even then he was coaching us.

You can't argue with the results. Alabama had been horrible the year before he came—didn't win a game. They had been bad for several years. He turned it around in a year with a winning record. In the first meeting we ever had with him, he told us we were going to win the national championship. I don't think any of us knew anything about the national championship. I know Auburn had won it in 1957, but back then nobody made anything of it.

He told us to stay in school and study, to make sacrifices, and to get ourselves in great shape to play 60 minutes. He told us we could never give up and that we had to be unselfish, to play as a team.

He was absolutely teaching us for life. He sort of boxed it up as a way to live your life, to be dedicated to whatever you are going to do—to try to do it right.

The mood of the campus changed while I was there as we got better each year. Even the teachers seemed to treat us a little better. Some of the teachers didn't want football players in their classes.

Billy Neighbors was one of the all-time great linemen in Alabama football history—a unanimous All-American in 1961 and the first Crimson Tide All-American for Coach Paul Bryant.

Every now and then a teacher would ask us to raise our hands if we were football players. I'd get up and leave. There was no sense staying in a class where that mattered.

I played both ways, like all of us did. Sometimes you'd never leave the game. Coach Bryant told me after I finished that I had averaged 58 minutes per game for three years. I never missed a game, although I only played a little bit in the first Georgia game when they beat us in Athens. I had a hip pointer.

I remember the games we lost. That game at Georgia in 1959; the Liberty Bowl at the end of the year because I played awful up there; and at Tennessee in 1960. We were 26–3–4 my three years.

I also remember Auburn never scored on us. We beat them 10–0, 3–0, and 34–0. One year they never got across our 40-yard line. Coach Bryant said they'd beat us if they did. They had that great kicker, Ed Dyas, who is a great guy, too. They only got across the 50 one time.

I was Lineman of the Week in the nation against Tennessee. We didn't read the papers, but somebody told me. But we had lost the game, and when we got back to practice, the coaches crucified us. And I graded 3 on offense and 5 on defense—out of 100. I'd made 12 or 14 tackles. But after I got that grade, that lineman award didn't mean anything.

Pat James graded me. He hated penalties, and I don't think I ever got one. I might have been called for one. But I never graded over 50 or 60 at Alabama. But by the time I was a junior, I had figured out that the grade didn't mean much.

But I thought about it when I went to the NFL and graded 90-something in my first game. And I never graded under 90 in eight years in the NFL. I told Coach James about that later. He just laughed.

Coach James actually took me and made a movie about how to block.

I didn't like bowl games. We voted against going to the Blue-bonnet Bowl, but Coach Bryant made us go. He let us vote, but that didn't mean anything. I never knew of anyone who voted to go. We went out and played Texas, and it ended in a 3–3 tie. I blocked a guy into the end zone, and Pat Trammell fell on top of me with the ball, but the officials didn't give us the touchdown. Coach Bryant asked me if I had blocked the guy into the end zone. I said I had. He said, "Next time block him out of the end zone." It was a bad call, but that happens.

The last game I played at Alabama was against Arkansas in the Sugar Bowl to complete our 11–0 national championship season. Coach Bryant told me later it was the best game I ever played at Alabama.

I was invited to go to New York to be on *The Ed Sullivan Show* and *The Bob Hope Show* for All-Americans. Coach Bryant and Pat Trammell went to Washington to meet President Kennedy. Pat was the offensive captain, and I was the defensive captain. They asked me to go meet the president, but I couldn't go because of those television shows.

That's a pretty big deal for a kid from Northport.

I'm like a lot of people who went to the university to play football. I wouldn't have been worth a damn without it. I wouldn't have gotten an education. I wouldn't have traveled anywhere. I wouldn't have become a broker. It got me name recognition.

I got to play eight years of pro football, four in Boston and four in Miami, on four good teams and four bad teams, and made All-Pro a couple of times. Of course, the money wasn't anything like it is now. I think in eight years I might have made a total of $600,000. That was more than the average person, but you certainly weren't set for life.

In the off-season I went to Huntsville, where my wife Susan is from, and I've worked for Wachovia Securities there since 1968. We raised our daughter, Claire, and our sons, Wes and Keith, in Huntsville. Wes and Keith also played at Alabama. My boys were full of Alabama and they were going to Alabama. But they were recruited by Coach Bryant like he didn't know them. He went to their games, came to our house. By then I had become much closer to Coach Bryant, and I'm glad I did.

I was on his first team, and Wes was on his last.

*Billy Neighbors was All-America in 1961 and won the Jacobs Award
as the best blocker in the SEC. He was selected as a member of the
Alabama Team of the Century and was selected to the Team of the
Decade for the '60s on both offense and defense. He was defensive
captain of the 1961 national championship team and was inducted
into the National Football Foundation Hall of Fame in 2003.*

---

## CORNELIUS BENNETT (INDUCTED 2005)

Only two Alabama players have been named first-team All-
American three times, and both were linebackers. Perhaps the
greatest of them all was Cornelius Bennett, who dominated oppos-
ing offenses under coach Ray Perkins in the 1980s. Bennett became
a starter early in his first season at Alabama, earning Freshman
All-America honors in 1983. He was first-year All-SEC and All-
America the next year, and first-team the three years after that.
He totaled 287 tackles (23 for loss), 15 sacks, six forced fumbles,
and three fumble recoveries in his Alabama career. He won the
Lombardi Award as the country's top defensive front-seven player
as a senior in 1986, when he totaled 61 tackles and 10 sacks, finished seventh in the Heisman Trophy balloting, and was named
SEC Most Valuable Player and SEC Defensive Player of the Year.
Bennett was responsible for one of the most famous individual
plays in Crimson Tide history when he knocked Notre Dame
quarterback Steve Beuerlein unconscious with "the Sack" in 1986.
Drafted No. 2 overall by the Indianapolis Colts in 1987, Bennett
played in five Super Bowls (four with Buffalo, one with Atlanta)
during a 14-year NFL career. He was a five-time Pro Bowler and
twice AFC Defensive Player of the Year.

## WOODROW LOWE (INDUCTED 2009)

What Cornelius Bennett was in the 1980s, Woodrow Lowe was a decade earlier. A four-year starter and three-time All-American, Lowe played on four consecutive SEC championship teams. He saw extensive playing time in 1972, the first year since World War II that freshmen were allowed by the NCAA to play on the varsity. Lowe set a single-season school record with 134 tackles in 1973, when Alabama won the national championship. He was named All-SEC and All-America that season and each of the two years afterward, finishing his career as part of Crimson Tide teams that went 43–5 overall and 27–1 in the SEC. Lowe was drafted in the fifth round by the San Diego Chargers in 1975, about which coach Bear Bryant said, "That's like getting a $50 gold piece for 50¢." Lowe played 11 years with the Chargers, totaling 21 interceptions and four touchdowns and missing just one game due to injury. He has served as an assistant coach in both college football and the NFL, and is now a successful high school coach at his alma mater, Phenix City Central.

---

## Crimson Tide in Their Own Words
# WOODROW LOWE
### LINEBACKER, 1972–1975

When people ask me why I went to Alabama instead of Auburn when I lived in Phenix City, just a few miles from Auburn, I have a simple answer. We had a flat tire. Auburn had invited me to a game, and I was going over with a buddy. But we had a flat tire, didn't have a spare, and had to hitchhike back to Phenix City to

Woodrow Lowe (47) earned his first of three All-America citations as a sophomore in 1973 as the Crimson Tide went undefeated in regular season play and won the national championship.

get help. I never made it to the Auburn game, and I never even met the Auburn coach who was supposed to be recruiting me.

I was being recruited by Pat Dye and Dude Hennessey for The University of Alabama. But I really wasn't that highly recruited. I didn't sign until about a month after everyone else had signed.

When I first started hearing from Alabama, my coach told me about Lee Roy Jordan. I went to the library and was able to do some research and found out what a great player he had been at Alabama, and that motivated me to want to be an Alabama linebacker.

And, of course, I knew what a great coach Paul Bryant was. And when I got there, I found out he was a lot greater than I suspected. One thing he talked about was character, and looking back, I can see we didn't have any players who weren't of high character. He talked to us about hard work, sacrifice, having confidence. He really stressed believing in yourself and how putting on that crimson jersey epitomized confidence. And he talked about the team, that no one person was bigger than the team. We had some stars, but I don't think even they knew it at the time.

I think it says something about Alabama that there has never been a Heisman Trophy winner, but there have been 12 Alabama teams that have been national champions. That speaks to team.

I think another key to success was that we never were down for long. If we had a setback, we bounced back. And we did it with sacrifice, hard work, and discipline. You're never far off from getting back on your feet if you know how to tighten your belt and get back to work.

It wasn't easy. It was an ordeal. But when you succeed, you have pride. I knew that I had been given the training and preparation to do whatever was necessary. That isn't conceit. But I was made to be confident that I was as good as anyone. We all know people who talk a good game. Coach Bryant and his staff taught us to play a good game. He told us when we made a good play to act like we were used to doing that. We didn't have to show out. We didn't have to tell anyone about it. If we were good enough, someone would tell us about it. And that is true.

I also believe I developed another trait. I didn't make much of an effort to get to Auburn after we had that flat tire back in 1971. But at the end of my career when we were about to play Penn State in the Sugar Bowl, I had to display great effort. And not in the game.

I went down to the lobby of the hotel to pay my incidentals because we checked out before the game. The university paid for our rooms and meals, but if we had phone calls or something like that, we had to pay for it ourselves. It was just a few dollars, but we had to take care of it before we left the hotel.

I could see the bus outside as I stood in line to pay my bill. Suddenly the bus started to move. I knew my bill wasn't very much, but I had a $20 bill in my hand and just gave it to the cashier with my key and took off running. Some of the players and even a couple of coaches saw me, and I could see they were laughing. I thought I would be in trouble, but I knew I would be in more trouble if I was late getting to the stadium. I just kept running. I was wearing my crimson blazer and a tie and felt like O.J. Simpson running through the airport in that television commercial that was popular at the time. Except I was running through the streets of New Orleans trying to catch the team bus. The bus would stop for a light, but just as I thought I might get to it, the light would change and off it would go again.

Fortunately, it wasn't very far to the Superdome. When the bus pulled up, I was pretty close to it. The players started coming off the bus, and I just mingled in with them. And I went out and played one of my best games, and we defeated Penn State. I don't know if Coach Bryant ever knew about me missing the bus. I think he probably did.

I had a lesson reinforced that day. I knew there were two time zones at Alabama. Central Time and Coach Bryant Time, and Coach Bryant Time was 15 minutes earlier.

I was fortunate enough to play 12 years with the San Diego Chargers. I have coached at the high school level and at the pro level, and I'm now coaching special teams at UAB. In everything I've done, I've taken the lessons I learned at The University of Alabama. My brother, Eddie, followed me to Alabama; my son, Woodrow, was a student coach there.

One thing that was unique about Coach Bryant was the way he stayed in touch with his former players. Each year before the start of the season, I'd get a telegram from him, a little note to let me know he was thinking about me and wishing me and the team good luck and reminding me to show class. I've got one of them framed and hanging in my house. I've talked to other former players like Joe Namath and Bob Baumhower, and he sent all of us those good luck notes at the beginning of every year. He never forgot his players, and no one who played for him will ever forget him.

> *Woodrow Lowe is one of two Alabama football players to be a three-time All-American, and he was also named Freshman All-America. He had 134 tackles for the 1973 national championship team. Lowe played 12 years in the NFL.*

*chapter 6*

# 20 MORE OF 'BAMA'S BEST

THERE SIMPLY ISN'T ENOUGH ROOM in the College Football Hall of Fame for all of Alabama's great players. Here are 20 men who might find their way into the game's hallowed halls one day. Either way, they're safely in the pantheon of Crimson Tide football heroes.

## SHAUN ALEXANDER, RB (1996–1999)

After a high school career that saw him rush for 6,657 yards and 110 touchdowns, Shaun Alexander actually sat out his freshman season at Alabama as a redshirt before bursting on the college football scene in 1996. He rushed for a school-record 291 yards and four touchdowns during a 26–0 victory at LSU that year but didn't establish himself as an every-down player until 1998. He began that season with a school-record five touchdowns against BYU and ended the year with 1,178 yards and 13 touchdowns as part of an All-SEC campaign. Alexander was an All-American and Heisman Trophy candidate his senior year, rushing for 1,383 yards and a school-record 19 touchdowns as Alabama won the SEC. He finished with a school record 3,565 yards rushing and 41 touchdowns. A first-round pick of the Seattle Seahawks in 2000, Alexander played nine years in the NFL, rushing for 9,453 yards

Shaun Alexander was a 1999 All-American and remains Alabama's all-time leading rusher with 3,565 yards.

and 100 touchdowns, including 1,880 yards and 27 scores in leading the Seahawks to Super Bowl XL in 2005.

## THOMAS BOYD, LB (1978–1982)

Thomas Boyd played during one of the most glorious times in Alabama football. During his four-year career, the Crimson Tide won three Southeastern Conference championships, two national titles, posted a 28-game winning streak, and never lost to either Auburn or Tennessee. Boyd was a three-year starter at linebacker, earning playing time as a freshman on Alabama's 1978 title team before moving into the starting lineup as the Crimson Tide repeated the following year. He was an All-American in both 1980 and 1981, including a career-high 120 tackles as a junior in 1980. Boyd finished his career with 324 tackles, a total that ranks second in school history since tackles became an official statistic in the 1970s. Boyd was an eighth-round draft pick of the Green Bay Packers in 1982 and later played with the Detroit Lions.

## LEROY COOK, DE (1972–1975)

There have been few defensive players in Alabama history more dominant than Leroy Cook, an All-America and All-SEC selection in both 1974 and 1975. He became a full-time starter as a junior and immediately became a star. The 6'4", 220-pound Cook totaled 81 tackles, six sacks, two forced fumbles, and three blocked kicks as the Crimson Tide went 11–1 and won the SEC title. He was even better as a senior, with 85 tackles, nine sacks, and four forced fumbles as Alabama went 11–1 and won the SEC again. Cook was also a contributor to the 1973 national championship team and four consecutive SEC titles. His promising NFL career was derailed when he suffered a knee injury during his senior season against Auburn, when a teammate jumped on his back while celebrating a big play. Cook was drafted by the Dallas Cowboys in the 10th round of the 1976 NFL Draft but never played a game in the pros due to the injury.

## BOBBY HUMPHREY, RB (1985–1988)

There was no more versatile running back in Alabama history than Bobby Humphrey, who finished an injury-shortened career as the Crimson Tide's career, single-season, and single-game rushing leader. The Birmingham native played extensively as a freshman in 1985 but became a true star as a sophomore. He set a school record with 1,471 yards and 15 touchdowns that season, earning All-SEC and All-America honors. Humphrey posted three games of 200-plus yards in 1986, including 284 yards against Mississippi State. He repeated his All-SEC and All-America recognition in 1987, when he rushed for 1,255 yards and 11 touchdowns to finish 10th in the Heisman Trophy balloting. Humphrey broke his foot early in the 1988 season and never returned to the field, finishing his career with 3,420 yards and 33 touchdowns rushing. He was drafted by the Denver Broncos and played four years in the NFL, starting in the 1990 Super Bowl against San Francisco. Humphrey was inducted into the Alabama Sports Hall of Fame in 2004 and was a 2011 nominee for the College Football Hall of Fame.

---

## *Crimson Tide in Their Own Words*

# BOBBY HUMPHREY

### TAILBACK, 1985–1988

I know that a lot of players who went to Alabama grew up fans of the Crimson Tide and were well aware of the great Alabama

Bobby Humphrey was a record-setting tailback for the Crimson Tide. Although he grew up in Birmingham and sold Cokes to attend Alabama games at Legion Field, he had little knowledge of 'Bama tradition until playing for the Tide.

football tradition. That didn't have anything to do with me selecting The University of Alabama. The great Alabama tradition was not a factor in my decision because I was not aware of it. I didn't grow up an Alabama fan. Now, I did like it when Alabama played its games in Birmingham and I could sell Cokes and get into the games to watch. But I was a city boy, from the projects. No one in my family had gone to Alabama or knew anything about Alabama and its tradition.

That said, it was one of the greatest decisions I ever made and something I am very, very proud of. While I didn't know anything about the tradition before I got to Alabama, when I did get there, I began to find out about it. And the more I learned, the more I wanted to know, and so I found out even more. That made me even more proud of the decision I had made.

I think I decided on Alabama because I thought it was the place I would have the best chance for early playing time. At the time, I think, Auburn had several good running backs returning. Alabama had Kerry Goode, a premier back to be sure, but Kerry had been injured.

I wanted to stay close to home and had decided I was going to stay in the state. I knew it was going to be either Alabama or Auburn. So I decided to go to Alabama because the chance to compete for playing time seemed better.

Once you have done it, you realize it means a lot to play for the Crimson Tide. There is something special about wearing the crimson and white and knowing you are a part of the best in college football. I look back and see that it was almost lucky that I ended up at Alabama and consider myself very fortunate.

Over the years, I have talked with a lot of football players from many, many colleges and universities, and I am convinced that no one has better fans than The University of Alabama. I have been amazed at the number of fans I have met and the places I have met them around the country. When I was playing in the NFL, I would see Alabama fans in the stadiums supporting me. I'm now coach of the Birmingham Steeldogs, and Alabama fans make up a great part of our fan base because I am part of the Alabama family.

Players from other schools are envious of the support that Alabama players get from Crimson Tide fans, who in my opinion also are a part of the Alabama family.

Alabama fans have great respect for the men who played football for the Crimson Tide. Most amazing, though, is the memories of the fans. The games sort of run together for me, but I have met many, many people who can tell me in detail about things that happened in games in 1985 and 1986 when I was a freshman and sophomore. They remember extraordinary details, and you know that you have given them something to be proud of.

After my playing career at Alabama, I played five years of professional football, three at Denver and two at Miami. I signed with Buffalo in 1995, but never played.

In 1997 I returned to the university to get my degree. And when I graduated in 1998, there were Alabama fans there to show their support for me as a student.

I worked for a semester in the Tuscaloosa County school system, then got the opportunity to coach the Birmingham Steeldogs in their first season in 2000.

*Bobby Humphrey was an All-American in 1986 and 1987 and named Alabama's Offensive Player of the Decade. In 1986 he rushed for a school record 1,471 yards. He was SEC Offensive Player of the Year in 1987. He was MVP of the Sun Bowl. He played in the NFL for Denver and Miami and coached in arena football from 2000 to 2005.*

## MARK INGRAM, RB (2008–2010)

Alabama finally got its first Heisman Trophy winner in 2009, its 115th season of college football. Ingram set a school record with 1,658 rushing yards in leading the Crimson Tide to a 14–0 record and the BCS national championship. He was the first running back since 1976 to win both the Heisman and the national title in the same season. The son of the former NFL star of the same name, Ingram came to Alabama to play for Nick Saban, the same man who coached his father at Michigan State. Serving as backup to Glen Coffee, Ingram rushed for 728 yards and 12 touchdowns as a freshman in 2008. He posted nine 100-yard games in 2009, including 116 yards and two touchdowns in the national title win over Texas. He was also a first-team All-American, the SEC Offensive Player of the Year, and won the Doak Walker Award as the country's top running back. His junior season was marred by a knee injury suffered in preseason camp that forced him to miss the first two games, but Ingram still rushed for 875 yards and 13 scores before leaving school to enter the NFL Draft. His career total of 42 rushing touchdowns is a school record, while his 3,261 yards ranks third behind Shaun Alexander and Bobby Humphrey.

## BOBBY JOHNS, DB (1966–1968)

One of only a handful of Alabama players to be named All-America more than once, Bobby Johns was one of the Crimson Tide's top defensive players of the 1960s. He started on Alabama's 1965 national championship team, totaling a team-high six interceptions. When the Crimson Tide went undefeated the following year—but did not win the national championship—Johns had four interceptions, including touchdowns against Vanderbilt and LSU. He was named first-team All-America that year and topped it off with three interceptions in a 34–7 Sugar Bowl win over

Nebraska. Despite just one interception as a senior in 1967, Johns repeated his All-America honors. Drafted by the AFL's Kansas City Chiefs, Johns instead elected to enter the coaching field, serving as an assistant at South Carolina, Eastern Kentucky, Chattanooga, Florida State, and Valdosta State, and was head coach at West Alabama from 1997 to 2000. Johns was inducted into the Alabama Sports Hall of Fame in 2010.

## JULIO JONES, WR (2008–2010)

One of the more hotly recruited players in Alabama football history, Julio Jones was a star before he even stepped on campus in Tuscaloosa. The 6'3", 210-pound Jones was SEC Freshman of the Year and a Freshman All-American in 2008, when he totaled 58 receptions for 924 yards and four touchdowns. Despite nagging injuries throughout the season, Jones helped Alabama to the national championship as a sophomore in 2009. He grabbed 43 passes for 596 yards and four scores, none bigger than a 73-yard catch and run to give the Crimson Tide the lead in a 24–15 victory over LSU. Jones enjoyed his best season as a junior, with a school-record 78 receptions for 1,133 yards and seven scores despite playing most of the season with a broken hand. He totaled 12 receptions for 221 yards in a victory over Tennessee and 10 catches for 199 yards in a loss to Auburn. After being named first-team All-SEC and second-team All-America, Jones was selected in the first round of the 2011 NFL Draft, No. 6 overall, by the Atlanta Falcons.

## BARRY KRAUSS, LB (1975–1978)

Barry Krauss was involved in perhaps the most famous play in Alabama football history, the goal-line stand against Penn State in the 1979 Sugar Bowl. With the Crimson Tide clinging to a 14–7 lead, Krauss stopped Penn State's Mike Guman just short of the end zone on fourth down to secure a national championship for Alabama. Krauss was named Most Valuable Player of the Game, as well as a 36–6 victory over UCLA in the Liberty Bowl two years earlier when he returned an interception for a touchdown. Krauss was a three-year starter for the Crimson Tide, and a first-team All-SEC and All-America selection as a senior in 1978. His interception on a two-point conversion secured a 21–20 victory over top-ranked Southern Cal in 1977, when he totaled a team-best 91 tackles to earn second-team All-SEC honors. As a senior, he finished second on the team with 112 stops. Krauss was a first-round pick of the Baltimore Colts in 1979 and played 11 years in the NFL. Most recently, Krauss has served as sideline reporter for Crimson Tide football on the radio.

## ANTONIO LANGHAM, CB (1990–1993)

Antonio Langham was perhaps the most gifted player on one of the most celebrated defenses in Alabama football history, the 1992 squad that carried the Crimson Tide to the national title. Langham scored touchdowns in three consecutive games that season, including a 27-yard interception return for the winning points in Alabama's 28–21 victory over Florida in the SEC Championship Game. The Town Creek native was an All-American as both a junior and a senior, and ended his Alabama career as the Crimson Tide's all-time leader with 19 interceptions. Langham won the 1993 Jim Thorpe Award as the top defensive back in college football and was a first-round pick of the Cleveland Browns in 1994. Langham is also a member of one of Alabama football's greatest families, with six of his cousins—Kerry, Chris, Pierre, Clyde Goode, Tarrant Lynch, and Steven Harris—all playing for the Crimson Tide between 1983 and 1997.

## MARTY LYONS, DT (1975–1978)

The defensive captain of Alabama's 1978 national championship team, Marty Lyons was a two-time All-SEC pick and an All-American as a senior. An athletic 6'6" and 250 pounds, Lyons totaled 59 tackles as the Crimson Tide went 11–1 in 1977. The following year, he piled up a team-high 119 tackles, including a career-best 16 in a 34–16 win over Auburn. Lyons was part of three SEC championship teams, with Alabama posting a 31–5 record during his tenure. He was part of the goal-line stand in the 1979 Sugar Bowl, famously telling Penn State quarterback Chuck Fusina, "You better pass," just before the decisive fourth-and-1 play. Lyons was drafted by the New York Jets in the 1979 NFL Draft and played 11 years with the team as part of the famed "New York Sack Exchange" defensive line that also included Mark Gastineau, Joe Klecko, and Abdul Salaam. [*Editor's note: Lyons was elected to the College Football Hall of Fame in May 2011.*]

## BOBBY MARLOW, RB (1950–1952)

Perhaps the first modern-style standout running back in Alabama football history, Bobby Marlow led the Crimson Tide in rushing three consecutive seasons. He rushed for 882 yards and six touchdowns as a sophomore in 1950, including 180 yards and four touchdowns in a 54–19 victory over Georgia Tech. He was a first-team All-SEC pick in 1951, when he totaled 728 yards and 12 touchdowns, including a 233-yard three-touchdown effort against Auburn. That yardage total was the highest in Alabama history for more than 30 years and remains the fourth-highest mark for a Crimson Tide back. Marlow rushed for a then–Alabama record 950 yards as a senior in 1952, when he was named SEC Player of the Year and a first-team All-American. Despite being selected in the first round of the 1953 draft by the New York Giants,

Marlow elected to play in Canada, playing eight seasons for the Saskatchewan Roughriders. He was a five-time CFL all-star and was inducted into the Roughriders Plaza of Honor in 1989. He died in 1985 at age 55.

## Joe Namath, QB (1962–1964)

One of football's all-time superstars, Joe Namath first made his name as Alabama's athletic and stylish quarterback in the early 1960s. He set a school record with three touchdown passes in his first college game, a 35–0 rout of Georgia in 1962. Alabama went 10–1 that year and won the Orange Bowl, beating Oklahoma 17–0. Namath was suspended late in the 1963 season but returned with an outstanding senior season despite a major knee injury suffered against North Carolina State in October 1964. Namath was named All-SEC and All-America that year, helping Alabama to the national championship. He came off the bench to throw two touchdown passes in the Orange Bowl against Texas but was stopped short of the goal line in the final seconds of a 21–17 Alabama loss. Namath was drafted by the New York Jets as the top overall selection in 1965 and signed for a then-record $427,000. He led the Jets to their lone championship in Super Bowl III, being named MVP of a 16–7 victory over the heavily favored Baltimore Colts. Namath retired in 1976 and later was an actor and television commentator. Inducted into the Pro Football Hall of Fame in 1985, Namath returned to Alabama and graduated in 2007, 42 years after leaving school 15 credits short of a degree.

## David Palmer, WR/KR (1991–1993)

Ask many Alabama fans who the most exciting player in Crimson Tide history was, and many will answer with David Palmer. "The

Deuce" (so named because he wore jersey No. 2), Palmer helped the Crimson Tide to the 1992 national championship and finished third in the Heisman Trophy balloting the following season. A high school quarterback in Birmingham, Palmer was an electrifying wide receiver and kick returner during his college career despite standing just 5'9" and weighing 170 pounds. He returned four punts for touchdowns as a freshman in 1991, including one in the Crimson Tide's Blockbuster Bowl victory over Colorado. Suspended the first three games of the 1992 season, Palmer returned a punt for the only touchdown of a 13–0 victory over Louisiana Tech that season. As a junior in 1993, Palmer caught 61 passes for 1,000 yards and seven scores and also played several games at quarterback when teammates were injured. He was a first-team All-American that season, and his third-place Heisman finish was the best in school history at the time. Palmer left school after his junior year to enter the NFL Draft and played seven seasons with the Minnesota Vikings.

## CHRIS SAMUELS, OT (1996–1999)

A three-year starter at offensive tackle, Chris Samuels was Alabama's first Outland Trophy winner as a senior in 1999. He was also first-team All-SEC, first-team All-America, and won the Jacobs Trophy as the SEC's top blocker that season, when the Crimson Tide went 10–3 and won the conference title. The 6'6", 291-pound "Big Sam" started 42 consecutive games at Alabama, clearing the way for All-America running back Shaun Alexander. A first-round pick of the Washington Redskins in 2000, Samuels played 10 seasons in the NFL, starting 141 games and being named to six Pro Bowls. Forced to retire in 2009 due to injuries, Samuels has stayed in the game to pursue a coaching career.

## ANDRE SMITH, OT (2006–2008)

Andre Smith inherited the mantle from Samuels as one of Alabama's all-time great offensive tackles, winning the Outland Trophy in 2008 as a junior. That season, the 6'4", 340-pound Smith led Alabama to a 12–2 record and the SEC West championship. Smith started three seasons at Alabama, being named Freshman All-America in 2006, first-team All-SEC and winner of the Jacobs Trophy in 2007, and first-team All-America in 2008. Smith left Alabama following his junior season and was a first-round pick by the Cincinnati Bengals.

## KEN STABLER, QB (1965–1967)

Part of Alabama's run of four All-America quarterbacks in the 1960s, Stabler was a star in both football and baseball for the Crimson Tide. Nicknamed "Snake" due to his running style, Stabler split time with All-American Steve Sloan on Alabama's 1965 national championship team and then became the full-time starter the following season. He led the Crimson Tide to an 11–0 record and a Sugar Bowl rout of Nebraska, but Alabama did not win the national championship. Stabler again stood out in 1967, though the Crimson Tide slipped a bit to an 8–2–1 record. He was a first-team All-SEC and All-America pick that year, and also went 10–0 as a left-handed pitcher. Stabler was drafted three times by major league baseball teams but stuck with football after the Oakland Raiders selected him in the second round of the 1968 draft. He played in the NFL until 1984, leading the Raiders to the Super Bowl championship in 1977. Stabler later served several years as Alabama's color commentator on the radio.

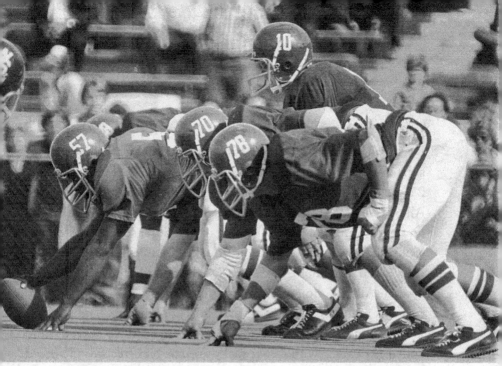

Dwight Stephenson (57) is considered the best center in the history of football. As a senior, he anchored the offensive line of the 1979 national championship team.

## DWIGHT STEPHENSON, C (1976–1979)

Alabama's Paul "Bear" Bryant and the Miami Dolphins' Don Shula both called Dwight Stephenson the greatest center they ever coached. Stephenson was a three-year starter for the Crimson Tide, earning All-SEC honors all three years and All-America twice. He helped Alabama to a 34–2 record, three SEC championships, and two national championships in his three years as a starter. He won the Jacobs Trophy as the SEC's top blocker during his senior season. Stephenson was drafted in the second round by Miami in 1980 and played eight years in the NFL before a severe knee injury ended his career. A starter in two Super Bowls, a five-time Pro Bowl selection, and a four-time All-Pro, he was selected to the Pro Football Hall of Fame in 1998 despite a relatively short career.

## DERRICK THOMAS, LB (1985–1988)

Derrick Thomas enjoyed one of the most dominant individual seasons in Crimson Tide history as a senior in 1988. Thomas posted 27 sacks, 88 tackles, and two forced fumbles, earning first-team All-SEC and All-America honors and being named Alabama's first-ever winner of the Butkus Award. That season, he posted five sacks against Texas A&M and four against Penn State. He also dominated as a junior, totaling 18 sacks and seven forced fumbles to earn All-SEC honors. Thomas' 52 career sacks are more than twice as many as any other player in school history. Thomas was a first-round pick of the NFL's Kansas City Chiefs in 1989 and ended his career with 126½ sacks and an NFL record 45 forced fumbles in 11 seasons. He was named to nine Pro Bowls, earned All-Pro honors twice, and was inducted into the Pro Football Hall of Fame in 2009. Thomas' career and life were cut short in 2000, when he died at age 33 a few weeks after being paralyzed in a car accident.

## PAT TRAMMELL, QB (1959–1961)

Though he was never a first-team All-American, Pat Trammell remains one of the most-admired players in Alabama football history. Trammell quarterbacked the Crimson Tide to three straight bowl games, including an 11–0 record and the national championship as a senior in 1961. He passed for 1,035 yards and eight touchdowns with just two interceptions as a senior, finishing sixth in the Heisman Trophy balloting. Trammell went 26–2–4 as a starting quarterback at Alabama, a winning percentage of .875. He passed up a chance at pro football to go to medical school but was diagnosed with testicular cancer while working on his residency in dermatology. Trammell died December 10, 1968, at age 28, leaving a wife and two young children behind. Bryant called

Pat Trammell was the first star quarterback of the Paul Bryant era and led the Crimson Tide to the 1961 national championship.

the day of Trammell's funeral "the saddest day of my life." The "A" Club Memorial Scholarship—later renamed the Paul Bryant Scholarship—was established in his honor by former teammates.

## TOMMY WILCOX, S (1979–1982)

After a stellar career as a high school quarterback, Tommy Wilcox moved to defensive back in college and was a four-year starter. He helped Alabama to the 1979 national championship, earning SEC Freshman of the Year honors when he totaled 49 tackles and four interceptions in the Crimson Tide's 12–0 run to the Sugar Bowl. Wilcox was also part of 39 victories, two SEC title teams, and three bowl wins. An All-American in both 1981 and 1982, Wilcox played key roles in both Paul "Bear" Bryant's record 315th victory over Auburn and his final victory in the Liberty Bowl over Illinois, and totaled 243 tackles and 10 interceptions in his Alabama career. An avid outdoorsman from Louisiana, Wilcox now hosts a popular hunting and fishing show on television.

## chapter 7
# MEMORIES, MYTHS, AND LEGENDS

ALABAMA FOOTBALL HISTORY IS FILLED with great plays and decisions that led to many a memorable victory. But there are also moments that, while often not directly related to who won or lost, are just as memorable. Here's a sampling of the greatest Crimson Tide football stories ever.

### THE TIDES THAT BIND

The Crimson Tide annals are filled with great brother and father-son teams—and even a few father-son-brother teams. First were the VandeGraaff brothers of Tuscaloosa: Adrian, Hargrove, and W.T. "Bully," Alabama's first All-American in 1915. The Mosleys of Blytheville, Arkansas—Herky, Russ, and Monk—also had a memorable run with the Crimson Tide in the 1930s and '40s.

It seemed like Paul Bryant's Alabama teams always had a Davis kicking field goals, and for many years they did. Columbus, Georgia, natives Tim, Steve, Bill, and Mike Davis all handled placements for the Crimson Tide between 1961 and 1975.

Two Rutledges from Birmingham quarterbacked the Crimson Tide to national championships in the 1970s, Gary in 1973 and Jeff in 1978. Woodrow Lowe was a three-time All-America linebacker in the mid-1970s; his younger brother, Eddie, was a standout defensive end on Bryant's last team in 1982.

Then there were the Goodes of Town Creek, the only four-brother letterman group in Alabama history. First came Kerry in 1983, followed by Chris in 1986, Pierre in 1987, and Clyde in 1989. Three of the Goodes' cousins—Antonio Langham, Tarrant Lynch, and Steven Harris—also played for the Crimson Tide in the 1990s.

In 2004 the Britts of Cullman were the first three brothers to all play for the Crimson Tide simultaneously since the VandeGraaffs had done so more than 90 years earlier. Wesley joined the Alabama team in 2000, followed by Taylor in 2003 and Justin in 2004.

There have been dozens of father-son combos through the years at Alabama, but only two three-generation families of lettermen. First were the Millers: grandfather Floyd in the late 1940s, father Noah Dean in the early 1970s, and sons Marc and Matt in the early 2000s. The Neighbors family—Billy, Wes, and Wesley—joined them when Wesley lettered in 2010.

Other great father-son duos include the Croyles (John and Brodie), the Tiffins (Van and Leigh), and the Castilles (Jeremiah and sons Tim and Simeon). James and Lance Taylor became the first African American father-son duo to letter at Alabama when Lance did so in 2001. They have since been joined by the Castilles and the Kings (Tyrone Sr. and Jr.).

But perhaps the greatest family in Alabama football history is the Hannahs of Albertville: father Herb and sons John, Charley, and David. Herb played for the Crimson Tide from 1948 to 1950 and later went on to the NFL's New York Giants.

John Hannah followed his father to Tuscaloosa and became an All-American in 1971 and 1972 (and later a Hall of Famer with the NFL's New England Patriots). Charley Hannah was an All-SEC defensive lineman in 1976, and youngest brother, David, started on back-to-back national championship teams in 1978 and 1979, earning All-SEC honors in the latter season.

"When I was growing up, my father encouraged me and my brothers, Charley and David, in athletics, but he didn't push us," John Hannah remembered. "In fact, he never coached us. I was four years older than Charley and six years older than David, which is a lot when you are a teenager, so we were never able to play together. When I was in the pros, I got to play against Charley once when he was at Oakland and once when he was at Tampa Bay. When I was at Boston, David got to come up for training camp and work as a ball boy. He got a lot of instruction on offensive line play from us players and coaches. But then he went back to Alabama, and they moved him to the defensive line."

---

## *Crimson Tide in Their Own Words*
# WESLEY BRITT
### OFFENSIVE TACKLE, 2001–2004

How close did I come to not having a final year of football at Alabama in 2004? Not what you might think. Some people might have thought I was going to turn pro after the 2003 season, but that wasn't an option. The reason I played in 2004 is because I was redshirted in 2000. And the reason for that was a timeout by Ole Miss during my first year at Alabama. I wasn't happy about being redshirted. I came in with big expectations. I was the second-team tackle on both the left and right. I was traveling to every game. They were preparing me to play. And I was about to go in the game against Ole Miss.

Wesley Britt missed half of his junior year with a broken leg but came back with an All-America season. He was joined on the 2004 team by brothers Taylor and Justin.

Neil Callaway was my offensive line coach. He had me put the headset on so he could talk to me from the press box. He told me the play and what he wanted me to do, because of the way Ole Miss was playing. He was giving me the steps.

Then Ole Miss called a timeout, and Coach DuBose and Coach Callaway decided to not send me in. They knew I was having good practices, and I think they wanted to play me because they thought I was good enough. But once we started losing, I think they decided not to waste the year.

I wanted to play. I've been playing organized football since I was in the second grade. But I knew that God had a plan and I would have the faith to realize that plan.

I've had an unusual career, with four head coaches and three position coaches. And I enjoyed it very much.

There was a time when it would have been unlikely that I would have been at Alabama. Growing up, we were Auburn fans. And then I went to a lot of Florida games, including the game in "the Swamp" when Alabama ended Florida's long home winning streak in 1999.

What really made Alabama different was the people. I'd go to Florida on a recruiting visit, and they'd look at the tag on my shirt and say, "We'd love to have you here." When I went to Alabama, the people didn't have to look at a nametag. They looked at my face and said, "Hey, Wesley. We can't wait to have you here. We can't wait to get you. You're an Alabama boy, and we have to have you." That made me feel at home.

I think the reason we were Auburn fans growing up—everyone except my brother Taylor—is because we didn't go to Alabama games. Then we got some tickets for Alabama games, and comparing Alabama to Auburn changed my mind. I began to fall in love with Alabama. By the time I was a high school senior, Alabama and Florida were the only choices.

I liked playing for Coach Fran and his offensive line coach, Jim Bob Helduser. He was a great motivator. We didn't really have a lot of technique in pass blocking or run blocking. He just wanted to see us get them on the ground. We learned a lot about becoming a physical football team.

They didn't care if the other team knew what was coming. We had a player transfer to Mississippi State, so when we played them, they knew all our audibles. We called a lot of plays at the line, and we'd hear their defense talking—"option right" or "belly left" or whatever. It didn't matter. We just ran over them because that's the kind of football we played.

We thought things were in pretty good shape. We had just had a 10-win season and had a lot of players back. And then Fran left. It was a hard process. We had just learned the system and were excited about having another year with it. The way he left kind of stripped away the foundation of what we were building.

I suppose that's the nature of the profession and that he did the best thing for himself and his family, but we were understandably let down.

Mike Price came in, and he loved the opportunity he had. He was living a dream. And then he had that rude awakening. The way we practiced was great. I don't know how he did it, but he had us practicing so hard without being forced. He had us practicing and competing and wanting to work and get better. And I'm talking about the whole team, everyone. We had a great spring, and all of a sudden he was gone, and we didn't have a head coach.

Coach Bob Connelly came in with Coach Price. He is a real technician. I learned a lot of technique in the final two years of my career. I know it was beneficial to take the technique I learned for pass blocking and run blocking to a chance in the NFL. I think I had a great base.

When Coach Shula came in, we didn't have a playbook the whole summer. It was up to us to do it ourselves. We couldn't pick up a playbook or take one with us. We had to get together and learn how to play with a new system. We didn't have the season that we felt we should or could, but we kept fighting. We never gave up. We never made excuses. We played hard for The University of Alabama.

Playing at Alabama prepared me for the next level. My five years at Alabama, I went against six defensive linemen in practice who are in the NFL right now. You don't find that at many other schools. The level of competition we play at in the SEC, the media and fan attention, and the atmosphere you play in week-in and week-out is something you can almost directly compare to the NFL.

One other thing that I think helped me get to the next level is Justin Smiley, who left after his junior year to go to the NFL. We are really good friends, on and off the field. And we pushed each other to be better. We competed in the weight room and in drills. I'd break a record in the weight room, and then he'd come behind me and break it, and so on. That competition made us both a lot better.

The one game I hear the most about is one I didn't finish. The 2003 Tennessee game, which we would eventually lose in five overtimes, was the game in which I suffered a broken leg in the first half. I was blocking on the end, and a linebacker dived for Shaud Williams and landed on my leg. When I was carted off the field, I wanted everyone to keep supporting the team and not worry about me, so I tried to give encouragement to my teammates and the fans. I was really pumping my fist for Coach Shula and the players, telling them to keep going, to beat Tennessee, but I heard the crowd roar and felt they were fired up, too.

I hope it showed the faith I have in the Lord and that that is the way I'll be remembered.

The two games I remember the most are beating Tennessee in Knoxville and beating Auburn in Jordan-Hare my freshman year. Nobody thought we could win that Auburn game, and we beat them 31–7. We were playing so physically and having a great time out there.

Against Tennessee, we knew what we did best, and that wasn't throwing the ball. We just wore away the Tennessee defense and plowed the linemen and linebackers. We just kept pounding the ball. They knew what was going on, and there was nothing they could do about it. That's the best feeling—being an offensive lineman and knowing before the snap that you're about to dominate.

I am very fortunate that I was able to play the 2004 season with my brothers, Taylor and Justin. That was amazing. I'm really thankful to have my name and theirs in the books at this tradition-rich school.

*Wesley Britt was captain of the 2004 team. He was winner of the Jacobs Award, voted by SEC coaches for the best blocker in the league. He was All-SEC and selected to play in the Senior Bowl.*

## The "Traitor"

It might be unthinkable for a star player from Tuscaloosa to go anywhere other than Alabama, but Joe Domnanovich did something similar with he spurned his hometown team, Notre Dame, and joined the Crimson Tide in the late 1930s.

Domnanovich became an All-America center with the Crimson Tide in 1942, but many in his hometown of South Bend, Indiana, never forgave him. As Domnanovich recalled:

When the *South Bend Tribune* found out I was going to Alabama, they ran a little cartoon of me with the Golden Dome in the background and me heading out with a suitcase that had "Traitor" written on it. Since I was from South Bend,

Joe Domnanovich, a native of South Bend, Indiana (home of Notre Dame), was an All-America center for the Crimson Tide in 1942 and was later selected to the All-Time Orange Bowl Team.

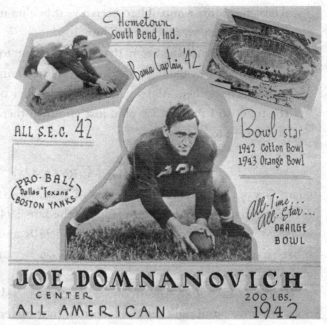

Hometown South Bend, Ind.

Bama Captain '42

ALL S.E.C. '42

PRO-BALL
Dallas 'Texans'
BOSTON YANKS

Bowl star
1942 Cotton Bowl
1943 Orange Bowl

All-Time...
All-Star...
ORANGE
BOWL

**JOE DOMNANOVICH**
CENTER 200 LBS.
ALL AMERICAN 1942

Indiana, almost everyone thinks I went to Alabama because of coach Frank Thomas, who had played at Notre Dame. But I had never heard of him until Alabama started recruiting me in 1938.

I thought I'd go to Notre Dame. I was named the most outstanding player at my high school my senior year. I had some hip problems and went over to Notre Dame because they had a trainer who was pretty well known. I went there and got treatment every week. But when the time came, I never heard a word from Notre Dame. So I went to work for a year.

Purdue and Indiana had talked to me, but I wasn't interested. In fact, I wasn't really interested in going to college. A guy from Gary, Indiana, came to see me about playing for

Alabama. Mort Kimball had been a year behind me at South Bend, and they were recruiting him, too.

Alabama was the team that always went to the bowl games. That was the big thing for me. Notre Dame didn't go to bowls back then. Alabama used to go to the Rose Bowl all the time, so I thought I would just go down there. So Mort and I went to Alabama.

## "TWO HANDS, GRYSKA!"

Clem Gryska has been an institution in Tuscaloosa for more than 60 years, first as an Alabama player in the late 1940s, later as an assistant coach under Paul Bryant in the 1960s and '70s, and for more than 20 years a fixture at the Paul W. Bryant Museum on campus.

It doesn't take long for anyone who meets Gryska to notice he does not have a full right hand. He lost all four fingers on that hand during a work accident as a young man in Steubenville, Ohio.

"I was working in a grocery store when I was 11 or 12 years old and lost my right hand in a meat grinder," Gryska said. "The doctor did a great job to save the thumb, or I wouldn't have been able to do anything. I wrote and called him until he passed away. If he hadn't done that, I would have been helpless."

Though the injury meant he was unfit for military service in World War II, Gryska didn't let his condition become a disability. Crimson Tide coach Frank Thomas coached in an all-star game near Gryska's hometown and eventually offered the young half-back a scholarship to play for the Crimson Tide.

Gryska lettered at Alabama in 1947 and 1948, playing on the Crimson Tide team that beat Auburn 55–0 in the reinstitution of the Iron Bowl his senior year. His missing digits led to at least one humorous exchange on the practice field.

"In 1947, after coach Red Drew took over for coach Frank Thomas, we switched our offense from the Notre Dame box to the wing T, a tight formation," Gryska said. "I had been a quarterback, which was really a blocking back in the box, but moved to right end in the T formation. We were having a practice session one day, and a pass was thrown to me. I dropped it. Coach Drew shouted, 'Two hands, Gryska, two hands!' That broke the team up. If I had two hands, I might not have been at Alabama."

Clem Gryska, who lost most of his right hand in a meat grinder accident as a youth, served Alabama as a player, assistant coach, and administrator. After his retirement from the athletics department, he moved to the Bryant Museum.

## TOO FULL OF ALABAMA

Tommy Lewis was a fine football player for the Crimson Tide in the early 1950s, the fullback in a backfield that also included the likes of Bobby Marlow, Bart Starr, Bobby Luna, and Corky Tharp. But if he is remembered for anything today, it is a bizarre occurrence during his last game at Alabama, the 1954 Cotton Bowl against Rice.

Lewis was the man who left the bench, minus his helmet, to tackle Rice's Dicky Moegle during a long run down the Crimson Tide sideline. Moegle was awarded a 95-yard touchdown on the play, and Rice went on to a 28–6 victory, but Lewis was forced to live with the shame of his infamous moment.

"I've never wanted to talk about the Cotton Bowl incident," he said more than 50 years later. "I knew the moment it was over that I would be hearing about it all my life. If there is one thing in my life I could take back, it would be that. I just didn't want that guy getting into our end zone. I'm still embarrassed by it. It's not my nature to do something like that. But I didn't want to lose my last game at Alabama, where I had dreamed all my life of playing. I'd do anything to keep from losing. And I did. But if I could take it back, I would.

"My teammates consoled me. My friends consoled me. They knew how I felt. And Alabama fans have been wonderful to me. I have never had an Alabama fan say that I had embarrassed him. But I embarrassed myself."

The play caused such a national stir that Lewis and Moegle later appeared together on *The Ed Sullivan Show*. Asked by the host why he did what he did, Lewis replied simply, "I'm just too full of Alabama."

Alabama guard Harry Lee, who was standing next to Lewis just before he charged off the bench, said everyone on the Crimson

Tide sympathized with their teammate. "I was the last person Tommy spoke to before he did it," Lee said. "In fact, he dropped his helmet, and it hit my foot. Later he apologized to Rice and Moegle and everyone else and said he was just too full of Alabama. And we understood because we all were.

"We all felt for Tommy and did all we could to protect him from photographers coming to our bench area trying to get a picture of him. They didn't get any pictures."

---

*Crimson Tide in Their Own Words*

# TOMMY LEWIS

### FULLBACK, 1951–1953

I've never wanted to talk about the Cotton Bowl incident. I knew the moment it was over that I would be hearing about it all my life. If there is one thing in my life I could take back, it would be that. I just didn't want that guy getting into our end zone. I'm still embarrassed by it. It's not my nature to do something like that. But I didn't want to lose my last game at Alabama, where I had dreamed all my life of playing. I'd do anything to keep from losing. And I did. But if I could take it back, I would.

My teammates consoled me. My friends consoled me. They knew how I felt. And Alabama fans have been wonderful to me. I have never had an Alabama fan say that I had embarrassed him. But I embarrassed myself.

I had wanted to play football for The University of Alabama since I was a little kid growing up in Greenville, Alabama. My father had been a great football player at Butler County High School, before there was a Greenville High School. I had seen

Tommy Lewis (42) is best known for his tackle from the bench in the Cotton Bowl, but he was an excellent fullback on powerful Alabama squads.

pictures of him in his leather helmet and heard the stories around town of what a player he was. Everyone knew him. He was considered a tough hombre.

We listened to Alabama football games on the radio when I was growing up. When I was a junior and senior in high school, I had a chance to be a junior counselor at Camp Mountain Lake near Tracy City, Tennessee. I didn't get paid anything, but I didn't have to pay to go, and it was a pleasant experience. The big drawing card for the camp was Harry Gilmer, who would bring kids up from Birmingham.

I admired every step Harry Gilmer took. After the regular camp activities each day, we'd have a football session. After it was over, I'd ask him to throw me a "Harry Gilmer pass." I'd run down the field and run either an out or a post, whatever he told me to do. And he would run out to his right and throw me that jump pass. That was almost more than I could stand, I was so happy. And you can bet I never dropped a Harry Gilmer pass.

There is no way to say how much I wanted to play for Alabama. I worked hard on my own to become a good football player. I don't know how in the world college football coaches found out about me playing in the little South Alabama town of Greenville, but I still have letters and telegrams from colleges that were recruiting me from around the country. One of them is from Coach Bryant at Kentucky. But I never gave a thought to any of them except Alabama. The day Alabama offered me a football scholarship, it made my world. It was the Crimson Tide for me!

Joe Kilgrow was the freshman coach for Coach Drew, and he recruited me for Alabama. And I was glad he did.

One of the men I played with at Alabama was Bobby Marlow. I tell people he is one of the main reasons I went to Alabama. Our Greenville team played his Troy team, and he just about killed all of us. I decided I wanted to play on his side. Bobby Marlow and I were about the same size, about 195 pounds, but he was twice as powerful. He was the halfback, and I was the fullback because they wanted me blocking for him. We also had Clell Hobson at quarterback and Bobby Luna at halfback. Looking back on it now, I thought that Happy Campbell, who was the backfield coach, might have had an easy job, but I'm sure that's not true. He was a great coach, and he was always very good to me.

Freshmen couldn't play for the varsity in 1950, and Alabama had a very fine varsity team. We played three freshman games, beating Georgia Tech, Georgia, and Auburn. The main thing I remember about my first year is one practice. Coach Drew had a separate practice field for the freshmen. But there was a tradition that each year the freshman team would "go across the fence," which meant we went to the varsity practice field for a scrimmage. We knew one day we'd get the call, but we didn't know when. One day Coach Drew said, "We're going across the fence." And so we ran—we ran everywhere—across to the varsity field. And we were scared to death because we knew there was a lot of quality talent and didn't know what they might do to us. But we held our own pretty well.

Alabama had made the transition from the Notre Dame box, but we still shifted to the box occasionally. I can remember playing an opening game in Crampton Bowl, and I can still hear the "2, 4, 7," which shifted us into what was a single-wing formation.

I was only a fullback my first two years, but in 1953 we went to one platoon, and I also played linebacker.

We had a good team in 1952 and went to the Orange Bowl to play Syracuse. In those days, the teams went to functions together. We didn't get all buddy-buddy, but we did mingle with them and get to know them, and they were very nice guys.

It was one of those days. The first team didn't play much over two quarters, but Bobby Luna and I had two touchdowns, and Bobby Marlow had one. Our defense scored; Hootie Ingram returned a punt for a touchdown; and, of course, everyone who went in was trying to score. You couldn't ask them to not try to score. And score is what they did. Bart Starr was the back-up quarterback to Clell Hobson, and he got us into the end zone.

There was not a soul on our team who wanted to run up the score on anyone. Red Drew was certainly not the kind of guy to run up the score. But we beat them 61–6.

After my playing career at Alabama, I played two years in the Canadian Football League. Bobby Marlow also played in Canada because it paid more than the NFL in those days. Bobby played for Saskatchewan, and I played for Ottawa. We were in different divisions and didn't play in the regular season, so I didn't have to play against him. But we played an exhibition game once. I took some of my teammates down to the train station to meet them coming in, and Bobby nearly beat me to death on the platform.

I always thought that many doors were opened for me in the business world because of my association with our great university. I consider membership in the "A" Club to be very special. I enjoyed being a State Farm agent in Huntsville for nearly 40 years, and I suspect having played football helped me to be successful. I wouldn't take "no" for an answer.

Even though my senior year did not end on a happy note, my joy at being a player for The University of Alabama has never diminished, and I will forever be grateful for that opportunity.

*Tommy Lewis was a three-year starter for Alabama and scored one touchdown in the Cotton Bowl and two touchdowns in the Orange Bowl.*

## BROOKER SUGAR

Perhaps the first great victory of Paul Bryant's coaching tenure at Alabama was the 16–15 comeback win over Georgia Tech on November 12, 1960. The game led to a humorous case of mistaken identity among the Crimson Tide's radio broadcast team and, eventually, its fans.

Tommy Brooker was the Crimson Tide's regular kicker that year, but he was coming off knee surgery, so Bryant planned only to use him in case Alabama needed to attempt a long field goal. So with Alabama lining up for a field goal at the Georgia Tech 6 and trailing 15–13 in the closing seconds, Bryant instead called on Richard "Digger" O'Dell.

"O'Dell got to kick it," Brooker said. "And he made it. The radio people, Maury Farrell and John Forney, thought it was me and announced that Brooker had won the game.... We didn't know about the radio mistake. We flew back to Tuscaloosa, and there were probably 5,000 people waiting for us. And all these

Tommy Brooker (81) kicked a field goal to beat Auburn 3–0 in 1960, but not the one to beat Georgia Tech 16–15 (kicked by Richard O'Dell). He still got credit for it, though.

college girls were there to give Brooker some sugar. They thought I'd won the game. I tried to tell them it wasn't me, that it was O'Dell, but they had heard it on the radio and knew it was me. By the time we got to the dorm, Richard was pretty upset that he wasn't getting credit. We finally got him up and went to the quad and had a pep rally. Word spread around, and everyone knew that O'Dell had won the game."

---

## *Crimson Tide in Their Own Words*

# TOMMY BROOKER

### END, 1959–1961

I know the first meeting we ever had with Coach Bryant when he was getting ready for his first season at Alabama in 1958 was the one when he talked about the long-range plans, how we would win the national championship if we did what he told us. I was a freshman, and all I could think about was that what he told us didn't make sense. He said, "If you don't have a good day—and all days won't be good days—then come back the next day and give 110 percent." And so we had the 110 percent rule. And I couldn't figure out how you could give more than 100 percent. In fact, I didn't know how you could know whether you had given 80 percent or 90 percent or 100 percent.

But I figured it out soon enough. I learned it on the practice field, in the drills. You'd find out that when you thought you had given all you could give, that somehow you could reach down and find a little more. And that was every day as we tried to survive.

Years later I realize that Coach Bryant taught us a lot. And you don't get it all at once. But over the years you'd have a situation and you'd think, *That's what Coach Bryant was talking about.* And you were better off for having that experience.

The reason I went to Alabama was I made them keep their word. Joe Thomas had recruited my brother, but my brother was signing with Detroit to play pro baseball, and so he went to Auburn because it was on the quarter system, which would be easier to work around baseball. That was when I was a sophomore in high school. Coach Thomas told me, "I'll be back to get you in two years." And two years later, he came back, and I told him I was taking him at his word and that I would sign with Alabama.

But before I signed, the Whitworth group was out. Pat James came to see me. He was coming in with Coach Bryant. He asked me if I was good enough to whip Auburn. I told him that was why I was going to Alabama.

When I got to Alabama, I thought maybe I had made a mistake. The first person I met was Jim Blevins. He had been in the service and was older and had tattoos. A few minutes later, one of the freshmen came in, and he had tattoos. Back then I thought only bad actors—really mean people—had tattoos, and I wondered if I was at the right place.

My freshman year we were the scout team for the varsity. We had a few freshman games, but we didn't have any plays except whatever we had been doing on the scout team that week. So one freshman game we'd play like Georgia Tech, and another game we'd play like Tennessee, and so on. We kind of made up plays.

We had a very smart quarterback on the freshman team. He understood what Coach Bryant wanted. I don't know why, but for some reason Pat Trammell and I were very close. He'd come by my room and get me to go with him to the drug store. He had a little TR7 sports car, the first one I ever rode in. I don't think I ever saw one in Demopolis. We'd go get cigars. He smoked Antonio y Cleopatra. I didn't smoke, but I'd go with him.

In the huddle with Trammell there was just one voice. If anyone tried to say anything, Trammell would kick him out of the huddle. I don't mean trying to get him to run a play or something. A guy might be blocking his man. But he couldn't say anything. Sometimes in a game someone would try to give Pat some information, and he'd spend all the huddle time cussing him out. And when I say cussing, I mean like a sailor. So we'd go to the line and he'd call the play there. It may have looked like an audible, but it was just getting a play called. Pat Trammell was the general when we were on the field.

I kept in touch with him right up until the time of his death. I was back in Tuscaloosa by then in the real estate and insurance business. He came by the office and showed me the scar where they had operated on him.

Pat died in 1968. Coach Bryant came up with the idea of an "A" Club Charitable Foundation, a way to help former players who might have catastrophic illnesses or other hardships. Coach Bryant told me to take care of it, and by the end of the year we had formed the corporation. I have been president of it since it was founded. I have tried to give it up but haven't been able to. We do have a large board, including a number of people who have been very successful in business, and we have helped a lot of families.

Although I was a tight end on offense and end on defense, I also worked on kicking. In 1959 Fred Sington missed a kick against Georgia Tech—we won the game anyway—and the next week Coach Bryant told me he might use me. And against Auburn I kicked a field goal to give us a 3–0 lead, and we beat them 10–0.

The next year we were playing Georgia Tech and I was coming off knee surgery. Coach Bryant told me that if we had a long field goal to win the game, he'd expect me to kick it, but if we just needed a short one he would use Richard O'Dell. Now how did Coach Bryant know that game was going to come down to a field goal? It did, and it was a short one. And O'Dell—"Digger" O'Dell we called him because a disc jockey had been buried alive in some promotion and his name had been Digger O'Dell—got to kick it. We were getting killed 15–0 at halftime, but came back and, with 16 or 17 seconds to play, had a chance to win. And he made it. The radio people, Maury Farrell and John Forney, thought it was me and announced that Brooker had won the game. It wasn't Brooker.

We didn't know about the radio mistake. We flew back to Tuscaloosa, and there were probably 5,000 people waiting for us. And all these college girls were there to give Brooker some sugar. They thought I'd won the game. I tried to tell them it wasn't me, that it was O'Dell, but they had heard it on the radio and knew it was me. By the time we got to the dorm, Richard was pretty upset that he wasn't getting credit. We finally got him up and went to the quad and had a pep rally. Word spread around, and everyone knew that O'Dell had won the game.

In the Auburn game, we were worried because they had a great field-goal kicker in Ed Dyas. Dyas was also their fullback, but he had broken his jaw a couple of weeks before our game. But coach told us we couldn't let Auburn across our 40 or we'd lose. We didn't let them across the 40.

I missed my first field-goal chance and thought that would probably be it for me. But Chief Smelley, who was the highway patrolman who escorted Coach Bryant, came over and told me not to worry about it, that we'd get another chance. I probably would have given up on myself without that pep talk. But I got another chance and made it, and we won 3–0.

After the season, Coach Bryant called me, Pat Trammell, and Leon Fuller into his office and thanked us for making good grades. He said we were the main reason the football team had a better grade-point average than the rest of the university, and particularly the fraternities. That was important to him. And he said he'd pay for us to go to graduate school, and I was able to get my master's degree in the off-season from pro ball.

After Alabama I went to Dallas. There were two teams there, the Texans and the Cowboys. I was with the Texans, owned by Lamar Hunt. I was a tight end, not a kicking specialist. But I did the kicking, and we won two or three games on field goals, and we won the AFL championship. We played what was the longest game in pro football against Houston, in Houston, on a muddy field. Len Dawson was my holder, and I can still remember him trying to get the mud out of my cleats before I kicked. We were at 2:54 in the sixth quarter when I made the kick, and we won the game.

We moved to Kansas City and got to play in the first Super Bowl, although it was called the NFL-AFL World Championship Game then. And there wasn't anything like the attention there is now, of course. We played pretty well with Green Bay for a half, but it got away from us in the second half. The best thing was the loser's check—$6,800.

I was back in town in the real estate and insurance business in 1971, and Coach Bryant called me and said, "It's stupid for you to be living here and me not utilize you." And he offered me a job as a part-time coach working with the kickers. I didn't go to meetings or anything, just met with the kickers at practice and worked with them. He would introduce me as his "shoes coach," because I just wore street shoes to practice. Or sometimes his "downtown coach." I could go to games. But between the 1978 and 1979

Sugar Bowls, they changed the rules to where I couldn't be on the sideline at games.

I love everything about the university and do anything I can for it. I go to football games, but I also go to basketball, baseball, gymnastics, everything.

*Tommy Brooker was a member of the 1961 national championship team as a tight end, defensive end, and kicker, and was one of two senior members of that team drafted to play pro football. He was an Academic All-American. He is president of the "A" Club Foundation and a member of the board of the First and Ten Club, a support group for athletes and former athletes.*

---

## GONE TOO SOON

A number of Crimson Tide players—very few, fortunately—have died while they were still active players. Starting lineman Tom Bible drowned during the summer of 1962, just before his senior year at Alabama.

Ray Perkins' Alabama team suffered back-to-back tragedies in 1986. Running back George Scruggs was killed in an April automobile accident that also seriously injured defensive back Vernon Wilkinson (Wilkinson sat out the 1986 season but returned to the team in 1987). Then in August, defensive lineman Willie Ryles collapsed on the practice field and later died from what was diagnosed as a blood clot in his brain.

But perhaps the most tragic story belongs to Pat Trammell, the star quarterback on Alabama's 1961 national championship team. He was an All-American as a senior but eschewed a professional football career in order to attend medical school. Trammell was working on his residency in dermatology when he was diagnosed

Paul Bryant always considered quarterback Pat Trammell (12) his favorite player. Trammell, who gave up a shot at pro football to pursue a medical career, died at age 28 from testicular cancer in 1968.

with testicular cancer in 1968. Just days after being given the game ball following Alabama's 24–16 victory over Auburn, he died at age 28.

"I kept in touch with him right up until the time of his death," former teammate Tommy Brooker remembered. "I was back in Tuscaloosa by then in the real estate and insurance business. He came by the office and showed me the scar where they had operated on him."

Trammell was cherished by Alabama coach Paul Bryant, who later wrote in his 1975 autobiography that Trammell's funeral was the saddest day of his life. He also called Trammell "the favorite person of my entire life."

Trammell left behind a wife and two young children, leading Bryant, Brooker, and several other former teammates to establish the "A" Club Charitable Foundation. Brooker is still on the foundation's board, part of which is distributing the Paul W. Bryant Scholarship, which, in honor of Trammell, allows any child or grandchild of a former Bryant player to attend the university tuition-free.

## "IT WAS A LEGAL PLAY"

What is considered among the most controversial moments in Alabama football history occurred in the 1961 game against Georgia Tech in Birmingham. The Crimson Tide led 10–0 in the fourth quarter when the Yellow Jackets were forced to punt.

Darwin Holt, Alabama's undersized but tough-as-nails linebacker, delivered a forearm to the face of Georgia Tech's Chick Graning as he turned upfield to block. The Yellow Jackets called the move a cheap shot, but the fact remains that Holt was not penalized.

Graning was later hospitalized, and Holt was vilified across the country for what was perceived as a dirty play. Atlanta sportswriters—and later magazines such as *Sports Illustrated* and the *Saturday Evening Post*—castigated Bryant for teaching such "brutality."

But nearly 50 years later, Holt maintained that his role in the incident, while unfortunate, was within the rules:

> I don't regret what I did. It was a legal play. I resent the
> fact that it's still there. The press just won't let it rest. I love
> the reputation I had of being one of the toughest guys who

played at Alabama. But that's not the same as dirty, and I was not a dirty player.

At first, Chick handled it well. I went to Atlanta to see him, and he took me around and introduced me to everyone. He said, "Hell, Darwin, if I hadn't been looking up in the stands, you wouldn't have got me." You can see in the film that he dropped down so the forearm that was to hit him in the chest got him in the face. Later, Chick decided it wasn't in his best interest to defend me.

Bobby Dodd, the Georgia Tech coach, probably made a mistake by not putting Chick in the hospital right after the game instead of taking him back to Atlanta. I only hit him. They nearly killed him because his head swelled up because they waited a day to hospitalize him.

Holt started two years at linebacker for the Crimson Tide, playing alongside the great Lee Roy Jordan as a senior in 1961. He said many years later that he believes the Graning incident cost him a spot on the All-America team and perhaps a shot at a coaching career.

## JOE WILLIE

Joe Namath was a hotshot recruit out of Beaver Falls, Pennsylvania, in the fall of 1961, but sat out that season because of NCAA rules prohibiting freshman from playing on the varsity. With All-American Pat Trammell directing the Crimson Tide offense that season, it's unlikely Namath would have made much of an impact that season had he been eligible.

But when Trammell graduated the following spring, the keys to the Alabama offense were in Namath's hands. Mal Moore was a fifth-year senior quarterback that year but couldn't hold off

Namath. "I introduce Joe as the man I brought out the very best in," Moore said. "He really had to strain to beat me out. I think I was first-team until he learned the snap count in the spring of 1962."

Namath went 21–3 as an Alabama starting quarterback despite a disciplinary suspension late in the 1963 season and a serious knee injury his senior year. He led the Crimson Tide to the national championship that year, though Alabama lost to Texas 21–17 in the Orange Bowl.

It was the last snap of his college career that still eats at Namath to this day. Though officials ruled that the Longhorns stopped Namath inside the 1-yard line on a quarterback sneak, he maintains he should have been awarded the game-winning touchdown.

"Over the years people have asked, 'Joe Willie, did you score a touchdown against Texas?'" Namath said. "My answer is that I did not because it was not ruled a touchdown. But I did get over the goal line. So many times over the years have I wished that I had had enough brains instead of being caught up in the situation to call timeout on third down to go over to talk to the man, to talk to Coach Bryant. The pain of losing that game was awful. But the next day I signed a contract with the [New York] Jets. The pain doesn't go right away, but signing that contract helped ease it a little."

## THE "FIX" THAT WASN'T

Namath's first college game also resulted in controversy of a different sort. He passed for three touchdowns in Alabama's 35–0 rout of Georgia in Birmingham on September 22, 1962.

The following spring, the *Saturday Evening Post* published a sensational story alleging that Bryant and Georgia athletics director Wally Butts had conspired to fix the game by discussing the

Bulldogs' plays over the phone. The *Post*'s primary source on the story was an Atlanta businessman who supposedly overheard the conversational when the telephone lines got crossed.

Bryant and Butts sued the *Post*'s publisher for defamation, and Bryant received a large out-of-court settlement. Namath wasn't called as a witness in the case, but would have had his testimony ready.

"I was the quarterback, and the quarterback called the plays," Namath said years later. "The coaches didn't call the plays. When the article came out, we had a team meeting, and Coach Bryant read it to us. He got to the part where it said, 'Georgia gained only 35 yards.' He stopped and said, 'That's too many yards.' It was a tense situation, but that broke us up."

## TRAILBLAZERS

The story of the racial integration of Alabama's football team is a complicated one. Bryant allowed a handful of African American players to walk on to the team as early as 1967 but did not actively recruit blacks until a few years later, evidently believing that state politicians—particularly governor George Wallace—would never allow it.

But once Bryant began to integrate the team, he did so at full speed. The first black football player to sign a scholarship with Alabama was halfback Wilbur Jackson in the spring of 1970. Speaking more than 30 years later, Jackson said he didn't realize the significance of the move at the time:

> It seems to surprise everyone that no one ever mentioned to me when I was being recruited that I would be the first black football player to sign with Alabama. If it ever came up, I don't remember it. I remember a few years ago talking to

Chuck Strickland, who was captain with me on our 1973 team, and telling him that it had been tough on me, so tough that I thought about quitting. He laughed and said, "We all thought about quitting because it was so tough."

I felt as though I was treated just like everyone else, and I also felt that is how it should have been. I didn't want anything given to me because I was black, but I didn't want anything taken away from me, either. As far as I could tell, I was treated no differently than any other player. It was a tough experience on the field, but it was tough on everyone. But when I had success, it meant everyone on the team had success. And when someone else had success, so did I.

Freshmen were not eligible to play on the varsity in 1970, meaning that Jackson was not the first African American football player in Crimson Tide history. That distinction goes to defensive end John Mitchell, who joined the Alabama team as a junior-college transfer in 1971 and started the season opener at Southern Cal (Jackson also played in the game, but Mitchell technically took the field first). Mitchell remembered his path to Alabama:

Growing up in Mobile, I knew all about Alabama and the great football stars like Joe Namath and Lee Roy Jordan. I knew all about the great wins and the national championships. I watched Alabama when they were on television and listened to the games on radio and watched *The Bear Bryant Show* on Sundays. Any kid would have wanted to go there.

But I couldn't go to Alabama. Alabama was not recruiting African American players when I finished high school at Williamson in 1969. And if they had been, I probably would not have been the one they would have taken because I was kind of a skinny kid.

I went to Eastern Arizona Junior College, where I got bigger and better. And I had my choice of a lot of schools when I finished after the 1970 season. I finally decided on Southern Cal. I made a recruiting visit there, and my hosts were Sam Cunningham and Charles Young. I met O.J. Simpson. And I really liked it. Coach John McKay had a great program, and I was excited about playing there.

Alabama didn't cross my mind. I didn't know Alabama had signed Wilbur Jackson in 1970. I thought Alabama was still all-white. I graduated in December and was back in Mobile when I got a call from Judge Ferrill McRae, an Alabama alumnus in Mobile. Alabama was interested in me. It seems that Coach McKay had told Coach Bryant they were going to sign an Alabama boy who was playing at Eastern Arizona. I realized my family had never seen me play in Arizona and would probably never see me play if I went to Southern Cal. But by my going to Alabama, they could drive up to Birmingham or Tuscaloosa and see me play. I really thought about that later when, after the first home game, I walked out of the dressing room and saw my parents waiting for me. It was one of the biggest moments in my life, and I know they were so happy to be able to see their son play for Alabama.

Jackson and Mitchell were the only two black players on the Alabama team that first season. But by 1974 the Crimson Tide had more than a dozen African Americans on its roster, including standouts such as Sylvester Croom, Calvin Culliver, Willie Shelby, Ozzie Newsome, Johnny Davis, Woodrow Lowe, and Mike Washington.

"We considered it an opportunity, not a chore," said Washington, an All-America cornerback in 1974. "We thought we would have the chance to prove that we could perform athletically and academically with the white guys. That was important."

Bryant also hired a handful of black assistant coaches in the 1970s, notably Mitchell in 1973 and Croom three years later. Croom would go on to become the first black head football coach in the SEC when he took the Mississippi State job in 2004.

The first black quarterback to see action for the Crimson Tide came five years later, when Michael Landrum took a handful of snaps during Alabama's national championship run in 1979. The team's first black starting quarterback was Walter Lewis, who made his first start under Bryant in 1981 and was an All-SEC selection under Ray Perkins as a senior in 1983.

"All of my friends weren't happy about me selecting Alabama," Lewis said. "A lot of them thought Coach Bryant would never play a black quarterback. I think there may have been some skepticism in my house, but when Coach Bryant visited, he erased any doubt. Coach Bryant said we bled the same blood and sweated the same sweat. There was a bond among the players. Coach Bryant wasn't concerned about your color. He was interested in producing and performing, and that's what the players wanted. I never thought being black was an obstacle at Alabama."

## THE USC MYTH

The year before Alabama integrated its team, the Crimson Tide lost to Southern Cal 42–21 in Birmingham. That game is not only famous for the exploits of Trojans running back Sam Cunningham but also for two myths that are propagated to this day.

First is that Alabama's loss that day embarrassed Bryant into integrating his football team. It's easy to shoot that myth down, in that Wilbur Jackson had already signed with the Crimson Tide and was watching from the Legion Field stands (freshmen were ineligible for varsity football play under NCAA rules at the time).

Second is the oft-told tale that Bryant brought Cunningham to the Alabama dressing room following the game and told his players, "This is what a football player looks like." Over the years, dozens of Crimson Tide players from the 1970 team, including nose guard Terry Rowell, have disputed that account.

"It was bad enough that we lost the game badly," Rowell recalled. "But what has made it worse is this myth about Coach Bryant bringing Sam Cunningham to our dressing room and telling us, 'This is what a football player looks like.' That just didn't happen, and I don't know why anyone would say it did. I can imagine that Coach Bryant went to Southern Cal's dressing room and congratulated them, and he may have said something to Cunningham there because Cunningham had a great game. But can you imagine Coach Bryant bringing another player into our dressing room and telling John Hannah and Johnny Musso, 'This is what a football player looks like'? Of course not. I will say that Cunningham doesn't say it happened."

What is without dispute is that any lingering doubts among fans and boosters as to whether or not the Crimson Tide *should have* racially integrated its team were probably doused forever on that night.

## THE FORGOTTEN STOP

When Alabama fans recall the Crimson Tide's famed goal-line stand against Penn State in the 1979 Sugar Bowl, most remember that it was Barry Krauss (along with Murray Legg, Rich Wingo, and David Hannah, among others) who tackled Mike Guman just short of the end zone on fourth down. Many will recall that it was

Crimson Tide defensive tackle Marty Lyons who taunted Penn State quarterback Chuck Fusina with, "You'd better pass," before that fateful play.

But a man who is often forgotten might have made the most important defensive play of that game. Two plays earlier on second-and-goal, Crimson Tide cornerback Don McNeal came seemingly out of nowhere to knock Penn State receiver Scott Fitzkee out of bounds inside the 1-yard line. Without McNeal's play, the goal-line stand on third and fourth downs would never have happened, and Alabama might not have won the national championship.

McNeal, who went on to play in two Super Bowls with the NFL's Miami Dolphins, remembers the play: "I was covering someone else in the end zone, but I saw the pass going to Fitzkee and broke on the ball," McNeal said. "This is where [secondary coach Bill] Oliver comes in. I didn't think. I just knew I had to make a perfect tackle or Fitzkee would fall in the end zone. The play I made was instinct, the result of hours and hours with Coach Bryant and Coach Oliver."

## THE KICK

Alabama has had a number of memorable game-winning field goals over the years: Richard O'Dell against Georgia Tech in 1960, Bucky Berrey against Florida State in 1974, Philip Doyle against Tennessee in 1990, Michael Proctor against Georgia in 1994, and Jamie Christensen against Ole Miss, Tennessee, and Texas Tech in 2005. But all those kicks pale in comparison to "the Kick," Van Tiffin's 52-yarder into the wind to beat Auburn 25–23 on November 30, 1985.

Tiffin was noted for his strong right leg, having hit from 57 yards against Texas A&M earlier that season and from 53 yards against Penn State in 1984. He also played his entire Alabama career without missing an extra point in 135 attempts.

But none of that prepared him for dashing onto the field with time running down against the Tigers that blustery day at Legion Field, after quarterback Mike Shula had led the Alabama offense down the field despite no timeouts, to set up for the winning kick. Tiffin recalled:

> Auburn didn't call a timeout, so everything was just rush, rush, rush. And that's the way I wanted it. I didn't want time to think about it. I never enjoyed having to wait through a timeout, even though by then I had gotten used to that and handled it better. But I'm glad Auburn didn't call a timeout, because I don't know how I would have handled it in that pressure situation.
>
> Kicking is a lot like hitting a golf ball or a baseball. When you don't feel anything, you know you've hit it good. And that's the way it was. I can just remember getting back and kicking it, not feeling it, and looking up, and there it was going right down the middle. I thought, *This can't be true. This can't be real.* Also, I could just feel Kevin Porter, the Auburn end, coming from the left side, and I knew it was going to be close. When I got out there on the field, it was: line set, snap. I was expecting more of a delay in snapping the ball, so I was just a little bit late getting to the ball. Kevin Porter was offside, so he was actually a little early. Had he not been offside, he might have blocked it.
>
> It was like it happened yesterday. That's all people remember me for, and that's okay. At least they don't remember me for missing that field goal. That would really be bad.

Tiffin was an All-American for the Crimson Tide as a senior in 1986, and many of his kicking records stood until they were broken by his son, Leigh, in 2009. Leigh Tiffin joined his father as an All-America selection that season and also won a national championship as a senior.

## "WE OWN IT"

The Alabama-Tennessee series has always been a streaky one, and Crimson Tide center Roger Shultz decided to have a little fun with that fact in 1990. Alabama entered the game at Neyland Stadium as a heavy underdog to the Volunteers despite having beaten them four straight years.

Shultz and the Crimson Tide made it five in a row with a 9–6 victory on Philip Doyle's last-second field goal. Asked for comment following the game, the notoriously gabby Shultz could not resist himself. He said, "We ought to have to pay property taxes on Neyland Stadium, because we own it." Shultz remembered how it happened:

> We had started that season with three straight losses, and Tennessee had not lost since we had beaten them the year before. I can remember Lee Corso on ESPN saying we would be like a high school team going into Knoxville. But we won the game, and I had finished my career having never lost to Tennessee.
>
> After that came out in the newspapers, Coach [Gene] Stallings said, "Man, why did you say that? We've got to go back and play them there in two years."
>
> I said, "I don't." I added, "It was pretty good, though, wasn't it?" And Coach Stallings said, "Yeah."

It must have stung them pretty good, because I still hear from Tennessee fans.

---

## *Crimson Tide in Their Own Words*
# ROGER SHULTZ
### CENTER, 1987–1990

I came to Alabama from Peachtree High School in Atlanta, Georgia, but I had lived in Alabama from 1974 to 1980, in the Center Point area and in Homewood. I played little league football, and our uniform jerseys were red with white numbers. In fact, I think every team in the league had red jerseys with white numbers. Everyone was an Alabama fan.

At the end of the season, everyone on the team got a copy of a letter from Bear Bryant about "What are you going to do to make your mark?" The letter had been photocopied about a million times, and you could barely read his signature, but to us it was like a personal letter from Coach Bryant.

They put out this poster with Coach Bryant pointing and saying, "The Bear Wants You," like the old Army recruiting posters, "Uncle Sam Wants You." I had it over my bed, and now my son has it over his bed. They didn't have nearly as much memorabilia as they do now, but I had everything "Alabama" I could get. Almost every day I wore something with Alabama on it. I still have an Alabama pillow my mother got for me in Tuscaloosa.

In 1980 I was in the sixth grade, but some of us were going to get to go with the high school team to Legion Field and sell Cokes for the Alabama-Auburn game. That would mean we could get

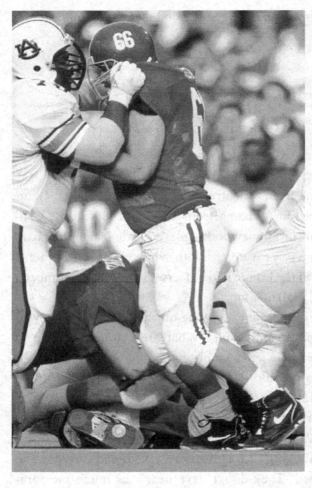

Roger Shultz (66) was a two-time All-SEC center for Alabama, but is as well-known for his humor as he was for his excellent offensive line play.

into the game. But there was a mix-up, and my name wasn't on the list. Three or four of us managed to scrounge up one ticket. Then we went to the gate and told the guy our mother had sent us out to get our coats. He let us all in on that one ticket.

We didn't have seats, so we stood around the fence. And they kept running us off. But I can remember how big Byron Braggs was. And we got to see Coach Bryant in person. That's also when

I learned that college students can get drunk. I had bought one of those big Alabama "Number One" hands with the finger sticking up, and an Auburn student took it away from me and tore the finger off.

Because of my father's job in hospital administration, we moved around a lot, finally ending up in Atlanta. My coach there told me if I worked really hard I might earn a scholarship to Furman. I thought, "Furman! I want to play for Alabama!" One of the doctors there, Dr. Milton Frank, had played for Coach Bryant, and he got Alabama to write me a letter when I was in the 10th grade—the first recruiting letter I ever got.

I was recruited by Coach Perkins, then played for Coach Curry and Coach Stallings. I had about three different coordinators and a handful of different offensive line coaches, although Coach Fuller was always there.

When I went on my recruiting visit and Coach Perkins offered me a scholarship, I said, "I'll take it." He said I didn't have to decide right then, and I told him I wasn't letting him take the offer back. The first person I met on that visit was Coach Gryska. What a great guy, then and now.

A lot of guys on that recruiting trip ended up signing with Alabama: Lee Ozmint, Chris Robinette, John Mangum, Charlie Abrams, Danny Cash, Robert Stewart, Gary Hollingsworth. We all felt like teammates from the first time we met.

I remember meeting Wes Neighbors and thinking, *I'm taller than he is, so I should be able to play here.* Of course, he was about the only one I was taller than.

Ohio State was recruiting me, too, and when I got back from my recruiting trip there, I told my father I might want to go to Ohio State. Dad had always said it would be my decision, but when I said that, he said, "No."

In a way it's a waste to have the opportunity to play football at Alabama when you are only 18 to 22 years old. I wish now I had paid more attention to things around me. It was so regimented—meetings, practice, meals, study halls, classes. I wish I had just taken a moment to stand in the middle of the field and look around at the full stadium.

Now I realize so much more what it means to pull on that crimson jersey, what it means to be a part of the greatest tradition in college football. It's funny that I don't remember many of the games I played in. In fact, I was redshirted in 1986 but made the trip to New York for the Kickoff Classic against Ohio State, and I remember that game. We beat Ohio State, but had to hang on when Derrick Thomas got two pass interference calls. Of course, he wasn't *the* Derrick Thomas then.

I was part of an SEC Championship team as a player, and then I stayed around for a couple of years as a graduate assistant and got a ring when we won the national championship in 1992. One of the most amazing things is to go to the "A" Club Room before a game and see all those national championship rings, some from back in the '60s and '70s.

They picked an All-Century Team at Alabama, and you could be an All-American and not even get mentioned for it. I knew a guy at another SEC school who didn't make All-America and made their Team of the Century.

Alabama is just different. If someone writes a book about college football, you can bet Alabama and Coach Bryant are going to be in that book. I have been across the country and even out of the country, and people comment on my size and ask if I played football. I say, "Alabama," and you can just see it register.

Think about how big it is for Auburn that Alabama went there to play a game? We went to Lafayette, Louisiana, to play a game, and they had parades, let school out, and I think maybe rededicated the town. Can you imagine if an Alabama player ever wins the Heisman Trophy? He'll be able to be elected governor.

I'd like to be recruiting for Alabama now. I'd tell all those prospects that I would guarantee if they go to Alabama and we go 13–0, we'll win the national championship.

I never had any goal other than to play college football for Alabama. I didn't have any goals beyond that. When I got to Alabama, I didn't even know what I wanted to major in. Shula and Neighbors were in business, and Hollingsworth was going into business, so I went into business. If they had been in painting, I guess I'd be a painter now.

People always said I was a hard worker on the football field, and I think that's the main thing I took from Alabama. The difference in real life is that you have to do it every day. And that's what I do. I go to work every day and do my job with a good attitude.

I'm associate athletics director for external affairs at Troy University. Before that I did some radio work, which I enjoyed, too. And I don't mind saying that I'd be thrilled if one day Mama called. I worry that she's lost my number.

*Roger Shultz was unanimous All-SEC center in 1989 and 1990, and selected to the 1991 Senior Bowl.*

## CAREERS CUT SHORT

As you might expect, Alabama football history is littered with players whose promising careers were cut short due to injury. Among those who either never lived up to their full potential in college or saw their NFL hopes diminished by injuries suffered during their Crimson Tide careers were Mike Fracchia, Jeff Rouzie, Mike

DuBose, Gary Rutledge, Calvin Culliver, Leroy Cook, Gene Jelks, Darrell Blackburn, Marvin Constant, and Antonio Carter.

Three other players deserve special mention here. One is running back Kerry Goode, who posted what is widely regarded as the greatest two and a half quarters of football in Crimson Tide history in the 1984 season opener against Boston College.

Goode, then a sophomore, rushed for a touchdown and caught a pass for another in the second quarter of that game, then returned the opening kickoff of the second half 99 yards for a touchdown. He went down with a season-ending knee injury midway through the third quarter, but not before compiling 297 all-purpose yards (68 rushing, 32 receiving, 197 on returns) in Alabama's 38–31 loss to the Doug Flutie–led Eagles. Goode returned to letter for the Crimson Tide in both 1986 and 1987, but never again showed the speed or elusiveness he had displayed before the injury.

The second player here is Tyrone Prothro, one of the more tragic figures in Alabama history. Prothro, who had already achieved Crimson Tide immortality with his body-twisting catch against Southern Miss early in the 2005 season, was on his way to perhaps winning the Heisman Trophy with the game he put together against Florida on October 1 of that year.

Prothro caught an 87-yard touchdown pass from Brodie Croyle on the Crimson Tide's first play of the game, added another scoring reception in the third quarter, and also had a punt return for a touchdown called back by penalty. But with Alabama leading 31–3 early in the fourth quarter, Prothro broke both bones in his lower left leg in grotesque fashion when he landed awkwardly attempting to catch a third touchdown pass in the Bryant-Denny Stadium end zone. Prothro underwent emergency surgery that night, but remained hospitalized for nearly three weeks after an infection set in. He never played for the Crimson Tide again.

Offensive lineman Kareem McNeal also saw his Alabama football career end abruptly, but not because of anything that happened on the field. He was visiting home in Tuskegee during the summer before his 1995 senior season when he was involved in a car accident that left him paralyzed from the waist down. McNeal, a starting tackle for the Crimson Tide in 1994 and a letterman on the 1992 national championship team, recalled the details and the aftermath of the accident some 10 years later:

> I was riding with my brother-in-law and a friend when our car left the road. We were all thrown out of the car. My brother-in-law had a cut on his back. My friend had a concussion. I had the worst injury.
>
> I don't remember the accident and don't remember the next week or so in the hospital. It was sometime after that I became aware of what was going on. My spinal cord had been crushed. I was paralyzed from the waist down.
>
> I definitely felt I had been dealt a bad hand. It was a rough time for me and my wife and my family. And it was rough for my friends and for my team.
>
> I had married my wife, Rene, the day after the SEC Championship Game in 1994, about seven months before the accident. Rene is from my hometown of Tuskegee. Seven years after the accident we had our sons, twin boys, Kevin and Carson.
>
> Coach Stallings came to visit me on several occasions in the hospital. I know he was there when I came out of surgery to fix my back, but I really can't remember much about that meeting. I had the surgery to straighten my back and put rods in it to hold it in place. That was at Carraway Hospital in Birmingham. I was in Carraway for about a month, then

I moved to Spain Rehabilitation. Coach Stallings came to see me regularly when I was there and was very encouraging.

I tried to stay positive, believing there would be a good outcome. And I have continued to stay positive. It's funny that I can remember in May before my accident that Christopher Reeve had his accident that paralyzed him. I remember thinking, *Oh, man! Superman!* And I remember feeling sad for him. And he became a great spokesman for people with spinal cord injuries and, I think, a lot of good has come from the attention he gave it. Naturally, I follow pretty closely the efforts being made. I think we're getting close to trying some promising work on people.

I was supposed to graduate in December 1995. That fall I went back to school, but I took it slow, taking some Internet classes and going at a slow pace. As it turned out, I took only one extra semester to earn my degree. I was graduated with a degree in human performance in May 1996. Then I went to work on a master's degree and earned that in 1999 in health education.

Not too long after I graduated, I had another surgery to remove the rods in my back. That was because I had become so active. I have stayed with a rehab program—swimming, stretching, and standing in a "stander" I have that keeps my legs accustomed to bearing my weight. The therapy is not as intense as it was the first three years after the accident, but I still do what I can.

I think having been a player helps when you face tough times. You can watch a football game and see the difficulties. A player puts in a lot of hard work, and I think I have continued to have a good work ethic and a good philosophy about life—things I learned on the football field.

*chapter 8*

# 'BAMA GOES BOWLING

EIGHTY-FIVE YEARS AFTER its first bowl trip, Alabama has put together a postseason history like no other team. Here's a rundown of all 58 Alabama bowl games, 33 of which ended in victory—an NCAA record for wins.

### JANUARY 1, 1926
#### The Rose Bowl, Pasadena, California
#### Alabama 20, Washington 19

In its first trip to what would become its home away from home over the next 20 years, Alabama overcame a 12–0 halftime deficit and 134 yards rushing by Washington star George Wilson to secure its first national championship. The big stars of the day for the Crimson Tide were quarterback Pooley Hubert and halfback Johnny Mack Brown, who accounted for three touchdowns in a 20-point Alabama third quarter. Hubert scored on a one-yard run and threw a 30-yard TD pass to Brown, who also caught a 59-yard strike from Grant Gillis as Alabama finished its perfect season at 10–0.

### JANUARY 1, 1927
#### The Rose Bowl, Pasadena, California
#### Alabama 7, Stanford 7

The Crimson Tide's second straight trip to Pasadena was not quite as successful, though Alabama still came away as co–national champion following a tie with West Coast powerhouse Stanford despite punting 13 times and being outgained 305 yards to 98 in the game. The Indians' George Bogue hit Ed Walker for a 20-yard touchdown to make it 7–0 through three quarters. The Crimson Tide got in position to tie the game in the fourth quarter, thanks to a blocked punt by Clarke Pearce that put the ball on the Stanford 14. Five plays later, Jimmy Johnson crashed into the end zone, and Herschel Caldwell added the extra point for the tie.

## JANUARY 1, 1931
### The Rose Bowl, Pasadena, California
### Alabama 24, Washington State 0

Wallace Wade's final Alabama team made it three national titles in six years with another dominant effort in Pasadena. The victim this time was Washington State, which turned the ball over seven times. Alabama's big offensive star was Monk Campbell, who rushed for 114 yards and touchdowns of one and 43 yards, while also kicking three extra points. Flash Suther added the other touchdown, a 61-yard reception from Jimmy Moore, during a 21-point second quarter. The Crimson Tide's final points came on a 30-yard field goal by J.B. "Ears" Whitworth, who would later be Alabama's head coach.

## JANUARY 1, 1935
### The Rose Bowl, Pasadena, California
### Alabama 29, Stanford 13

Frank Thomas had replaced Wade as coach in 1931, but his first trip to Pasadena yielded similar results to his predecessor. Alabama dominated a powerful Stanford team—which had given up only 14 points all season coming in—thanks to a quick-striking passing attack led by Dixie Howell and Don Hutson. Stanford took a 7–0 lead after one quarter, but the Crimson Tide took control with a 22-point second period. Hutson, who ended the day with 164 yards on eight receptions, caught touchdown passes of 54 and 59 yards. Howell rushed for 111 yards and two scores, and also threw for 160 yards and one score to Hutson. For the fourth time in 10 years, Alabama claimed the national championship.

## JANUARY 1, 1938
### The Rose Bowl, Pasadena, California
### California 13, Alabama 0

Alabama left the Rose Bowl a loser for the only time when it met the California Golden Bears on New Year's Day 1938. Cal's Vic Bottari was the day's big star, rushing for 137 yards and two touchdowns on the day. Alabama managed 180 yards of offense (including 70 yards on 16 carries by fullback Charlie Holm), but turned the ball over eight times, including fumbles at Cal's 2- and 7-yard lines. Alabama's shutout loss is one of just two in bowl history for the Crimson Tide.

## JANUARY 1, 1942
### The Cotton Bowl, Dallas, Texas
### Alabama 29, Texas A&M 21

For the first time, Alabama traveled somewhere other than Pasadena for a bowl game, heading to Dallas instead, less than a month after the bombing of Pearl Harbor thrust the country into World War II. The Crimson Tide managed just 75 yards of offense and one first down, but jumped out to a 29–7 lead thanks to 12 turnovers by the Aggies. Jimmie Nelson ran a punt back 72 yards for a touchdown, and also scored on a 21-yard run following an A&M fumble. Holt Rast added a 10-yard interception for a touchdown in the fourth quarter.

## January 1, 1943
### The Orange Bowl, Miami, Florida
### Alabama 37, Boston College 21

Alabama's first trip to the Orange Bowl resulted in a comeback victory, as the Crimson Tide fought off a 14–0 deficit to prevail over the Eagles. Monk Mosley and Johnny August threw touchdown passes to get Alabama back in the game, and Bobby Tom Jenkins' 40-yard run and a 25-yard field goal by George Hecht gave the Crimson Tide the lead for good at 22–21 just before halftime. Alabama piled on 15 second-half points on two touchdowns and a safety to claim the 16-point victory. Halfback Mike Holovak was a solo star in defeat for Boston College, scoring all three touchdowns.

## January 1, 1945
### The Sugar Bowl, New Orleans, Louisiana
### Duke 29, Alabama 26

In the Crimson Tide's final wartime bowl game, a Duke team loaded with Navy trainees scored the day's final nine points to score the victory. George Clark led a 336-yard Duke rushing attack with 114 yards and two scores, the last a 20-yard run to put the Blue Devils on top with less than a minute to play. Alabama had one last shot, but Duke captain Gordon Carver tackled Crimson Tide end Ralph Jones on the 26-yard line as the final gun sounded. The Crimson Tide got a big day in defeat from freshman Harry Gilmer, who was 8-for-8 for 145 yards and one score passing.

## January 1, 1946
### The Rose Bowl, Pasadena, California
### Alabama 34, Southern California 14

Alabama's final 20th century trip to the Rose Bowl was a memorable one, as the Crimson Tide buried a Southern Cal team that had been undefeated in eight previous Rose Bowl appearances. Alabama got 113 yards rushing and a receiving touchdown from Gilmer and a pair of touchdown runs from Hal Self, but defense carried this game for the Crimson Tide. Alabama limited Southern Cal to three first downs and 41 total yards, including just six on the ground. The following year, the Rose Bowl signed an exclusive agreement that would limit participation to teams from the Pac-8 (now the Pac-10) and Big Ten conferences until 2002.

## JANUARY 1, 1948
### The Sugar Bowl, New Orleans, Louisiana
### Texas 27, Alabama 7

For the first of five straight times, Alabama would emerge from a postseason matchup with Texas tasting disappointment. The first bowl meeting between the two teams was among the most decisive, as the Longhorns got 183 yards and a touchdown passing and 51 yards and another score rushing from future NFL star Bobby Layne. Alabama's lone touchdown came on an eight-yard, second-quarter pass to Ed White from Harry Gilmer, who was playing the final game of a record-setting Crimson Tide career. Texas also scored two defensive touchdowns, a blocked punt recovery in the third quarter and an interception return by Lewis Holder in the fourth.

## JANUARY 1, 1953
### The Orange Bowl, Miami, Florida
### Alabama 61, Syracuse 6

The first televised Orange Bowl was a laugher, as the Crimson Tide recorded the biggest blowout in its postseason history. Alabama piled up a school bowl record 586 yards of total offense, including 300 passing. Bobby Luna rushed for two touchdowns and kicked seven extra points for the Crimson Tide, which also got a pair of scoring runs from Tommy Lewis. Star halfback Bobby Marlow even got into the act despite a broken toe, rushing for a two-yard score in the second quarter. Adding non-offensive touchdowns were Hootie Ingram on an 80-yard punt return and Buster Hill on a 60-yard interception return.

## JANUARY 1, 1954
### The Cotton Bowl, Dallas, Texas
### Rice 28, Alabama 6

A Cotton Bowl record 265-yard, three-touchdown performance by Rice's Dicky Moegle was overshadowed by an infamous play from Alabama fullback Tommy Lewis in the second quarter. With Rice leading 7–6, Moegle broke free down the right sideline, where Lewis came off the bench to tackle him. Officials awarded a 95-yard touchdown to Moegle, who had already scored on a 79-yard dash earlier in the quarter. Lewis scored Alabama's only touchdown on a one-yard run in the first quarter, but would go on to lifelong infamy following his illegal tackle in the Cotton Bowl.

## DECEMBER 19, 1959
### The Liberty Bowl, Philadelphia, Pennsylvania
### Penn State 7, Alabama 0

Paul "Bear" Bryant got Alabama to its first bowl in six years in his second season as coach, meeting Penn State in the Crimson Tide's first postseason game not played on New Year's Day. At a cold and windy Franklin Field in Philadelphia, Alabama was shut out for one of only two times in school bowl history. Penn State scored the game's only points in the second quarter, thanks to Galen Hall's 18-yard scoring pass to Roger Kochman. It was the first of 25 consecutive bowl trips for the Crimson Tide.

## DECEMBER 17, 1960
### The Bluebonnet Bowl, Houston, Texas
### Alabama 3, Texas 3

Bryant's second bowl trip also ended in something of a disappointment, as the Crimson Tide and Longhorns ended in a field-goal deadlock. Tommy Brooker put Alabama on top with a 30-yard boot in the third quarter, while Texas' Dan Petty connecting from 20 yards away to tie the game with 3:44 to play. After forcing a Crimson Tide punt, the Longhorns had a chance to win following a pass interference call on the final play of regulation that put the ball on Alabama's 18. With one untimed down remaining, Texas went for a game-winning field goal, but Petty's 35-yard boot went wide left.

## JANUARY 1, 1962
### The Sugar Bowl, New Orleans, Louisiana
### Alabama 10, Arkansas 3

The Crimson Tide secured its first national championship under Bryant by beating the Razorbacks in New Orleans on New Year's Day. Alabama quarterback Pat Trammell passed for just 20 yards in the game, but rushed for 69, including the only touchdown of the day, a 12-yard run in the first quarter. Fullback Mike Fracchia was a workhorse for the Crimson Tide, rushing for 124 yards on 20 carries to earn the Miller-Digby Award as the game's outstanding player. The Alabama defense did the rest, surrendering just 168 total yards and forcing four turnovers. The Crimson Tide finished the season having allowed just 25 points in 11 games, with six shutouts.

## JANUARY 1, 1963
### The Orange Bowl, Miami, Florida
### Alabama 17, Oklahoma 0

A late-season loss to Georgia Tech ended any hopes for a second straight national championship, but the Crimson Tide made up for that disappointment with another memorable bowl victory in Miami. In a historic meeting between perhaps the two greatest college coaches of the mid-20th century, Alabama's Bryant outdid Oklahoma's Bud Wilkinson behind a smothering defense and two first-half touchdowns. Lee Roy Jordan, the Crimson Tide's All-America linebacker, compiled an astounding 31 tackles. Sophomore Joe Namath threw a 25-yard touchdown pass to Richard Williamson in the first quarter, and Cotton Clark ran 15 yards for another score in the second to give Alabama more than enough points.

## JANUARY 1, 1964
### The Sugar Bowl, New Orleans, Louisiana
### Alabama 12, Ole Miss 7

The Crimson Tide posted its third straight New Year's Day bowl win, a remarkable one in many ways. First off, Alabama was without star quarterback Joe Namath, who had been suspended for breaking training rules late in the regular season. Steve Sloan, an inexperienced sophomore, was given the reins of the Crimson Tide offense. Then, the day saw a rare New Orleans snowfall, which blanketed the field at Tulane Stadium. That made for tough sledding for both offenses, and Alabama did not reach the end zone. It didn't matter, as senior Tim Davis booted field goals of 31, 46, 22, and 48 yards to give the Crimson Tide a 12–0 lead. The Rebels got a late touchdown, but Alabama stopped them twice inside the 10 to secure the victory.

## JANUARY 1, 1965
### The Orange Bowl, Miami, Florida
### Texas 21, Alabama 17

The first night game in Orange Bowl history turned out to be one of the most closely fought games in postseason history and among the most disappointing losses ever for the Crimson Tide. Senior quarterback Joe Namath, having played through a severe knee injury for much of the season, came off the bench in relief of Steve Sloan and very nearly led Alabama—which had already been crowned national champions on the strength of an undefeated regular season—to victory. Namath passed for 255 yards and two touchdowns. Along with a fourth-quarter field goal, these pulled the Crimson Tide to within four points. Jimmy Fuller's interception gave Alabama one last chance, but Namath was stopped just short of the goal line on fourth down as Texas held on for the victory.

## JANUARY 1, 1966
### The Orange Bowl, Miami, Florida
### Alabama 39, Nebraska 28

The Crimson Tide validated its second consecutive national championship—and third in five years—with a dominant performance in Miami. With Joe Namath having gone to make his mark in pro football, Steve Sloan was the unquestioned leader for the Alabama team this time. He passed for 296 yards and two touchdowns as the Crimson Tide rolled up 519 yards of total offense. Split end Ray Perkins, who would go on to be Alabama's coach nearly 20 years later, set an Orange Bowl record that stood for a quarter century with nine receptions for 159 yards. Steve Bowman and Les Kelley combined for three touchdowns to lead a 296-yard Alabama rushing attack.

Alabama split end Ray Perkins makes a leaping grab of a Steve Sloan pass during the Tide's 39–28 victory over Nebraska to take the 1966 Orange Bowl after winning the 1965 national championship. *Photo courtesy of Getty Images*

# JANUARY 2, 1967
### The Sugar Bowl, New Orleans, Louisiana
### Alabama 34, Nebraska 7

The Crimson Tide did its part to get in position for a third straight national championship by smashing the Cornhuskers for the second consecutive year. Kenny Stabler compiled 252 yards of total offense and two touchdowns to win the game's most outstanding player award as Alabama posted 436 yards of offense. Ray Perkins had another huge day as a receiver, with seven receptions for 178 yards and a score. But Alabama's 11–0 season did not do enough to impress poll voters as the Crimson Tide finished No. 3 in the final polls behind Notre Dame and Michigan State, who had played to a 10–10 tie late in the regular season.

## JANUARY 1, 1968
### The Cotton Bowl, Dallas, Texas
### Texas A&M 20, Alabama 16

An eight-year postseason drought for the Crimson Tide would start at the hands of a former assistant coach and a Tuscaloosa area native. Alabama took leads of 7–0 and 10–7, but could not hold on as Gene Stallings' Texas A&M team scored back-to-back touchdowns to go on top 20–10 midway through the third quarter. Kenny Stabler's seven-yard run—his second TD of the game—pulled Alabama to within four points with 3:55 to play. But an interception by Northport native Curley Hallman, the Crimson Tide's third turnover of the game, ended Alabama's comeback hopes in the final seconds.

## DECEMBER 28, 1968
### The Gator Bowl, Jacksonville, Florida
### Missouri 35, Alabama 10

A rushing yards disparity of 402 to –45 led to one of the more decisive losses of Bryant's career. Alabama stayed within 14–10 early in the fourth quarter, but Missouri pushed across three late touchdowns thanks to two turnovers and a shanked punt. The Crimson Tide's only touchdown came on a 38-yard interception return by Donnie Sutton in the second quarter. Quarterback Terry McMillan was the game's big star for Missouri despite not completing a pass, rushing for touchdowns of four, five, and two yards.

## December 13, 1969
### The Liberty Bowl, Memphis, Tennessee
### Colorado 47, Alabama 33

Quarterbacks Scott Hunter and Neb Hayden led the Crimson Tide in a wild offensive shootout in Memphis, a game in which Alabama led 33–31 going into the final quarter. But it was Colorado's Bob Anderson who carried his team to victory, scoring a pair of touchdowns in the fourth quarter—the Buffaloes also got a safety in the final period—as Alabama got outscored 16–0 in the final 15 minutes. The Crimson Tide's Hayden threw two touchdown passes, including one to Johnny Musso, who also rushed for a touchdown.

## December 31, 1970
### The Bluebonnet Bowl, Houston, Texas
### Alabama 24, Oklahoma 24

The Crimson Tide played in two Bluebonnet Bowls 10 years apart, and both ended in ties. The second time was at least a better offensive showcase than the 3–3 tie with Texas following the 1960 season. Scott Hunter threw a pair of touchdown passes and caught another on a halfback pass from Johnny Musso for Alabama, which led 24–21 in the final minutes. Oklahoma's Bruce Derr kicked a 42-yard field goal to tie the game, leaving Alabama 59 seconds to try for the win. The Crimson Tide drove as far as the Oklahoma 17, but the Sooners' John Shelley blocked Richard

Following Texas A&M's 20–16 upset win over 'Bama in the 1968 Cotton Bowl, Paul Bryant gave his former player and Aggies coach Gene Stallings a surprise "Bear hug" at midfield.

Ciemny's last-second field goal, and the two teams walked off the field in a deadlock.

## JANUARY 1, 1972
### The Orange Bowl, Miami, Florida
### Nebraska 38, Alabama 6

Alabama returned to glory during the 1971 regular season, unveiling the wishbone offense to run through the SEC season undefeated. The Crimson Tide's good fortune would not last through the bowl season, however, as the Cornhuskers dealt national championship contender Alabama its most decisive postseason defeat ever. The game-breaking play came on a 77-yard punt return by Nebraska's Johnny Rodgers on the final play of the first quarter. The Cornhuskers ripped off four straight scores before Terry Davis finally put the Crimson Tide on the board with a three-yard run in the third quarter.

## JANUARY 1, 1973
### The Cotton Bowl, Dallas, Texas
### Texas 17, Alabama 13

The Crimson Tide has had many frustrating bowl losses to the Longhorns over the years, but perhaps none was more gut-wrenching than the 1973 Cotton Bowl. Alabama led 10–0 after one quarter, 13–3 at halftime and 13–10 midway through the fourth quarter before the inevitable Texas comeback. First the Longhorns' Terry Melancon intercepted Terry Davis in the end zone to kill a potential game-clinching scoring chance for the Crimson Tide. Then Texas quarterback Alan Lowry bolted 34 yards for a touchdown with 4:22 to play to give the Longhorns the lead, a run on which the Alabama faithful claimed—and television replays appeared to confirm—that he stepped out of bounds near the 10-yard line. Nevertheless, the play stood, and Alabama's bowl drought extended to six straight.

### DECEMBER 31, 1973
**The Sugar Bowl, New Orleans, Louisiana**
**Notre Dame 24, Alabama 23**

In perhaps the most-anticipated college football game of all-time, the two titans of college football met for the first time on New Year's Eve in New Orleans. The game would prove to be the classic it had been billed as, but Alabama came out on the short end. Undefeated and top-ranked Alabama—which had already been declared national champion by one poll—led 17–14 in the third quarter and 23–21 in the fourth before Notre Dame's Bob Thomas gave his team a one-point lead with 4:12 remaining. Alabama punted to the Notre Dame 1 with the game entering its final three minutes, leading to a gutsy, game-winning call by the Irish. Tom Clements completed a 35-yard pass to Robin Weber to get Notre Dame out of the hole and run crucial seconds off the clock for the victory.

### JANUARY 1, 1975
**The Orange Bowl, Miami, Florida**
**Notre Dame 13, Alabama 11**

Top-ranked Alabama suffered its second-straight postseason loss to Notre Dame, this time costing it a shot at a national championship. The Fighting Irish jumped out to a 13–0 lead in the second quarter, but the Crimson Tide battled back behind Danny Ridgeway's 21-yard field goal and Richard Todd's 48-yard touchdown pass to Russ Schamun—plus a two-point pass to George Pugh—to pull within two points in the fourth quarter. Alabama got the ball back in the final two minutes and drove to the Notre Dame 38, but Todd's pass was intercepted by the Irish's Reggie Barnett to end the threat. Todd hit 13 of 24 passes for 223 yards in the game, six for 68 yards to freshman Ozzie Newsome and five for 126 yards to Schamun.

## DECEMBER 31, 1975
### The Sugar Bowl, New Orleans, Louisiana
### Alabama 13, Penn State 6

In the first postseason game played at the Louisiana Superdome, the Crimson Tide finally ended nearly a decade of bowl frustration. It wouldn't come easy, however, against seventh-ranked Penn State. Once-beaten Alabama led 3–0 at halftime, but Penn State tied the game at 3 in the third quarter. The Crimson Tide finally got into the end zone early in the fourth quarter on Mike Stock's 11-yard touchdown run. The two teams traded field goals to make it a 13–6 Alabama lead, and the Crimson Tide stopped the Nittany Lions on fourth-and-1 with 1:15 left to clinch the win. Richard Todd had a huge day for Alabama, completing 10 of 12 passes for 205 yards to earn the game's most outstanding player award.

## DECEMBER 20, 1976
### The Liberty Bowl, Memphis, Tennessee
### Alabama 36, UCLA 6

On a brutally cold day in Memphis—a game dubbed the "Refrigerator Bowl" by those in attendance—Alabama dominated from the start against overmatched UCLA. Barry Krauss, who would be named the game's MVP, scored the Crimson Tide's first touchdown on a 44-yard interception return. Johnny Davis and Rick Watson rushed for scores, Tony Nathan threw a 20-yard halfback pass to Jack O'Rear for another touchdown, and Bucky Berrey kicked three field goals as Alabama built a 30–0 lead. Only a

61-yard scoring run by UCLA's Theotis Brown in the fourth quarter prevented the shutout.

## JANUARY 2, 1978
### The Sugar Bowl, New Orleans, Louisiana
### Alabama 35, Ohio State 6

The Crimson Tide won its second Sugar Bowl in three years with a dominant win over Ohio State, a game that matched up coaching legends Bryant and Woody Hayes. Alabama built a 21–0 lead behind a touchdown run by Tony Nathan and two scoring passes by Jeff Rutledge, and then put the game away with fourth-quarter scores by Nathan and Major Ogilvie. By the time the game was over, the only drama remaining was whether or not third-ranked Alabama would win the national title following losses by top-ranked Texas and No. 2 Oklahoma. But Notre Dame once again dealt the Tide a postseason disappointment, vaulting into the final top spot after beating Texas in the Cotton Bowl. Alabama, 11–1 for the fifth time in seven years, had to settle for No. 2.

## JANUARY 1, 1979
### The Sugar Bowl, New Orleans, Louisiana
### Alabama 14, Penn State 7

The Crimson Tide beat the Nittany Lions in the Superdome for the second time in four years, but this time it was for all the marbles. No. 2 Alabama upset top-ranked Penn State thanks to one of the more memorable goal-line stands in school and college football history. Touchdowns by Bruce Bolton and Major Ogilvie offset Scott Fitzkee's score for the Nittany Lions, setting up the decisive fourth quarter. Penn State recovered a fumble at Alabama's 19 with 7:57 left, and soon drove inside the 10. Don McNeal kept Fitzkee out of the end zone on second down, and then the Crimson

Tide stopped running backs Matt Suhey and Mike Guman' on back-to-back plays to preserve the seven-point lead and ultimately the national title.

## JANUARY 1, 1980
### The Sugar Bowl, New Orleans, Louisiana
### Alabama 24, Arkansas 9

Alabama secured its second straight national championship—and final one under Bryant—but this time didn't have to sweat it out. Arkansas took an early lead on an Ish Odonez field goal, but the undefeated and top-ranked Crimson Tide scored 17 straight points to all but put the game away by halftime. Major Ogilvie rushed for two touchdowns as part of an MVP performance, and Billy Jackson ran for 120 yards out of Alabama's potent wishbone attack. The Razorbacks scored a touchdown in the third quarter to make it 17–9, but Steve Whitman's 12-yard score in the fourth quarter put a cap on a 12–0 finish for the Crimson Tide.

## JANUARY 1, 1981
### The Cotton Bowl, Dallas, Texas
### Alabama 30, Baylor 2

After falling out of the national championship race with November losses to Mississippi State and Notre Dame, the Crimson Tide clinched its ninth 10-win season in 10 years by pummeling the Bears in Dallas. Alabama rolled up 241 yards rushing, including scores by Major Ogilvie, Don Jacobs, and Mark Nix, plus three field goals by Peter Kim. The Crimson Tide defense, meanwhile, did not allow a point and forced seven turnovers. Baylor's only score came on a first-quarter safety when Crimson Tide quarterback Walter Lewis was trapped in the end zone.

---

## Crimson Tide in Their Own Words
# MAJOR OGILVIE
### HALFBACK, 1977–1980

When I had the opportunity to go to The University of Alabama and play football for Coach Bryant, it was not a time of rebuilding. My first year, 1977, was his 20th year at Alabama, so things were in place. The tradition was established, the routines were set, and everyone knew Coach Bryant's system of hard work, discipline, teamwork, and all the rest that went into success. I've always considered myself lucky to be able to go to Alabama at that time.

It was not a complicated situation. Coach Bryant explained things in basic terms. We learned about hard work and never quitting and telling the truth and being honest with yourself. Do those things and you had a chance—and I emphasize chance—to be successful. Because as he told us, sometimes you can believe in something and work for it and you may still come up short. And in that case, you circle the wagons and try a little harder. I have thought of these lessons in business and in raising a family.

After you have been out of it for a while, it's fun to talk about how you just survived. I know that it wasn't fun at the time. But we learned that we could do more than we thought, that when we were fatigued, we could go on, could take another step, and then another one and another. And that is a lesson that stays with you, one of many that I am so grateful for. But you don't realize that lesson until later, and you are not truly grateful to Coach Bryant until it is too late to thank him.

Major Ogilvie (42) raced for a 22-yard TD to start Alabama to a 24–9 victory over Arkansas in the 1980 Sugar Bowl and secure the 1979 national championship. Ogilvie was the first man in college football to score TDs in four consecutive bowl games.

I don't know if any of us could be fully prepared for Alabama football when we arrived as freshmen. I knew something about winning, because my high school teams were very successful. In six years of playing high school and college football, my teams had a record of 71–4. Our Mountain Brook teams won two state championships; at Alabama we won two national championships. And that was a lot of fun. But getting started at Alabama was starting over no matter how successful you had been in high school. We all had to adapt to the new situation.

The four losing games I played in were at Alabama. But that was over a four-year period, and we were playing tough schedules. Our nonconference games in those days were against Nebraska, Southern Cal, Notre Dame, Washington, and Missouri, which were very good, and teams like Miami, Georgia Tech, Virginia Tech, and Louisville, which weren't as good then as they are now.

Like most players, I remember the losses. But we won 44 games, which was one of the best records of any four-year group in Alabama football and college football history. I don't remember all the wins, but I remember the significant ones, the championship games.

We played to win, and we wanted to win national championships. We played in a lot of big games, and I enjoyed those. I think our teams had an attitude of going out, playing the best we could, and seeing where the chips fell. Most of the time we were on the right side of the scoreboard.

The 1979 Sugar Bowl game against Penn State was one of those games you are proud to say you were a part of and that you made whatever contribution you could. That was the toughest and best football game I ever played in. Penn State had a great team and they were well-coached. It was the hardest-hitting game I ever played in. It seemed as if the game was meant to go our way.

Another tough game that year was the Nebraska game to open the season. They were a really good team. They had beaten us the year before and then we had lost a lot of people from that 1977 team, Ozzie Newsome and Johnny Davis, for instance. Our 1977 team had done well and actually had a chance to win the national championship. Then we came back and started the season with a win over Nebraska. That was a real confidence-booster for us.

Even though we were ranked No. 1, we needed something for our confidence. In our first three games, we were playing top 10 teams, and then we were going to Washington. Typically, Alabama teams got stronger as the year went on. In 1978 we had to be pretty good from the get-go.

People seem to think we just coasted through the 1979 season, maybe because we beat Arkansas pretty decisively in the Sugar Bowl for the national championship. We did win a lot of games handily, but we had tough games that year against Tennessee and LSU.

One of the things about being lucky to be in the right place at the right time was something I was never aware of until after it happened. They've started keeping records on just about everything. The only thing that matters in football is the team, but they keep individual things that don't really matter, and one of them was my scoring touchdowns in four consecutive bowl games. That really says more about the team than one person. It doesn't mean anything to me compared to those national championship trophies.

I was probably destined to go to Alabama. My uncle, Hayden Riley, was on the staff at Alabama, a football recruiter and basketball and baseball coach. So I knew about the caliber of programs, that Alabama was a place where it was important to win. And that was of interest to me. From an educational standpoint, I was interested in accounting, and Alabama had a good accounting school. I was recruited by two really great guys in Coach Mal Moore and Coach Bill Oliver.

All of those things made Alabama the right place for me. But even if somewhere else had those things, Alabama had Coach Bryant. And who would want to pass up the opportunity to play for him? It was something for a young person to be excited about, and it's still exciting for me today.

After my Alabama playing career, I was drafted by San Francisco. I was one of the last ones cut, and that was it for me. I came back to Birmingham, where I have worked ever since. I'm now with Block USA.

*Major Ogilvie was a four-year letterman, All-SEC performer, and captain of the 1980 Crimson Tide. Ogilvie was the first man in college football history to score touchdowns in four different bowl games—three Sugar Bowl games (two national championship games) and one Cotton Bowl, all 'Bama wins.*

---

## JANUARY 1, 1982
### The Cotton Bowl, Dallas, Texas
### Texas 14, Alabama 12

Bryant's last great team—which shared the SEC title with Georgia—suffered yet another head-scratching postseason loss to the Longhorns. Alabama led 10–0 early in the fourth quarter on the strength of Walter Lewis' six-yard touchdown pass to Jesse Bendross and Peter Kim's 24-yard field goal, but the Crimson Tide could not hold the lead. Robert Brewer ran for a 30-yard touchdown on a quarterback draw with 10:22 left to make it 10–7, then Terry Orr's eight-yard score with 2:05 to play gave the Longhorns a 14–10 lead. Texas' William Graham intercepted Walter Lewis on Alabama's ensuing play to all but end the Tide's hopes. Alabama would add a late safety, a play on which Texas punter John Goodson intentionally stepped out of the end zone.

## DECEMBER 29, 1982
### The Liberty Bowl, Memphis, Tennessee
### Alabama 21, Illinois 15

The Crimson Tide—which suffered three frustrating losses in November—sent Bryant out a winner on another cold day in Memphis, holding off a late Illini rally to give their coach his 323rd victory. Ricky Moore, Jesse Bendross, and Craig Turner scored touchdowns for Alabama, and Jeremiah Castille intercepted three Illinois passes to lead the Crimson Tide defense. Tony Eason—who was knocked out of the game due to injury for a time—threw a third-quarter TD for Illinois but saw his last pass intercepted by game MVP Castille as Bryant ended his career with a record of 323–85–17.

---

## Crimson Tide in Their Own Words
# JOEY JONES
### SPLIT END, 1980–1983

Not long after the 1982 football season had ended, I was walking down the hall near the locker room. I heard Coach Bryant yell at me and went jogging back where he was about to get on the elevator. He told me to ride upstairs with him. He said he knew I liked to fish and that when it warmed up in the spring, he wanted me to go down to his son's lake in Greene County and do some bass fishing with him.

You can imagine how excited I was. The coach-player relationship Coach Bryant had with us was great, but he had just retired, and I thought about how it would be to know him at a different level, to sit down and talk to him on a personal basis. And I was flattered that he had wanted that, too.

And then he died just a couple of weeks later.

Like almost everyone who played for Alabama, I came to Alabama in great part because of what Coach Bryant had accomplished. But it was the entire Alabama tradition, how Alabama football had represented the state so well. Alabama players always seemed to exhibit so much more class, and you knew that came from the leadership.

In those days, a team could give out 30 scholarships, and I guess I got the 30th one. During the recruiting process, I didn't meet with Coach Bryant a lot, and I'm not sure he knew who I was. After I signed, I heard he looked at me and then had a few choice words for the coach who signed me—Bobby Marks; that I was too small, that I wouldn't be able to play here.

My freshman year was rough. I was about sixth string. And Coach Bryant made some remarks in the newspaper that I was too small a target for the quarterback.

But my sophomore year, a bunch of receivers got hurt, and he pretty much had to start me. As luck would have it, I scored a touchdown and had a pretty good game. The next week we played Kentucky, and I had another good game and also started returning punts. The following Monday, Coach Bryant told me not to dress out. He said I had been in a couple of physical games and was beaten up. I wasn't hurt, but it was his way of telling me I had finally made it. He winked at me and told me to sit out practice. My confidence meter was sky high after that.

I had a pretty good year. In the wishbone, we didn't catch a lot of passes, but I kind of made the 12 I caught that year pay off. I averaged over 30 yards per catch and had one against Vanderbilt for an 81-yard touchdown.

Anyone who played football for Alabama is honored to have been a small part in the tradition created by hundreds of coaches

Joey Jones (4) was considered too small to be an effective wide receiver, but he led Alabama in receiving for three consecutive years, from 1981 to 1983.

and players through the years. When you are playing, it means a lot to pull on that crimson jersey; 30 years later it still means something. I have great respect for those who played before me, those I played with, and those who have played since. I also sense respect from others for those who played for the Crimson Tide.

It means a lot to me to have a tie to the university, to be an alumnus. Alabama alumni and fans are everywhere, and it's always a treat to meet with them.

I was fortunate after my Alabama playing career to have an opportunity to play with the Birmingham Stallions and then with the Atlanta Falcons. I wanted to be a high school coach and so got into the business as an assistant coach at Briarwood Christian, then got a head coaching opportunity at Dora.

There was a time when I thought I needed to do something to make more money than I could in coaching and got out for a while. But I found myself going to watch practices in the afternoons and going to games on Friday nights. I was fortunate enough to get back into coaching in 1996 at Mountain Brook.

*Joey Jones was invited to play in both the Senior Bowl and the East-West Shrine Game following his Crimson Tide career. He was Alabama's leading receiver in 1981, 1982, and 1983. Jones coached many years in high school and has been head coach at the University of South Alabama since 2008.*

---

## DECEMBER 24, 1983
### The Sun Bowl, El Paso, Texas
### Alabama 28, SMU 7

With new coach Ray Perkins on the sideline, the Crimson Tide advanced to its 25th consecutive bowl, playing for the first time in El Paso. Alabama built a 28–0 halftime lead behind running back Ricky Moore, who finished with 113 yards and two touchdowns rushing. Quarterback Walter Lewis scored on a one-yard run and also threw a 19-yard touchdown pass to Joey Jones. SMU avoided the shutout on Lance McIhenny's 15-yard touchdown pass to Marquis Pleasant in the third quarter.

## DECEMBER 28, 1985
### The Aloha Bowl, Honolulu, Hawaii
### Alabama 24, Southern California 3

After seeing its quarter-century bowl streak end due to a 5–6 record in 1984, the Crimson Tide returned to the postseason with a vengeance the following year. Making its first football trip to Hawaii, Alabama thumped long-time rival USC 24–3 thanks to three second-half touchdowns. The game was tied 3–3 at half-time, but the Crimson Tide finally got into the end zone on Craig Turner's one-yard run in the third quarter. Alabama added late scores on a 24-yard pass from Mike Shula to Clay Whitehurst and a 14-yard flanker reverse by Al Bell.

## DECEMBER 25, 1986
### The Sun Bowl, El Paso, Texas
### Alabama 28, Washington 6

All-America linebacker Cornelius Bennett said good-bye to Crimson Tide football with a memorable performance in what also proved to be Ray Perkins' final game on the Alabama sideline. Bennett led a Crimson Tide defense that limited Washington to 62 rushing yards and no touchdowns. Sophomore Bobby Humphrey rushed for 159 yards and two touchdowns, and also caught an 18-yard score from Mike Shula. The Tide's other touchdown came on a 32-yard pass to Greg Richardson from Shula, who threw for 176 yards in the game.

## JANUARY 2, 1988
### The Hall of Fame Bowl, Tampa, Florida
### Michigan 28, Alabama 24

Bill Curry's first bowl game as Alabama coach also marked the Crimson Tide's first-ever meeting with the Wolverines and its first postseason trip to Tampa. The game turned into an off-season shootout, as Alabama overcame a 14–3 halftime deficit to take a 24–21 lead with 4:49 left to play following Bobby Humphrey's 17-yard touchdown run and Jeff Dunn's two-point pass to Clay Whitehurst. Michigan won the game with 50 seconds left, when quarterback Demetrius Brown connected with John Kolesar on a 20-yard touchdown pass. Humphrey rushed for 149 yards and two touchdowns in a losing effort for the Crimson Tide.

### DECEMBER 24, 1988
#### The Sun Bowl, El Paso, Texas
#### Alabama 29, Army 28

The Crimson Tide made its third trip to El Paso in six years and came away with a thrilling victory and a record-setting performance by its quarterback. Senior David Smith completed 33 of 52 passes for 412 yards, all school postseason records. He threw touchdown passes of seven yards to Marco Battle and 23 yards to Greg Payne, but the Crimson Tide still trailed 28–20 entering the fourth quarter. Philip Doyle kicked his third field goal to pull Alabama to within five with 7:25 to play, and then David Casteal burst into the end zone for the winning touchdown with 4:01 remaining. Freshman safety Charles Gardner stopped Army's final drive with a late interception.

### JANUARY 1, 1990
#### The Sugar Bowl, New Orleans, Louisiana
#### Miami 33, Alabama 25

Despite ending the regular season with a loss to Auburn, Alabama still had an outside shot to win the national championship when it faced Miami in its first Sugar Bowl trip in 10 years. Alabama's high-flying passing attack kept the game tight at 20–17 by halftime, but Miami got back-to-back touchdown passes from Craig Erickson to lead 33–17 early in the fourth quarter. The Crimson Tide got a nine-yard touchdown pass from Gary Hollingsworth to Prince Wimbley and a two-point pass to Lamonde Russell to pull within eight, but could not recover an onside kick and went down in defeat to the eventual national champions. In Bill Curry's last game as Alabama coach, Hollingsworth passed for 214 yards and three scores.

---

## Crimson Tide in Their Own Words

# GARY HOLLINGSWORTH

### QUARTERBACK, 1989–1990

You know what it means to be Crimson Tide? It means trying to explain to your children why someone would want Daddy's autograph. They have no clue. It is pretty amazing. I was lucky to go to Alabama, and then it took some bad luck for Jeff Dunn for me to have an opportunity.

Although I wasn't a big Alabama fan growing up, Alabama was the first school to show any interest in me as a prospect, and that meant a lot to me. Rockey Felker was recruiting North Alabama and had seen several games in which I had played. He was actually recruiting players on the teams we were playing against, but when he reported back after his scouting trips, he mentioned the quarterback from Hamilton. After that happened a few times, Coach Perkins said, "Well, Rockey, don't you think we ought to be recruiting him?"

I didn't really have that great of an appreciation for Alabama football when I first got to Tuscaloosa because I hadn't followed it that much. But once I got there, I quickly realized the tradition. I particularly realized what an honor it was to be a quarterback at The University of Alabama, where people like Joe Namath and Kenny Stabler had played. That's pretty big to me now, and it was huge when I was 18 years old.

In 1989 it was pretty much acknowledged that we could be written off if anything happened to Jeff Dunn. He was our only experienced quarterback. I had been redshirted as a freshman in 1986, then didn't play in 1987 or 1988. I threw one pass in our opening game, and then against Kentucky in our second game, Jeff hurt a knee.

The season was a satisfying one for me personally. I was able to come in and keep going what Jeff had started. We won a share of the SEC championship.

I like to think that I had the confidence I could do the job. That's part of football, that the back-ups are ready to step up and play. Everyone on the team has proven something to the coaches or he wouldn't be there. Sometimes guys aren't ready when the opportunity comes. But in football, and in a lot of other things, you never know when it's coming, and you have to be prepared as best you can. I think I've taken that from football to my business career.

It's possible that I wouldn't have been ready if the opportunity had come earlier. It worked out very well for me from the standpoint that I didn't play my first three years. A lot of guys, I think, are put in situations in which they're forced to play earlier, and sometimes they're not ready. I got to travel with the team a good bit. I got to go to Neyland Stadium and experience it without having to be the quarterback playing in Neyland Stadium. The same was true for Death Valley at LSU and some other places. You aren't under the gun, but at the same time you get to experience and feel what it's like. So then to play as a junior finally, I think I was better prepared for what I encountered than some of the guys who have to play the first time they ever go to Neyland Stadium. I think that can be hard sometimes.

I'm glad I got the opportunity and that it went the way it did. There's a satisfaction there because I could have had some opportunities probably to go play at some other schools and played earlier and maybe played more, but to look back and know that you're a part of one of the greatest traditions in college football is tremendous. It gives me great satisfaction to have been able to be a part of that and compete at that level.

I really enjoyed my time at Alabama. And I enjoyed living in Bryant Hall. We had a good group of friends. Once you finish, you stay in touch with a handful, but people begin to spread out and have families and careers, so you don't see or talk to one another. And this was a group of guys who were almost inseparable for four or five years.

There is one thing as a quarterback I know I am not remembered for, and that is running. But I remember one run. We played an unlikely game, playing at Southwestern Louisiana. I ran a naked bootleg and gained about 25 or 30 yards, which was easily the longest run I ever had in my career. I went out of bounds in front of their bench. And all of our linemen and the rest of the guys started laughing. I think it offended their team because they didn't really know how big the joke was. It wasn't that we were laughing at them; it was that I ran 30 yards.

In 1989 Bo Jackson won the Alabama Sports Writers Association professional athlete of the year award, and I was the amateur athlete of the year. Bo wasn't able to be there, so Coach Dye was there and accepted the award for him. Coach Dye told a story about an Auburn spring game that Bo wasn't participating in. All the kids wanted to go see Bo play in the game, and they were disappointed when he didn't play, Dye said. So Bo came up with the idea to get a bunch of kids on the field and he would race them. To make it fair, Bo gave the kids a 50-yard head start, and Bo went on to win the race.

When I gave my acceptance speech, I said that Coach Stallings had decided to hold me out of our spring game, too. And, I said,

Gary Hollingsworth (14) was an unheralded quarterback who was elevated to first team in 1989 when Jeff Dunn was injured. He took advantage of the situation to lead 'Bama to the SEC championship and earn Player of the Year.

we had a similar event. Except in my case the kids gave me a 50-yard head start.

One of the most interesting games we played was the Mississippi game in Jackson in 1989. They got up 21–0 in the first quarter, but then we scored 62 straight points. We led 48–21 at halftime. We also outscored Tennessee 47–30. I threw a lot of passes to my fullback, Kevin Turner. And in 1990, after starting the season with three straight losses, it was satisfying to come back and beat Tennessee, LSU, and Auburn.

After finishing at Alabama, I went to the Houston Oilers as a free agent, but I had been in athletics long enough to know when I didn't belong. I came back to Alabama, and since 1991 I've been with Cavalier Home Builders in Addison where I'm sales manager.

*Gary Hollingsworth was All-SEC and captain of the 1990 team. He holds Alabama records for completions in a game (32 against Tennessee). He also holds the Tide mark for all-purpose yards per game for a career (170.9). He was SEC Offensive Player of the Year in 1989.*

---

## JANUARY 1, 1991
### The Fiesta Bowl, Tempe, Arizona
### Louisville 34, Alabama 7

In its first bowl trip under Gene Stallings, Alabama couldn't continue the late-season momentum that saw it claim victories over Tennessee and Auburn. The Crimson Tide's opponent in Arizona was an up-and-coming Louisville team coached by Howard Schnellenberger, a former assistant at Alabama in the 1960s who led Miami to a national championship in 1983. The Cardinals scored four touchdowns in the first quarter, two on scoring passes by Browning Nagle (who threw for 451 yards on the day) and another on a blocked punt by Ray Buchanan. Alabama got its only points in the second quarter on an interception return by Charles Gardner, but Louisville held the Tide scoreless in the second half to secure the 27-point win.

### DECEMBER 28, 1991
#### The Blockbuster Bowl, Miami, Florida
#### Alabama 30, Colorado 25

The Crimson Tide ended the regular season on a nine-game winning streak, securing a bowl trip to south Florida for the first time since the 1975 Orange Bowl. The opponent was defending national champion Colorado, who built leads of 12–10 and 19–16. But Alabama had the best player on the field, wide receiver/return specialist David Palmer. The freshman scored touchdowns on a 52-yard punt return and a five-yard pass from Jay Barker, and had a third score called back due to penalty. Barker threw three touchdown passes, including a 12-yarder to Kevin Lee that put the Tide up for good late in the third quarter.

---

## *Crimson Tide in Their Own Words*

# JAY BARKER
### QUARTERBACK, 1991–1994

It was funny that almost no one expected us to win against Miami in the national championship game in the New Orleans Superdome at the end of the 1992 season. When we were preparing for the game, a reporter said to me, "Do you know what you're stepping into? This is like David going up against Goliath."

Jay Barker was quarterback of Alabama's 1992 national championship team as a sophomore and finished his career with a record of 34–2–1 as a starter.

I said, "Well, I know who won that battle."

I believe the thing that defines Alabama football is the national championship. It is the great part of Alabama football tradition. And while the opportunity to play for the national championship is huge for the players and coaches, I believe it is most apparent in our fans.

I was fortunate enough to be a part of a lot of big moments as an Alabama football player, but probably nothing compares to running onto the field as a sophomore quarterback about to play against the No. 1 team in the nation with Gino Torretta, the Heisman Trophy winner, quarterbacking Miami. I can't even remember my feet hitting the turf, I was so nervous.

And then the most electrifying situation in my life was the Alabama crowd. Alabama fans filled the Superdome on January 1, 1993. I think Alabama fans turn into a new species when the national championship is on the line. That is when you see the true fans. They are home and in their comfort zone in that atmosphere.

Miami had the nation's longest winning streak, and almost all the talk was about Miami. But we thought we would win the game. Before the game, Coach Stallings told me that he didn't think we would have to pass much to win, that we could run it just about every down. We saw a weakness that we could run right at them. They were very fast if you tried to go wide, but after looking at the films, we saw we could beat them. And it worked out just about like Coach Stallings said it would.

To us it seemed like it was right winning against everything that was so wrong. And we did it the right way: with sportsmanship. I've always believed that the game was good for Miami, too, because they seemed to have a change in attitude that was for the better.

After that game, we were all so excited and, really, spent. But of course, everyone wanted to go out and celebrate. I went back to my room to get changed and decided to lay down on the bed and watch the highlights on television. I fell asleep. There was a banging on the door, and when I first woke up I thought maybe I had just dreamed the game. But then I realized how sore I was and knew that we had played.

It had seemed the city was covered with Miami fans before the game, although there were certainly more Alabama fans in the Superdome. But when we went to eat that night you could hardly find a Miami fan.

I can still remember the cry of an Alabama fan that night. "'Bama's back!" And that probably brought as much joy to me as it did to him.

I have never seen the replay of the televised version of the game. I have gone through the coaching video. Between plays, the camera goes to the stands, and I have paused it to see how happy our fans are. I love to see people happy, and if I had a small part in that happiness, it means a lot to me. I've thought I might never look at the television version because I've got it in my mind how the game went, and I don't want that to change. But someday I'll probably watch it.

There are some games that would obviously be big ones, and that Miami game ranks at the top. Certainly our 29–28 comeback win over Georgia in a night game at Bryant-Denny Stadium in 1994 and the Citrus Bowl win over Ohio State at the end of that season were big.

But I also remember games like the comebacks against Mississippi State in 1992 and 1994.

The 1992 season was incredible. It is very, very difficult to go undefeated. Certainly we had some outstanding players, but we also had a lot of guys who were—for lack of a better term—role players. There were a lot of pressure moments, but I don't think we recognized them because it was the job that had to be done. How was I not nervous facing a must-make fourth-and-10 against Tennessee? I don't know, but I wasn't. In looking back, I have great respect for what my teammates and coaches did.

Other than the Miami game, it seems more people remember our comeback against Georgia than any other game. That was a humbling night for me. What most people don't remember is that I was benched, the only time in my career I was taken out of a game because I wasn't playing well. Coach Stallings took me aside and said, "Let's get over here and take a look." It was what I needed, and Coach Stallings figured it out.

The 1995 Citrus Bowl in Orlando was the last game in my college career. I think Ohio State had about six first-round draft choices. They had an excellent team, and we were kind of the Cardiac Kids type of team. And we lived up to our name. I don't think any quarterback could have a greater thrill than the last play of his college career being to throw a pass to Sherman Williams that went for a 50-yard touchdown in the final minute to win the game. That gave us a four-year record of 45–4–1, the best of any class in Alabama history.

It's great to remember the wins, but there are so many things we got out of being Alabama football players. I tell my kids the same thing Coach Stallings told us: "You'll never go wrong by doing right." That sticks with you. Our coaches cared about me as a person, how I was going to measure up as a husband and a father and a worker.

You hear Alabama players talk about "gut checks," that you are going to have them in life. And you learn that at Alabama. You learn about high expectations. You learn to be a team player.

I can never give back to Alabama football what it has given to me. Alabama football has impacted just about everything I have done, and there is not a day in my life that passes that someone doesn't say something to me about playing at Alabama. I think that's true for almost everyone who has pulled on that crimson jersey.

I've had a lot of men I have looked up to, and many of them are the products of athletics. And I always hoped that things I did off the field would live longer than what I did on the field. The greatest example of that is John Croyle, who has done so very much good in taking care of the children at his ranches.

John invited me up several years ago, and while I was there he asked if I would throw with his son, Brodie, to try to help him out. I threw a few with him, then said, "John, I don't want to mess him up."

I have the greatest admiration for Bart Starr, who played at Alabama, and Mike Kolen, who played at Auburn, as men of integrity.

I never wanted to appear "holier than thou," but I hoped that what was in my heart would shine through. It's a fine line. I believe that championship trophies are important, and I was competitive and wanted to win every game. But relationships last for eternity, and I like to think they made me a better person.

I was born to be an Alabama football player. My dad loved Coach Bryant and Alabama, and we grew up cheering for the Tide and going to games when we could. At age five I was telling my friends that I was going to play for Coach Bryant. I honestly think my class was about the last one that identified itself as the Bryant Generation. We didn't just wear the jersey. We represented it.

I almost wasn't an Alabama player. I only played one year of quarterback in high school, and Coach Curry's staff was not recruiting me. But when Coach Curry left and Coach Stallings got the job, my prayer had been answered. Before that, I was afraid I was headed to Auburn. But Coach Stallings called me the night he was hired.

I still see a number of my old teammates, but right now we're focused on the games our children are playing. Maybe soon we'll be sitting down and talking about our Alabama careers more. Meanwhile, it is wonderful to continue to be embraced by the fans for our accomplishments as Alabama football players.

I've been fortunate to stay close to sports and close to people as an on-air personality on WJOX radio in Birmingham and through speaking engagements and endorsements. And we have FaithWorks, a company involved in restaurants, real estate, and charitable foundations, and Nspira, a merchant services in the hospital field.

*Jay Barker had the best record of any Alabama starting quarterback, 34–2–1, and was an All-American and winner of the Johnny Unitas Golden Arm Award as the nation's best quarterback in 1994.*

## January 1, 1993
### The Sugar Bowl, New Orleans, Louisiana
### Alabama 34, Miami 13

The Crimson Tide's first national championship of the post-Bryant era was one of the more dominant defensive performances in school history. Facing a vaunted Miami passing attack led by Heisman Trophy winner Gino Torretta, Alabama unveiled an innovative defensive scheme that featured 11 men on the line of scrimmage at times. The Crimson Tide never trailed, did not allow an offensive touchdown, and forced three turnovers. One of those was a 31-yard interception return for a touchdown by George Teague, whose most memorable play didn't even count in the official statistics. With Alabama on top 27–6 in the third quarter, Teague ran down Miami receiver Lamar Thomas and stripped the ball away from behind to kill the Hurricanes' will once and for all (the play didn't count because the Crimson Tide was ruled offside on the play). Derrick Lassic was named game MVP after rushing for 135 yards and two touchdowns.

## December 31, 1993
### The Gator Bowl, Jacksonville, Florida
### Alabama 24, North Carolina 10

The Crimson Tide wasn't able to win a second straight national championship, but did reel off its second bowl victory in less than a calendar year when it scored three straight touchdowns to pull away from the Tar Heels. Quarterback Brian Burgdorf, playing in place of the injured Jay Barker, scored on a 33-yard run to tie the game at halftime. Burgdorf, who was named the game's MVP, threw two second-half touchdown passes, an eight-yard strike to Tarrant Lynch in the third quarter to give Alabama the lead, and a 10-yard toss to Chad Key with 6:34 remaining to put the game away.

## January 2, 1995
### The Citrus Bowl, Orlando, Florida
### Alabama 24, Ohio State 17

The once-beaten Crimson Tide scored its fourth consecutive bowl victory, turning back fellow national power Ohio State thanks to late heroics from seniors Jay Barker and Sherman Williams. The teams were tied 14–14 through three quarters, then the Buckeyes took the lead on Josh Jackson's 34-yard field goal with 8:41 left. Michael Proctor's 27-yard boot tied the game again with 4:29 left, and a defensive stand gave the Tide the ball back with one last chance to win. With 50 seconds to play, Barker connected with Williams over the middle, and the senior tailback did the rest, racing 50 yards to the end zone for the win. Williams ended the day with 321 yards combined rushing and receiving, a school bowl record.

## JANUARY 1, 1997
### The Outback Bowl, Tampa, Florida
### Alabama 17, Michigan 14

After a one-year bowl absence due to NCAA sanctions, the Crimson Tide was able to give retiring coach Gene Stallings his 70th victory in seven years. Alabama scored its first-ever win over Michigan in the process, overcoming a 6–3 halftime deficit thanks to a pair of touchdowns early in the fourth quarter. First came Dwayne Rudd's 88-yard interception return, which put the Tide up 10–6. Then came Shaun Alexander's 46-yard gallop, giving Alabama a 17–6 advantage. Michigan pulled to within three on a nine-yard TD pass from Brian Griese to Russell Shaw and a two-point conversion with less than a minute to play. But Alabama's Chad Goss recovered the onside kick to clinch the win.

## DECEMBER 29, 1998
### The Music City Bowl, Nashville, Tennessee
### Virginia Tech 38, Alabama 7

The inaugural Music City Bowl got away from the Crimson Tide in the second half, as the Hokies scored four unanswered touchdowns to turn a 10–7 game into a laugher. Virginia Tech forced four turnovers, blocked two punts, and got three touchdown runs from Lamont Pegues and one each from Al Clark and Shyrone Stith. Alabama's lone touchdown came on a five-yard pass from Andrew Zow to Michael Vaughn in the second quarter. The game was played in a freezing downpour at Vanderbilt Stadium, unquestionably turning it into one of the more miserable days in Alabama football history.

### JANUARY 1, 2000
#### The Orange Bowl, Miami, Florida
#### Michigan 35, Alabama 34 (OT)

Alabama won its first SEC championship in seven years under Mike DuBose during the 1999 regular season, but couldn't overcome Michigan's passing game in one of the more exciting Orange Bowls ever. On the first day of the new millennium, the Wolverines' Tom Brady threw three touchdown passes to David Terrell, and four overall. Alabama got three rushing touchdowns from Shaun Alexander and a 62-yard punt return by Freddie Milons to tie the game at 28. The Tide's Phillip Weeks blocked a field goal on the last play of regulation to send the game into overtime. Michigan scored first in overtime on Brady's 25-yard pass to Shawn Thompson to go up 35–28, and then Andrew Zow hit Antonio Carter for a 21-yard score to pull Alabama to within one. But Ryan Pflugner missed the extra point, and the Tide lost by one.

---

## Crimson Tide in Their Own Words

# ANDREW ZOW

### QUARTERBACK, 1998–2001

It was an unlikely trip from Lake Butler, Florida, to Tuscaloosa. When I was first being recruited, it was the three Florida schools showing interest. Then, just before the start of my senior season, I tore my anterior cruciate ligament. That knee injury ended any interest the Florida schools had in me. Auburn and Alabama were recruiting me, and I committed to Auburn. Jeff Rouzie was recruiting me for Alabama and asked if I would reconsider because Alabama really needed a quarterback. Auburn had recruited me as a linebacker, but I wanted to be a quarterback.

I didn't take my commitment to Auburn lightly. I had given my word. But I had doubts. After talking with my family and my girlfriend—who is now my wife—and praying, I changed my mind. I told Auburn that I was going to Alabama because they had promised me a legitimate chance to play quarterback. Auburn then said they would give me a shot at quarterback, too, but I had made my decision.

It made me feel good when at the first practice at Alabama I threw a ball and Bruce Arians, who was the quarterbacks coach, said, "There's a quarterback." That's what I wanted to be.

Growing up in Florida, I didn't know too much about the Alabama tradition, or at least the specifics of it. But when you hear people say, "Alabama football," you know they are talking superior. Alabama was one of those teams that you expected to win the national championship every few years. And since we had won three straight state championships in high school, I had championship aspirations. I really thought we'd be in the hunt, and I wanted to be a part of that.

You also heard what a classy program Alabama has. That was a big part of my decision. Even the people in Florida who weren't Alabama fans knew that Alabama was a prestigious place, a great school to be associated with.

It meant a whole lot to me to put on that uniform. An Alabama football player can't help but think about Coach Bryant and the great players who have gone before. A quarterback can't help but think about Joe Namath and Ken Stabler playing on the same field.

When you get to Alabama, you know you are in a family atmosphere. That's players, but it's also students and fans. You feel a lot of people are behind you. When you finish playing at Alabama, the fans don't forget you. They continue to be supportive. Alabama fans make me feel that I did something that made them feel better about their school or that entertained them. It's a pleasure to give autographs to fans who are so much for you and for Alabama. I talk to friends who played at other schools, and they don't get that from their fans, particularly when their playing days are over.

After I finished playing at Alabama, I gave the Canadian Football League a short try at Montreal, then went home to Lake Butler, where I coached and taught school. But for the past two years I've been back in Alabama with my own business, Andrew Zow & Associates, in Birmingham. A main reason I came back to Alabama was the support I received as a Crimson Tide player.

And this is for a guy who quarterbacked that 2000 team that was so disappointing. A moment in the UCLA game was so typical of that season. My roommates were Jason McAddley and Shaun Bohanon. Shaun had a bad game against UCLA, fumbling a couple of times. And we were going into the huddle and Shaun said, "Give me the ball, Drew. I'm going to score this time." Really determined. Jason was a little skeptical, but I called Shaun's number. And he fumbled. You can bet it wasn't funny then, but we think back to the look on Shaun's face and now we can laugh.

I prefer to remember better times. I certainly enjoyed my last trip to "the Swamp," Florida Field. One of my best friends, Gerard Warren, was at defensive end for Florida. He was taunting me that we couldn't run at him. I threw a few passes and completed them for long yardage. As I jogged downfield, I said to him, "We might not be able to run, but we're sure passing it." And a little later we

Andrew Zow had committed to Auburn as a linebacker, but when he had a chance to be a quarterback at Alabama, he went with the Crimson Tide.

had a nice run with Shaun Alexander running and Chris Samuels blocking to win the game in overtime.

*Andrew Zow ended his Alabama career as the school record-holder for career yards passing (5,983), total offense (5,958 yards, including minus-25 rushing), and career plays (1,020 on 852 passes and 168 rushes). He also threw a then–school record 12 consecutive completions against Ole Miss in 2000. He was a 2001 captain.*

## DECEMBER 27, 2001
### The Independence Bowl, Shreveport, Louisiana
### Alabama 14, Iowa State 13

The Crimson Tide won four straight to end Dennis Franchione's first season as head coach, including a narrow one-point win over the Cyclones in Shreveport. Iowa State led 13–7 entering the final six minutes, but Alabama's Waine Bacon blocked a punt to give the Tide the ball at the Cyclones 29. Andrew Zow hit Terry Jones on a 27-yard touchdown with 4:44 remaining to give the Crimson Tide a one-point lead on Neal Thomas' extra point. Iowa State had a shot to win, but Tony Yelk's 47-yard field goal attempt with 44 seconds remaining sailed wide to give Alabama its record 29th bowl victory.

## DECEMBER 31, 2004
### The Music City Bowl, Nashville, Tennessee
### Minnesota 20, Alabama 16

The Crimson Tide returned to the postseason for the first time in three years in Mike Shula's second season as head coach. Alabama's opponent was a Minnesota team that featured a pair of 1,000-yard rushers in Marion Barber and Laurence Maroney. The Tide struck first after recovering an early fumble, getting Le'Ron McClain's two-yard touchdown reception from Spencer Pennington to lead 7–0. But the Golden Gophers controlled the rest of the action behind 292 combined yards from Barber and Maroney, including 187 and a touchdown on 37 carries by Barber. Back-to-back touchdowns and a Rhys Lloyd field goal gave Minnesota a 17–14 halftime lead, and the Gophers withstood a late Alabama drive to clinch the four-point win.

## JANUARY 2, 2006
### The Cotton Bowl, Dallas, Texas
### Alabama 13, Texas Tech 10

Alabama returned to Dallas for the first time in nearly a quarter-century, playing in a New Year's bowl for the first time in six years. The Crimson Tide picked up an early touchdown on Brodie Croyle's 76-yard touchdown pass to Keith Brown in the first quarter, but couldn't get into the end zone the rest of the day. A late comeback by Texas Tech tied the game at 13 late in the fourth quarter, and Alabama took over at its own 14 with a chance to drive for the win. Several key completions put the ball into Texas Tech territory, and Jamie Christensen delivered a wobbly 45-yard field goal as time expired to give Alabama the victory and a 10-win season.

## DECEMBER 28, 2006
### The Independence Bowl, Shreveport, Louisiana
### Oklahoma State 34, Alabama 31

With interim coach Joe Kines having replaced Shula at the end of the regular season, the Crimson Tide lost in a wild shootout despite a fourth-quarter comeback. Alabama trailed 31–17 following Bobby Reid's touchdown pass to Adrian Bowman early in the final quarter, but the Tide's Javier Arenas pulled his team to within a touchdown on an 86-yard punt return for a touchdown. Alabama used a little razzle-dazzle to tie the game, with offensive tackle Andre Smith hauling in a short pass from John Parker Wilson (a play technically ruled a lateral) and rumbling into the end zone for a two-yard score. Oklahoma State still had time left on the clock, however, and drove for Jason Ricks' 27-yard field goal to win the game.

## DECEMBER 30, 2007
### The Independence Bowl, Shreveport, Louisiana
### Alabama 30, Colorado 24

The Crimson Tide returned to Shreveport in Nick Saban's debut season, but this time came out with a victory thanks to a standout passing day from John Parker Wilson. The junior threw for 256 yards and three scores, the last a 31-yard strike to give Alabama a 27–14 halftime lead. Leigh Tiffin gave the Tide a 30–17 lead on a 26-yard field goal with 4:36 left in the game, but Colorado battled back to pull to within six on Cody Hawkins' 14-yard pass to Tyson DeVree with less than three minutes remaining. Alabama ran the clock down to one second before turning the ball over on downs at the Colorado 20, and the Buffaloes' lateral-filled final play was stopped well short of the end zone.

## JANUARY 2, 2009
### The Sugar Bowl, New Orleans, Louisiana
### Utah 31, Alabama 17

Playing in New Orleans for the first time since its national championship–winning victory over Miami 16 years earlier, the SEC West champion Crimson Tide fell flat against the unbeaten Utes. Quarterback Brian Johnson led Utah to three touchdowns in the first quarter on the way to a stunning upset of Alabama. The Crimson Tide did cut the lead to 21–17 early in the third quarter after back-to-back touchdowns by Javier Arenas and Glen Coffee, but the Utes scored the game's final 10 points.

## JANUARY 7, 2010
### The BCS National Championship Game, Pasadena, California
### Alabama 37, Texas 21

Alabama's first postseason trip to Pasadena since 1946 paid off big-time, as the Crimson Tide won its first national championship in 17 years in the same place it won its first four. Texas led 6–0 after one quarter, but Alabama scored 24 consecutive points in the second quarter to take control. The biggest plays were a 49-yard run by Trent Richardson and a 28-yard interception return by defensive end Marcel Dareus. Texas rallied to cut 'Bama's lead to 24–21 behind backup quarterback Garrett Gilbert, but the Tide got two late touchdowns to take home its first BCS title.

## JANUARY 1, 2011
### The Capital One Bowl, Orlando, Florida
### Alabama 49, Michigan State 7

Losses to LSU and Auburn late in the regular season knocked the Crimson Tide out of the national championship race, but Alabama took out its frustration on the Spartans on New Year's Day. The Crimson Tide led 28–0 at halftime and 42–0 after three quarters on the way to its biggest blowout bowl win since the 1953 Orange Bowl. Alabama running backs Mark Ingram and Eddie Lacy combined for 145 yards and four touchdowns rushing, while linebacker Courtney Upshaw was named Most Valuable Player after a two-sack performance.

*chapter 9*

# THE CHAMPIONSHIP
# SEASONS

ALABAMA HAS MADE A HABIT of playing for championships over the years, 13 times coming out as the No. 1 team in the country. Still, the Crimson Tide has had a number of near-misses. Here's a look back at those Alabama teams that were truly championship material.

### 1925

Alabama's 1925 season didn't come totally out of nowhere. The Crimson Tide had been 8–1 and 10–1 in 1919 and 1920 under Xen Scott, and then 8–1 with its first Southern Conference championship under Wallace Wade in 1924.

Alabama returned star players such as Pooley Hubert, Johnny Mack Brown, and Grant Gillis the following year, though Georgia Tech was widely considered the conference favorite. But the Crimson Tide rolled through the regular season, winning nine straight games and outscoring its opponents 277–7.

Among the Crimson Tide's wins was a 7–0 defeat of Georgia Tech on October 24 in Atlanta. Brown scored the game's only touchdown, taking a punt back 55 yards in the second half.

Alabama upended Mississippi State 6–0 the following week and then routed Kentucky, Florida, and Georgia in succession. The Crimson Tide then became the first southern team to be invited to the Rose Bowl but was considered a major underdog to a powerful Washington team on New Year's Day in Pasadena.

Led by star halfback George Wilson, the Huskies took a 12–0 lead into the locker room at halftime. No doubt inspired by a rousing halftime speech from Wade, the Crimson Tide stormed back to score three times in the third quarter—including a pair of long touchdown receptions by Brown—to secure a 20–19 victory.

Of Alabama's victory, famed New York sportswriter Damon Runyon wrote, "It was a great team that the South sent to California to take its part in the Tournament of Roses, probably the greatest that ever came out of the South."

There was no Associated Press or coaches' poll in those days, but Helms, Billingsley, Football Research, and the National Championship Foundation were among those ranking services that declared the Crimson Tide national champions.

## 1926

Hubert, Brown, and Gillis were all gone in 1926, but Alabama still boasted a strong team led by Herschel Caldwell, Red Barnes, and All-America end Hoyt "Wu" Winslett. The Crimson Tide again rolled through the regular season undefeated to win the Southern Conference championship, this time outscoring its opponents 242–20.

The closest regular-season game came on October 23 in Birmingham, a 2–0 victory over Sewanee. Early in the fourth quarter, tackle Freddie Prichard blocked a punt, with the ball rolling out of the end zone for a safety and the only points of the game.

Alabama earned its second straight Rose Bowl bid, this time matched up against undefeated Stanford and legendary coach Glenn "Pop" Warner. The game ended in a 7–7 stalemate, with Alabama's Jimmy Johnston—a Tuscaloosa native—scoring from a yard out in the fourth quarter to tie the game.

Alabama football first became a national sensation under coach Wallace Wade (center, with tan suit and hat), who led the Crimson Tide to back-to-back Rose Bowl appearances after the 1925 and 1926 seasons.

Fred Digby of the *New Orleans Item* wrote of the Crimson Tide, "The Alabama team brought new glory to the South and southern football when it came from behind to tie the Stanford Cardinals [sic] at Pasadena on Saturday. Almost every expert in the East and West thought Stanford was too good for the Crimson Tide.... The entire South should be proud of the Alabama team, for it exemplifies the spirit of the southland."

The Crimson Tide and the Cardinal (as Stanford was unofficially known before 1930 and again after they dropped the nickname "Indians" in 1972) were both undefeated and once tied, and would share the national championship. Stanford was No. 1 under the Dickinson System, while Alabama was declared champion by the Helms Foundation.

## 1930

The Crimson Tide had some relatively lean years in the late 1920s—failing to win more than six games in any season from 1927 to 1929. But Wallace Wade's final team might have been his greatest, and it gave him his third national championship in six years.

Behind quarterback John "Monk" Campbell, fullback John "Hurri" Cain, tackle Charles "Foots" Clement, and All-America tackle "Football Freddie" Sington, the Crimson Tide not only led the college football world in colorful nicknames, but rolled through the regular season at 9–0. Alabama allowed just 13 points all season, six to Tennessee in an 18–6 victory and seven to Vanderbilt in a 12–7 win.

That earned Alabama yet another Rose Bowl bid, where the Tide faced Washington State. The game turned out to be a complete mismatch, as the Crimson Tide forced seven turnovers and scored three second-quarter touchdowns on its way to a 24–0 victory.

*The Corolla*, the University of Alabama yearbook, proclaimed the Crimson Tide "Champions of the Universe." An anonymous author (perhaps wishfully) wrote, "Wallace Wade and his peerless 1930 team have made the word 'Alabama' a household phrase throughout the world, from England's foggy Thames to Mother India's sacred Ganges, from Brazil's copper Amazon to Nippon's snow-capped Fujiwara, the Crimson Tide rolls on."

Alabama was awarded the national championship by Parke Davis and Football Research, but Wade would not be around for the afterglow, as he left Tuscaloosa in a dispute with president George Denny to take the coaching job at Duke. The Blue Devils' football stadium is named in his honor.

## 1934

Frank Thomas' first three Alabama teams went a combined 24–4–1, but regular season losses doomed their hopes of another championship or Rose Bowl bid. That changed in 1934, as the Crimson Tide won its second straight Southeastern Conference title with a 9–0 regular season.

Led by the All-America passing combination of halfback Dixie Howell and end Don Hutson (with junior Paul "Bear" Bryant lined up at the other end), the Crimson Tide won all but one game by at least 20 points. The only nail-biter was a 13–6 win in Birmingham against Tennessee, in which Howell's all-around play earned him praise as the South's top back by Volunteers coach Robert Neyland.

Alabama was again bound for Pasadena to face Stanford after the season, as always traveling by train. End Ben McLeod, a backup to Hutson, remembered the trip some 70 years later: "The Rose Bowl was quite a deal. We left Tuscaloosa on Friday morning and arrived in Pasadena on a Monday morning. We stopped in San Antonio, Texas, for a full practice and stopped again in Tucson, Arizona, for a walk-through. Bill Young, a tackle, suffered an appendicitis attack and was operated on in Del Rio, Texas, and, of course, he missed the game."

Howell and Hutson put on another show in the Rose Bowl, as Howell rushed for a pair of touchdowns and threw another.

Frank Thomas' Alabama team traveled by train to the 1935 Rose Bowl and returned to Tuscaloosa as heroes across the state and the Southeast following a 29–13 victory over Stanford.

Hutson caught that 59-yard aerial, as well as a 54-yarder from Joe Riley, as Alabama won 29–13.

The *Los Angeles Times'* Bill Henry wrote, "Like arrows from Robin Hood's trusty bow, there shot from Howell's unerring hand a stream of passes the like of which have never been seen in football here on the Coast. Zing. Zing. Zing. They whizzed through the air and found their mark in the massive maws of Hutson and Bryant, 'Bama ends."

Two years before the advent of the AP poll, Alabama was voted national champion by four bodies, including Dunkel and Williamson.

## 1941

Alabama was in fact awarded a national championship by Houlgate in 1941, so the school counts it among its 13 titles. But it is something of a dubious claim.

Thomas' Crimson Tide went 9–2 that season, but got shut out by both Mississippi State (14–0) and Vanderbilt (7–0), and finished third in the SEC. Alabama did boast a number of top-flight players, including end Holt Rast and linemen Don Whitmire and Joe Domnanovich, but even those on the team weren't sure they deserved a national title.

"We didn't know it until a long time after, but that 1941 team was awarded a national championship," fullback Don Salls said years later. "I moved back to Tuscaloosa in 2001, and I'd see [longtime assistant coach] Clem Gryska at church. And Clem has all those national championship rings. I wanted one and was going to buy one. But in 2003 at a reunion of some of my players from Jacksonville State, they presented me with a 1941 national championship ring. They didn't give rings in those days, so I have the only one. One of my Jacksonville players, Duck Hodges, was a representative for Balfour, which makes those rings."

Still, the Crimson Tide did end the 1941 season in a memorable way, beating Texas A&M 29–21 in the Cotton Bowl on New Year's Day. World War II had begun less than a month earlier after Japan bombed Pearl Harbor.

"We played in the Cotton Bowl against Texas A&M, which was considered the No. 1 team in the nation by a lot of people," Domnanovich said years later. "That was a big event for us. Statistically, we didn't beat them, but we ran all over them."

## 1961

Paul "Bear" Bryant's rebuilding plan was in full force by 1961, as his first class of recruits was now in its senior year. Alabama's team that year featured such stars as quarterback Pat Trammell,

Alabama won the first of six national championships under coach Paul "Bear" Bryant (third from right) in 1961, going 11–0 and beating Arkansas in the Sugar Bowl.

linebacker Lee Roy Jordan, tackle Billy Neighbors, fullback Mike Fracchia, and end Bill Battle, along with one of the most stifling defenses in college football history.

Alabama rolled through the regular season at 10–0, allowing only 22 points and shutting out its last five opponents, including a 34–0 win over Auburn. Led by Jordan, the Crimson Tide allowed just three touchdowns and forced 36 turnovers.

Bryant had vowed to his players upon taking the Alabama job that they would play for a national championship if they followed his plan. He delivered on his promise four years later.

"Somehow I knew we'd win the national championship in 1961," linebacker Darwin Holt said. "We had great coaches and great players. And it was sort of like the Marines. Coach Bryant wanted only a few good men. Not everyone can be a Marine, but those who are, are the best at what they do, and they thrive on the challenge to be tough enough every day. Playing for Coach Bryant wasn't for everyone, but the only ones who ever said anything bad about him were the quitters."

Alabama capped its first national championship in 20 years— and first of six under Bryant—with a 10–3 victory over Arkansas in the Sugar Bowl. Unlike in some previous years, there was no disputing who the national champion was. The Crimson Tide was ranked No. 1 by 14 different polling services, including the Associated Press, United Press International, and the National Football Foundation.

## 1964

Bryant's machine was running smoothly by 1964. The Tide had gone 30–3 in the preceding three years, with New Year's Day bowl victories in all three seasons. But slip-ups during the regular season—a 7–6 defeat to Georgia Tech in 1962 and losses of

10–6 to Florida and 10–8 to Auburn in 1963—had cost Alabama opportunities for another national title. With senior quarterback Joe Namath having been reinstated following a lengthy suspension his junior year, the Crimson Tide's hopes were high for 1964.

Alabama rolled through the regular season unbeaten, though Namath suffered a knee injury during a 17–14 victory over Florida on October 24 that would affect him the rest of the season. With junior Steve Sloan starting and Namath coming off the bench, the Crimson Tide beat Mississippi State, LSU, Georgia Tech, and Auburn down the stretch to end the regular season and clinch the SEC title.

That set up an Orange Bowl showdown with Texas, which was 9–1 and had won the Southwest Conference title. The AP and UPI both awarded the national title before the bowl games, meaning the Crimson Tide was already a championship team before it even took the field against the Longhorns on New Year's night in Miami.

The game was a true classic, with Alabama falling 21–17 despite a Herculean effort from Namath. The gimpy-kneed senior threw for 255 yards and two scores, but was stopped by Texas' Tommy Nobis just short of the goal line in the final seconds.

"One of my greatest disappointments came in the Orange Bowl in my last game," Namath said. "Late in the game we had an opportunity to win, and I fouled up on the goal line. We had first-and-goal at the 6 and gained four yards on a first-down run. And I guess we gained about a yard on second and a little less than a yard on third. On fourth down we went with the surest play, a quarterback sneak. It wasn't disrespect of Texas. It was a belief that we could knock them off the ball and get it in. We were taught around here that if you couldn't blow someone out for a yard, maybe you didn't deserve it."

# 1965

Namath and other stars such as linemen Dan Kearley and Wayne Freeman were gone in 1965, but the Crimson Tide still returned a loaded team featuring Sloan, running back Steve Bowman, linemen Paul Crane and Jerry Duncan, end Ray Perkins, and kicker David Ray. Still, Alabama played like anything but national championship contenders early in the season.

The Tide lost its opener at Georgia in controversial fashion, an 18–17 loss in which the Bulldogs scored on a hook-and-lateral play as time expired. To this day, many involved in the game claim—as photographic evidence appears to show—that Pat Hodgson's knee was down before he shoveled the ball to Georgia teammate Bob Taylor on the game-winning play.

Alabama then shut out Tulane, but slipped past Ole Miss 17–16 and later tied Tennessee 7–7 when backup quarterback Ken Stabler inadvertently threw the ball away on what he believed to be third down (it was fourth down). The Crimson Tide re-gathered itself to blow out four of its final five opponents—with a 10–7 nail-biter at Mississippi State, the only close game—to finish 8–1–1 and earn a bid to the Sugar Bowl against third-ranked Nebraska.

"Coach Bryant had a way of making things work out. I don't know how he did it, but I'm convinced he was able to make things come around to the way we needed," Sloan remembered. "They were waiting until after the bowl games to choose the national champion, and we were ranked about fourth. But a couple of teams in front of us lost that afternoon in bowl games, and that night we were playing Nebraska for the championship."

Indeed, UCLA beat top-ranked Michigan State in the Rose Bowl, and LSU stunned No. 2 Arkansas in the Cotton Bowl, leaving the door open for Alabama to win the national title. The Crimson Tide thumped Nebraska 39–28—behind two touchdown passes from Sloan to Perkins—and waltzed away with its second straight national title, its third in five years.

## 1973

In the eight years between its eighth and ninth national championships, Alabama football had undergone numerous major changes. The sport was integrated in the South a few years before, with the first African American players joining the Crimson Tide in 1971.

That was the same year Bryant radically changed his team's offensive philosophy, moving from a pro-style passing attack to the run-heavy wishbone. The Crimson Tide won back-to-back SEC titles the first two seasons with the offense, but fell flat in the clutch each time.

The 1973 team was loaded offensively, with such stars as quarterbacks Gary Rutledge and Richard Todd, halfback Wilbur Jackson, split end Wayne Wheeler, and linemen Sylvester Croom and Buddy Brown. The Crimson Tide blitzed through the regular season at 11–0, winning by such blowout scores as 66–0 over California, 44–0 over Vanderbilt, 42–21 over Tennessee, 77–6 over Virginia Tech, 35–0 over Mississippi State, and 35–0 over Auburn.

A UPI national championship already in-hand, the Crimson Tide could lay ultimate claim to being the best team in the country—and perhaps one of the top teams of all-time—if it could win its first-ever meeting with Notre Dame in the Sugar Bowl on December 31. It wasn't to be.

Alabama led 17–14 in the third quarter and 23–21 early in the fourth. Notre Dame took the lead on Bob Thomas' field goal with 4:12 remaining, then converted a third down deep in its own end on a 35-yard pass from Tom Clements to Robin Weber to clinch the victory and the AP national title.

"That was a heartbreaker," Wheeler said years later. "That was the best team we had while I was there. Losing that game left us with kind of a hollow feeling. You don't feel like national champions when you don't win the last game."

## 1978

It is remembered largely for one play, but Alabama's 1978 national championship was the culmination of one of the more impressive runs in school history. After narrowly missing out on titles in 1974, 1975, and 1977, Alabama entered the 1978 season ranked No. 1 in the country. With stars such as quarterback Jeff Rutledge, running back Tony Nathan, center Dwight Stephenson, defensive linemen E.J. Junior and Marty Lyons, linebacker Barry Krauss, and cornerback Don McNeal, the Crimson Tide was loaded with All-Americans and future NFL standouts.

Alabama beat Nebraska and Missouri in its first two games, but stumbled in Week 3, a 24–14 loss to Southern Cal in Birmingham. That knocked the Crimson Tide out of the top spot, but the team won eight straight down the stretch—including road victories at Washington and Tennessee—to climb back to No. 2 by the time it secured a Sugar Bowl bid against top-ranked Penn State.

Alabama led 14–7 in the fourth quarter, but Penn State picked up a fumble and drove for what seemed to be a sure score. McNeal made a great play on second-and-goal to keep Scott Fitzkee out of the end zone, and then Matt Suhey was stopped short of the goal line on third down.

That set up the play everyone remembers, with Krauss leading the charge to stuff Mike Guman on fourth down. Alabama held on for victory and had won its 11th national championship on the field.

"So, yes, [Guman] went over the top, and I was the one who hit him," Krauss said years later. "But that was because of what the defensive line had done. It was Coach Bryant's plan that the defensive line would take out the interference and let the linebackers make the play. And then Murray came in and pushed us back, keeping the back from twisting and maybe falling into the end zone. Everyone was involved. It was the epitome of Alabama defense, which was teamwork at its best."

---

## Crimson Tide in Their Own Words
### E.J. JUNIOR III
#### Defensive End, 1977–1980

Coach Bryant only came out of the tower for four reasons: practice was over; some dignitary, like the governor, was visiting practice; someone was hurt; or he was going to chew someone out. One day Coach Bryant started down the tower steps, and we all looked around to see if we knew the reason. We knew it was too early for practice to be over. We looked over by the tunnel to see if there was a limousine parked outside, and there wasn't. No one seemed to be injured. That left only one possibility. And he was walking my way.

I was a freshman, practicing with the second-team defense. And I knew I was about to be chewed out. Coach Bryant looked at me and said, "E.J., go over there and put on a white jersey and get in there with the first defense." I was shocked. I guess I just stood there, because he said, "Did you hear me?"

I said, "Yes, sir," and sprinted over to the manager. By the time I got to the track that went around the practice field, Coach Bryant

E.J. Junior III wasn't sure if he was going to be good enough to hold on to his starting job at Alabama, but he was a first-round draft choice in the NFL.

had chewed out the guy who had been in front of me—chewed him up and spit him out.

And I was on first-team defense!

Coach Bryant was not happy about the way we had played the week before against Nebraska in Lincoln. The defense had not played well, and we had lost 31–24. And he didn't like the way our ends had played, because he told the ends, "I could take two freshmen and do better than what you did." And later that day, I was a freshman moving to first-team defense. At the other end, another freshman, John Mauro, got moved up to first team.

We were getting ready to play Vanderbilt, and I thought maybe he was just moving me up because we were going to be playing in Nashville, my home town. But that didn't explain Mauro, who was from South Bend, Indiana, going to first team, too. It wasn't about geography.

I started against Vanderbilt and then pretty much started every game the rest of my Alabama career. But you were never comfortable about your position. I turned my knee against Mississippi State, didn't play much against LSU, and watched Dewey Mitchell have a heck of a game. We had John Knox and Wayne Hamilton, too. We were interchangeable, and it was difficult to tell who was the starter and who wasn't.

I think that helped us win games. That was partly because there wasn't much difference—if any—between the first-team guys and the guys who gave them a break in games, so that was pretty tough on the opponent. And the other reason is that you had to keep pushing if you wanted to keep your job, and that made us all better. Once you got a taste of first team, you didn't want to go back to second team. I never forgot the chewing out of the guy whose place I took on first team.

It's funny that when I was growing up I hated Alabama. I guess it was because they beat everyone, including the team I wanted to win. It was sort of the way so many people hated the New York Yankees when they were winning all those championships. I was probably for Vanderbilt and Tennessee and Tennessee State. But as I thought about it more, I realized that everyone wants to be a winner, and Alabama was a winner.

As I began to get interested in Alabama football, I discovered that it wasn't just football where Alabama excelled. They were good in basketball and baseball and track. I was going into engineering and discovered that Alabama's engineering program was considered among the best in the country. I liked the social life, which was enough to be good but not so much as to be able to get me in trouble. It was away from home, but not too far away.

And then there was Coach Donahue. I made a trip to Alabama on a weekend when there was no football game so I could really see the campus and talk to people. Coach Donahue met with me and my parents, and he sold them when he said, "I can't promise you that he'll start. I can't even promise you he'll play. That's up to him. But I can promise you he'll have the opportunity to get a quality education, and I can promise you that we will teach him about hard work, because we're going to work his tail off."

Playing at Alabama is an experience I'll never forget. It was about the tradition. I learned about character from Coach Bryant. Class. How to push yourself beyond your limits. We were the first to hold up four fingers at the beginning of the fourth quarter. Everybody else does it now, but what that meant was that the fourth quarter belonged to us because we were so well-conditioned and so well-disciplined. In the fourth quarter, we were going to dominate. Coach Bryant could take a group of players who were good and make them great. He could take average players and make them good. Everybody had an opportunity to grow. He treated us all the same way.

And he was the reason we played as a team, not like a bunch of stars. Everyone understood his role.

One of the most shocking things I ever heard was from my position coach, Sylvester Croom. Going into my senior year, he said, "If you play like you are capable of playing, you could be a first-round draft choice." I had no idea I might be able to play professional football, even though I knew I was getting some mention for All-America going into my senior year.

And Coach Bryant had a way of keeping your feet on the ground. One day he said, "You're supposed to be an All-American? I haven't seen him play yet." And that lit a fire under me.

Coach Bryant taught us to be good football players, and it was a special experience to play for him. But I know we didn't get the vintage Coach Bryant. He was much more mellow when I was playing for him. Not that he didn't command respect, but it was nothing like the stories I had heard from guys who played for him earlier. But just because he had changed with the times, the one thing that didn't change was the winning. We were 44–4 over my four years, a record that wouldn't be broken until the '90s by Coach Stallings' teams.

We learned to work hard. In fact, the defining moment for everyone who played defense came on the goal-line stand against Penn State in the Sugar Bowl to win the 1978 national championship. When we were in the huddle preparing for that fourth-down play, the leaders of that defense—Marty Lyons and Barry Krauss and Murray Legg—laid it out. They said this is what we had worked for, this was that old-fashioned gut check, this was why we had sweated on the practice field in those 100-play scrimmages, this is what it is all about.

We learned that it takes hard work and discipline in everything. It's how you raise your kids, it's how you do your job. You can push or you can be average. You can be complacent or you can be great. It's up to you.

I've been licensed and ordained as a pastor. I'm the assistant pastor at a small ministry called International Prayer Village. I've worked in the school system with a mentoring program for four years as an administrator, and I was an executive director for a year with the Overtime Youth Center, which is Alonzo Mourning's youth program. I have been assigned to coach with the Rhein Fire in NFL Europe and could return to coaching in the NFL.

*E.J. Junior III was an All-American in 1980, SEC Defensive Player of the Year, and a finalist for the Lombardi Trophy in 1980. The three-time All-SEC selection was the fifth player drafted in the first round and played for the St. Louis and Phoenix Cardinals, Miami Dolphins, Tampa Bay Buccaneers, and Seattle Seahawks.*

## 1979

Even though it had won the national championship the previous year and returned numerous star players—Stephenson, McNeal, and Junior among them, Alabama was not ranked No. 1 to start the 1979 season. Southern Cal held the top spot in the preseason, with the Crimson Tide checking in at No. 2.

Alabama beat its first five opponents by a combined 209–9 margin, including wins of 45–0 over Baylor, 66–3 over Vanderbilt, and 40–0 over Florida. The Crimson Tide jumped into the top spot following Southern Cal's 21–21 tie against Stanford on October 13 and finished the regular season 11–0 for the first time since 1974.

"That was a very good football team," McNeal said. "We didn't feel sorry for our opponents that year, but we knew they were at our mercy. In fact, we made it look so easy in 1979 that no one talks about that team."

McNeal might be exaggerating slightly, as Alabama had to rally from 17 down to beat Tennessee on October 20 and in the fourth quarter to beat Auburn 25–18 on December 1. That shaky showing in the Iron Bowl—which came with quarterback Steadman

Shealy playing on a bad knee—cost the Tide in the polls, as Ohio State jumped the Tide for the top spot headed into the bowls.

Alabama entered its Sugar Bowl showdown with No. 6 Arkansas knowing a victory would result in a national title, as Southern Cal had beaten Ohio State by a single point in the Rose Bowl earlier in the day. Major Ogilvie rushed for two touchdowns as the Tide rolled 24–9 and handed Bryant his sixth—and last—national championship.

## 1992

The 1980s were a difficult time for Alabama football. Not only did Bryant retire and die soon after, but several Crimson Tide teams failed to live up to their potential as the school went the entire decade without a national championship.

Gene Stallings, a Bryant protégé, had coached the Crimson Tide to an 11–1 finish and a top five final ranking in 1991, his second season. Still, Alabama entered the 1992 season ranked No. 8 nationally, making it a fringe national title contender at best.

While the teams in front of them began to lose one by one, Alabama—spearheaded by a dominant defense featuring All-Americans Eric Curry, John Copeland, and Antonio Langham—just kept winning. The Crimson Tide vaulted into the No. 2 spot when top-ranked Washington lost to Arizona on November 7, setting up a Sugar Bowl matchup with No. 1 Miami on New Year's Day.

Alabama entered the game as a heavy underdog, picked to lose by virtually everyone. Everyone, that is, except the Crimson Tide players and coaches. "Were all gathered in the tunnel, preparing to take the field," Curry said years later. "And when they announced us, it was showtime. We were insane. It was like a big-time fight, Tyson vs. Holyfield, or a barroom brawl. And it was like the roles were reversed. We were hyped up like you would expect Miami to be, although not in an in-your-face way like Miami. Miami was intimidated before the kickoff. They lost the game before the first snap. They weren't ready."

Alabama dominated from the outset, going on to win 34–13 behind three turnovers and a pair of rushing touchdowns from Derrick Lassic. The Crimson Tide finished 13–0 for the first time in school history and had its 12th national championship.

## 2009

Alabama had to wait quite a while to win its 13th national championship. It would be 17 years before the Crimson Tide ended the year No. 1, and the team had five coaching changes in that time.

Nick Saban took over the program in 2007 and quickly returned the Crimson Tide to the top of the college football mountain. Alabama went 12–2 and won the SEC West in Saban's second season, and entered 2009 ranked No. 5 in the country.

Alabama beat Virginia Tech 34–24 in the season opener and then temporarily took over the top spot in the BCS rankings following a 20–6 victory over South Carolina on October 17. The Tide fell to No. 3 following a 12–10 win over Tennessee the following week, but rolled through the rest of the regular season and then smashed top-ranked Florida 32–13 in the SEC Championship Game.

That put Alabama back in Pasadena for a bowl game for the first time in 64 years, facing Texas—a team it had never beaten—in the BCS Championship Game. After some early struggles, the Tide surged to a 37–21 victory, claiming its 13th national title.

"To be a part of this tradition, it's amazing," defensive end Brandon Deaderick said following the game. "We're in the history books. We're actually part of those lists of great teams at the

University of Alabama. I'm so excited. It's amazing. To be at the bottom of the totem pole in the SEC [in 2006], and to make the move up and have this chance, it's just great. I can't really put it into words."

---

HAD FATE SMILED A LITTLE MORE, the Crimson Tide could have claimed a few more national titles over the years. Here are eight more Alabama teams that just missed ending up No. 1.

## 1945

Alabama's "War Babies" trashed all comers in the first season following World War II, outscoring its opponents 396–66 in the regular season. Led by All-Americans Harry Gilmer and Vaughn Mancha, the Crimson Tide then crushed Southern Cal 34–14 in the Rose Bowl.

But a championship wasn't to be. Army, a virtual all-star team during the war years, held the No. 1 ranking the entire season despite not playing in a bowl game. The Tide finished No. 3.

## 1962

The Crimson Tide had no one to blame but itself for not winning a second straight title in 1962. Joe Namath and Alabama were ranked No. 1 and carrying an 18-game winning streak when it traveled to Atlanta to face Georgia Tech on November 17. But it was a forgettable day for the Tide, which lost 7–6. Namath threw four interceptions, and Bryant refused to kick a game-tying extra point in the fourth quarter, opting to go for two and the win. Alabama failed on the two-point conversion attempt and lost by a point.

The Crimson Tide would go on to rout Auburn 38–0 two weeks later, then beat Oklahoma 17–0 in the Orange Bowl. Alabama finished No. 5 in the final rankings.

## 1966

Alabama finished one of its greatest-ever seasons in bitter disappointment, as a chance at a third straight national title came up short despite the Crimson Tide doing everything it could on the field. Alabama went 11–0, outscored its opponents 267–37, and beat Nebraska 34–7, yet finished No. 3 in the final rankings.

Notre Dame and Michigan State, which had entered the season ranked as the top two, tied 10–10 to end the regular season. Neither played in a bowl game yet held onto the top two rankings in the final poll.

The theories as to why Alabama was dismissed by national voters are numerous, with many theorizing that the Crimson Tide—and southern football in general—were being penalized for being late to racially integrate. Whatever the reason, it was tough to swallow for Alabama quarterback Ken Stabler.

"I had watched as a kid as Pat Trammell won a national championship, then watched Joe Namath and Steve Sloan win national championships, and I thought 1966 was my turn," Stabler said years later. "We made a pretty good run, but we didn't get there. It was disappointing, but I believe we did all we could do."

## 1975

Alabama finished perfect in the regular season in 1971, 1973, and 1974, only to lose in the bowl game, but its 1975 national title hopes got derailed in the first week. The Crimson Tide lost 20–7 to Missouri in the season opener and never got back higher than No. 3 in the country despite winning its final 11 games.

Alabama beat Penn State 13–6 in the Sugar Bowl, which wasn't enough to push the Crimson Tide past Oklahoma and Arizona State for the top spot. But that win was still a significant one, as it snapped a nine-year bowl winless streak for the Crimson Tide.

"It was my last Alabama game, and we wanted to go out with a win," quarterback Richard Todd said. "Alabama had lost—or at least failed to win, since there had been a tie in there—every bowl game since the 1966 team beat Nebraska in the 1967 Sugar Bowl. And we heard a lot about that."

Though it didn't end in a title, the 1975 season was also significant for another reason. It marked the fifth straight year Alabama won the SEC championship, a streak unmatched in conference history.

## 1977

Though Alabama lost in Week 2 at Nebraska in 1977, the Crimson Tide played its way back into the national championship race by winning its final nine regular season games. Third-ranked Alabama entered New Year's Day needing a little help to win the title.

Everything appeared to line up for Alabama, as Notre Dame beat No. 1 Texas in the Cotton Bowl, and Arkansas beat second-ranked Oklahoma in the Orange Bowl. The Crimson Tide, meanwhile, crushed No. 9 Ohio State 35–6 in the Sugar Bowl, and had to wait on the poll results.

The voters instead went with Notre Dame, which had been ranked No. 4 before beating Texas. For the third time in five years, the Fighting Irish had dealt the Crimson Tide a bitter pill in early January.

"I thought we had it won in 1977," Alabama wide receiver Ozzie Newsome said years later. "After the [Sugar Bowl], we had a van to go to Mobile for the Senior Bowl. Johnny Davis, Bob

Cryder, a player from Ohio State, and I drove over together. While we were driving, we heard on the radio they had voted Notre Dame the national champion. It made that trip twice as long. We just couldn't believe it."

## 1980

Led by All-Americans E.J. Junior and Thomas Boyd, Alabama was again chasing a third straight title in 1980. The Tide was ranked No. 1 in the country and had won 28 straight games by the time it pulled into Jackson, Mississippi, to face Mississippi State on November 1.

But the Crimson Tide's championship dreams died there, as Mississippi State shocked Alabama 6–3 in what is still regarded as the greatest win in Bulldogs history. Alabama quarterback Don Jacobs fumbled on the 1-yard line in the final minutes to secure the loss.

Alabama would lose 7–0 to Notre Dame two weeks later and then beat Auburn 34–18 to end the regular season. A 30–2 win over Baylor in the Cotton Bowl gave the Crimson Tide a 10–2 final record, but it ended up sixth in the final rankings.

## 1986

Alabama never seriously threatened for a national championship in 1986. The Tide lost three games that year and never achieved the top ranking in the country.

But Ray Perkins' team might have been the victim of over-scheduling. The Tide played nonconference games against Ohio State, Notre Dame, and Penn State that year, in addition to the SEC gauntlet against Florida, LSU, Tennessee, and Auburn.

Led by All-Americans Bobby Humphrey and Cornelius Bennett, Alabama made it as far as 8–0 before losing to eventual national champion Penn State 23–3 on October 25. The Tide also lost to LSU and Auburn down the stretch before rebounding to beat Washington 28–6 in the Sun Bowl to salvage a 10–3 season.

## 1994

Alabama's 1994 team wasn't ever really in the national title race, not entering the top five until mid-November. But it probably came within a point of at least being in the argument.

Alabama made it through the regular season at 11–0, though it was ranked behind fellow unbeatens Nebraska and Penn State at that point. There was no guaranteed No. 1 vs. No. 2 bowl match-up in those days, so the Crimson Tide would have probably needed losses by both the Cornhuskers and Nittany Lions on New Year's Day (and both won) to gain consideration for No. 1.

It turned out not to matter, as Alabama lost 24–23 to Florida in the SEC Championship Game. The Crimson Tide then beat Ohio State 24–17 in the Citrus Bowl to finish 12–1 and ranked No. 5 in the final rankings.

"One of the most exciting games I ever played in was the Citrus Bowl at the end of the 1994 season," offensive lineman Kareem McNeal said years later. "That was a really big win for our seniors because it gave Alabama a 45–5–1 record over four years, the best four-year record in Alabama history."

*chapter 10*

# ALABAMA'S GREATEST PLAYERS SPEAK

THE LAST WORD IN THIS BOOK will be from the players themselves. In the following pages, more than eight decades' worth of Crimson Tide greats will describe what Alabama football means to them.

## HOWARD CHAPPELL, HB (1931–1933)

I was always interested in guiding students to the university, and particularly football players. I'd tell them that if you played football at Alabama, you would be playing for a school known for its football. The university put out engineers and doctors and lawyers, but when you think about Alabama, the first thing that comes to mind is football.

## BEN McLEOD, FB (1935–1936)

I didn't really go to the University of Alabama to play football, but it's one of the best things that ever happened to me. I know I owe everything to the university. At least eight members of my family have attended Alabama, including my brother, who got his doctorate there, and youngsters from our family continue to attend.

## JOE DOMNANOVICH, C (1941–1942)

They didn't make much out of being an All-American. I don't have any idea how I was selected. I just read about it in the newspaper.

Howard Chappell
was on coach Frank
Thomas' first Alabama
Crimson Tide team.

Afterward they sent me a sweater. Long after my playing career, it was amazing how many people knew that Joe Domnanovich had played football for Alabama.

## HARRY GILMER, HB (1944–1947)

Alabama prepared me for a life in football. If you add it up, after Alabama I played for nine years, coached for 27 years, and scouted for 11 more. Add that up, and it's 47 years in pro football. I always enjoyed returning to Tuscaloosa to scout Alabama players. I have great respect for and loyalty to Alabama, and I am appreciative of the great record in football there.

## VAUGHN MANCHA, C (1944–1947)

I fell in love with the University of Alabama at an early age, when I was playing football at Ramsay High School in Birmingham. There were so many things I appreciated about the opportunity I had. I was a poor kid, but I was lucky enough to have the skills to play for Alabama, which meant I was going to get three meals a day and not have to sleep with my big brother any more. And I was lucky enough to have a coach, Frank Thomas, who stressed education. I've tried to apply the lessons I learned from Coach Thomas throughout my life as a player, coach, administrator, and professor.

## HARRY LEE, G/LB (1951–1954)

After [World War II] we moved back to Alabama, to Birmingham, and I became even more of a fan. I got to see a lot of Alabama games in those days. And I started to learn about the history and tradition of Alabama football, the bowl games and championships. And it seemed to me that it would mean something special to wear that crimson jersey. I took it as a great compliment to Alabama when I read that General [Robert] Neyland at Tennessee had told his team, "You never know what a football player is made of until he plays against Alabama."

## TOMMY LEWIS, FB (1951–1953)

There is no way to say how much I wanted to play for Alabama. I worked hard on my own to become a good football player. I don't know how in the world college football coaches found out about me playing in the little south Alabama town of Greenville, but I still have letters and telegrams from colleges that were recruiting me from around the country. One of them is from Coach Bryant at Kentucky. But I never gave a thought to any of them except

Alabama. The day Alabama offered me a football scholarship, it made my world. It was the Crimson Tide for me!

## Cecil "Hootie" Ingram, CB/QB (1952–1954)

Alabama didn't have to recruit me. I had been practicing to be an Alabama player since I was in about the fourth grade. And I spent a lot of time on the Alabama practice fields watching as a kid. I got letters from other schools, but I was never going anywhere else. One day during basketball season, Coach Crisp asked me when I was going to sign. I told him I didn't know I had an offer. He told me to come by his office the next day, which I did. He then sent me to coach Lew Bostick's office to sign the scholarship. Coach Bostick told me it was out on the table, to fill it out and sign it. And I did. Years later when I was working for the Southeastern Conference, I went back in the files and found my scholarship papers that I had filled out myself.

## Bart Starr, QB/CB (1952–1955)

While maturing I realized Alabama was very, very special and highly regarded around the nation for its athletics achievements. I appreciated the history and tradition of the football program. After moving to the professional level, I could appreciate it even more. When Coach Bryant came in a few years later, he raised the bar tremendously. I am very proud to be an alumnus, even though we experienced some embarrassing disappointments during those two years. Lifetime friendships were developed with teammates and other students.

## Fred Sington Jr., T (1958–1959)

There is nothing like having played football for the University of Alabama. I loved it, and many, many other people love it. And

Bart Starr did not have the best of college careers because of injuries and coaching changes, but became a Pro Football Hall of Fame quarterback for Vince Lombardi and the Green Bay Packers.

it's a good feeling to be a part of the greatest tradition in college football.

## TOMMY BROOKER, E/K (1959–1961)

After the [1960] season, Coach Bryant called me, Pat Trammell, and Leon Fuller into his office and thanked us for making good grades. He said we were the main reason the football team had a better grade-point average than the rest of the university, and particularly the fraternities. That was important to him. And he said he'd pay for us to go to graduate school, and I was able to get my master's degree in the off-season from pro ball.

## BILLY NEIGHBORS, T (1959–1961)

I'm like a lot of people who went to the university to play football. I wouldn't have been worth a damn without it. I wouldn't have gotten an education. I wouldn't have traveled anywhere. I wouldn't have become a broker. It got me name recognition.

## DARWIN HOLT, LB (1960–1961)

I'll never forget the first time I saw Tuscaloosa. I was raised in Gainesville, and the nearest thing to a river we had was the Red River, which was just a little ditch unless it flooded. When I came to the University of Alabama in 1959, I drove all night and came across the Black Warrior River the next day. I thought there must have been a flood. Although I was out of the state for a while, I loved Alabama so much I couldn't wait to be back here and make this my home. And I appreciate the way the people of this state have supported me.

## LEE ROY JORDAN, LB (1960–1962)

Everything I've ever done is because of a big boost I got from attending the University of Alabama. And I feel very fortunate that people still recognize me and think good thoughts about the teams we had. I've tried to be a good ambassador for the university because I am very proud to be an Alabama graduate.

## MAL MOORE, QB (1961–1962)

When Coach Bryant took the Alabama job after the 1957 season, two of his assistants, Jerry Claiborne and Elmer Smith, came to Dozier to see me. We just talked for a few minutes in the driveway— I didn't even know enough to invite them into the house—to confirm that I would be at Alabama. That had not been a hard decision for me. My father was a huge Alabama fan. He had loved Alabama going back to the Rose Bowl days. And so I grew up pulling for Alabama. I can remember Saturday afternoons around a dove field listening to Alabama games on a truck radio. We'd pull for Alabama like the devil. Alabama had some tough times my last three years in high school, but we were still Alabama fans. I was looked at by Georgia, Auburn, and Alabama, and there was no question where I was going. And I am so thankful the opportunity came my way.

## JOE NAMATH, QB (1962–1964)

To be Crimson Tide is an honor because of the history and tradition. I never felt I did anything except be with a great bunch of guys. But being any part of it makes you humble because of the greatness that was there. And to be a small part of it makes you want to know about it, to learn about it. And you appreciate what other people have done. The tradition of the university is about people. And other people associate you with your university.

## PAUL CRANE, C/LB (1963–1965)

Playing at Alabama has given me a reference point. Part of it is that people remember you, even that far back, which is nice. But the personal reference point is the hard work, commitment, and dedication it took to play for Coach Bryant and Alabama. Each of us has a period in his or her life that has a profound effect or results in a huge change. For me that period was my time as a player at Alabama. It has served as the reference point for the rest of my life.

## STEVE SLOAN, QB (1963–1965)

Playing football at Alabama in the mid-'60s was sort of like being in the brotherhood of coal miners. You didn't know if you were going to get out of that mine or not. It was a tough process. But the winning made it fun. Both at the time and ever since, I felt honored to be a part of the team and to play for Coach Bryant and the assistant coaches. They were all so dedicated, and I was fortunate to be a part of it.

## JIMMY FULLER, OL (1964–1966)

When I was being recruited, the players from that 1961 national championship team and the 1962 team would come by my house, guys like Bill Battle, who was from West End, and Billy Richardson, from Jasper. I think the players and ex-players made the biggest impression on me because they had so much class. They were the type of persons I wanted to be.

## RAY PERKINS, E (1964–1966)

It worked out great that Alabama would be the only school that recruited me because Alabama was the only school I was interested in. I had wanted to go to Alabama since I was a sophomore in high school. The most meaningful things about my time as a player at Alabama were the people I played with, the coaches I played for, and of course, Coach Bryant. I love the memory of Coach Bryant because he meant a lot to me as a coach and later as a friend. The most meaningful thing about my time as coach was the players. And I still hear from a lot of them and keep up with a lot of them. That is rewarding.

## JERRY DUNCAN, T (1965–1966)

I was extremely fortunate to come along at the right time to have the opportunity to play for Alabama. I wasn't really a very good football player, although I was probably a decent athlete. I played at Sparta, North Carolina, a very small program with 25 or 30 guys on the team in the smallest county in the state. And I found out later that Coach Gryska was sent up to sign me without even talking to my coaches or looking at film. I never did know what Coach Bryant had heard about me. It was an extraordinary time to be given the opportunity to play for Coach Bryant and the great assistant coaches we had. It was a fantastic journey.

## KEN STABLER, QB (1965–1967)

I was young and dumb and wild, and when I became a disciplinary problem, Coach Bryant disciplined me. At the time I couldn't see it, but he was teaching me a life lesson. I was close to throwing everything away, and he saw something worth saving. He suspended me, then gave me the opportunity to get back. Don't think I got off light. I got the hell beat out of me at practice, but he didn't let me throw it away.

## JOHNNY MUSSO, RB (1969–1971)

When I was 11 years old, I knew what I wanted to do. And I was able to live a childhood dream. I never lost the wonder of it. The reality of playing for Alabama never left me. I couldn't believe I was lucky enough to be wearing that crimson jersey and playing for Coach Bryant. It never lost its magic. Every time I slipped on that jersey, it was a wonder.

## TERRY ROWELL, NG (1969–1971)

I have nothing but fond memories of my time at Alabama. I know they have had great teams at Alabama, national championships before I came and national championships after I was there. But I wouldn't swap places with anyone. With the exception of two or three players—Johnny Musso and John Hannah and Jeff Rouzie when he was healthy—we didn't have anything resembling an

John Hannah is one of the greatest O-lineman in football history. An All-American at Alabama, he went on to a Pro Football Hall of Fame career with the New England Patriots. His father, uncle, and two brothers also played football for the Tide.

NFL player. But we played hard. We were motivated. And we had the greatest coach of all time.

## JOHN HANNAH, G (1970–1972)

The biggest thing you remember is the relationships you developed and the friendships you made with your teammates. Even though I may not stay in touch that much, there is still that bond. We had great players like Johnny Musso and Jim Krapf and real characters like Bearcat Brown, Wayne Hall, Steve Bisceglia, and Joe LaBue. It was just a great bunch of guys like John Croyle and Steve Sprayberry and on and on and on. I think about them all the time and what they meant to me.

### WILBUR JACKSON, HB (1971–1973)

I never thought about playing professionally until my junior year when I got a letter from the Dallas Cowboys. But my goal was to play football for Alabama and to get an education. As it turned out, I did get that professional football opportunity. One thing I learned is that it was a lot easier to play pro ball than it was to play at Alabama. The Alabama practices were a lot tougher than the games. And we were winning. I wondered sometimes what the practices would be like if we were losing. But, of course, it paid off.

### JOHN MITCHELL, DE (1971–1972)

I don't know if any of them have a greater appreciation for Alabama than I do. I was a little African American kid who knew nothing and who was nurtured by and learned from Coach Bryant. He gave me my opportunity. Any success I have had, I owe to him. There is no way I could ever repay the University of Alabama.

### WAYNE WHEELER, SE (1971–1973)

Playing football at Alabama was the best experience of my life. I never had one regret since the day I chose Alabama. My family and everyone else didn't really want me to go out of state, so I kind of went against everyone when I signed with Alabama. But for me, it was the best decision I've ever made. It was everything I expected it to be, and I played with the greatest players and coaches I could have ever asked for.

### WOODROW LOWE, LB (1972–1975)

When people ask me why I went to Alabama instead of Auburn when I lived in Phenix City, just a few miles from Auburn, I have a simple answer. We had a flat tire. Auburn had invited me to a game, and I was going over with a buddy. But we had a flat tire, didn't have a spare, and had to hitchhike back to Phenix City to get help. I never made it to the Auburn game, and I never even met the Auburn coach who was supposed to be recruiting me.

## MIKE WASHINGTON, CB (1972–1974)

There were a lot of days I wanted to go home, but I felt a responsibility to take advantage of the opportunity the university had given me. I didn't want to disappoint my mother and grandmother and all the people who were rooting for us to make it. As much as I wanted to leave sometimes, there were many more times that I was glad to be there. We were having a great time. We had a great run of winning football games. If I had it to do all over, I'd do it the exact same way.

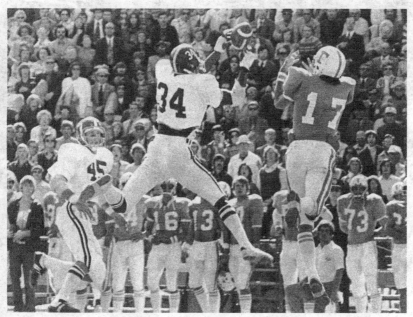

Mike Washington (34) was an All-America cornerback who had eight interceptions as 'Bama won one national championship and three SEC titles.

## RICHARD TODD, QB (1973–1975)

We had a lot of fun playing in those days. We had a great bunch of guys, excellent coaches, and we had really good teams. We were the premier team in the Southeastern Conference. We won the SEC championship every year I was there. It was fun to be able to do that at your state university. I think we understood then, and I know we understood later, that we were part of a great tradition by playing football for Alabama. I think the one other thing that stood out alongside tradition was the emphasis on class, on doing things the right way.

Richard Todd (14) was a wishbone quarterback who could hand off to a big fullback like Calvin Culliver (33), pitch to a halfback, or keep it himself for a run or pass.

## BOB BAUMHOWER, DT (1974–1976)

When I went to the [Miami] Dolphins, another defensive lineman, A.J. Duhe from LSU, and I were the first two picks. The guys playing our positions had gotten into a little trouble, so we went right to first team, which was sort of being thrown to the wolves. And while coach Don Shula was tough, I never felt that I wasn't prepared to do whatever it took to get the job done because of my Alabama background.

## GUS WHITE, NG (1974–1976)

I still remember my first class at Alabama. It was an English class. The teacher said, "You football players think you're going to get something. You get nothing." And she was true to her word. It wasn't a cakewalk. And that's the way it was on the football field. Nothing was given. And I've always liked that. All I've ever asked for is an opportunity, and I think I've made the most of those opportunities.

## OZZIE NEWSOME, SE (1974–1977)

After your career has been over a few years, you can look back and see that you were a part of an historic time. But at the time a place in history was the last thing on your mind. It was just playing football. Every day was a matter of making sure you gave your best effort. We had so many good players that I was just concerned with maintaining my place on the depth chart. It was a matter of that day, that practice, maybe that period of practice. I can also look back and see how my time at Alabama has been helpful to me. Coach Bryant stressed priorities, which is the team. We learned what initiative is. He encouraged us to be as good as we could be because we wanted to, not because of outside motivation.

And we learned that when we win, there is enough for everyone. Everyone can share in the glory when you win.

## Barry Krauss, LB (1976–1978)

I didn't realize at the time what I was a part of. We had great football teams at Alabama. When I got to professional football, I realized how great Coach Bryant was. The best lessons I learned were at Alabama. There is no question that the greatest experience of my life was playing football for Coach Bryant at the University of Alabama. It is something I am very proud of and something I think about every day.

## Marty Lyons, DT (1975–1978)

I have nothing but fond memories of my days at Alabama. It starts with the players. There was a closeness that is difficult to describe. We practiced hard, we played hard, and we did things together off the field. And there was accountability. When we were in a big game, we knew we could trust one another.

## Don McNeal, CB (1976–1979)

I didn't know a lot about college football when I was growing up in Atmore. I guess I was an Alabama fan more than any other team, but I wasn't a real fan. I just knew about the Crimson Tide and about Bear Bryant. Lou Ikner and I had been on the Escambia County championship team. I went to Tuscaloosa, and Lou took me out to a fraternity party. I met the coaches and the players and started finding out more about the tradition of Alabama. They had all those pictures of All-Americans. I was impressed—by the tradition and by the people. I was still deciding. Tennessee called and Auburn called. But then Coach Bryant called, and when he

Don McNeal (28) was recruited as a possible wide receiver, but when he made an interception, he became a dangerous return man.

called, that was it. You wanted to be a part of that success. It was a no-brainer.

## STEADMAN SHEALY, QB (1976–1979)

I was sitting in our living room in Dothan with Doug Barfield, who was Auburn's head coach. Vince Dooley of Georgia was out front of the house in his car waiting for Coach Barfield to leave so he could talk to me. The phone rang, and my mother came in and said, "It's Coach Bryant."

I went to the phone, and he said, "What jersey have you always wanted to wear?"

"Crimson," I answered.

## DWIGHT STEPHENSON, C (1976–1979)

I had a great, great time at Alabama. We really did have fun. We didn't want to lose a game. We thought if we lost we were personally responsible. And practices after a loss weren't too good. Fortunately, we usually won 34 out of 36 games. It was fun to know when we had the game won, a great, great feeling. And that's because we gave it everything we had.

## E.J. JUNIOR, DE (1977–1980)

Playing at Alabama is an experience I'll never forget. It was about the tradition. I learned about character from Coach Bryant. Class. How to push yourself beyond your limits. We were the first to hold up four fingers at the beginning of the fourth quarter. Everybody else does it now, but what that meant was that the fourth quarter belonged to us because we were so well-conditioned, so well-disciplined that in the fourth quarter we were going to dominate. Coach Bryant could take a group of players who were good and make them great. He could take average players and make them good. Everybody had an opportunity to grow. He treated us all the same way.

## MAJOR OGILVIE, RB (1977–1980)

One of the things about being lucky to be in the right place at the right time was something I was never aware of until after it happened. They've started keeping records on just about everything. The only thing that matters in football is the team, but they keep individual things that don't really matter, and one of them was me scoring touchdowns in four consecutive bowl games. That really says more about the team than one person. It doesn't mean anything to me like those national championship trophies.

## JEREMIAH CASTILLE, CB (1979–1982)

Everyone talks about football teaching life lessons. It's true. What you learn on the football field can be applied to how you live your life off the football field. If you work in corporate America, you learn to be a team player. If you have your own business, you learn to be a self-starter. If you are raising a family, you apply the lessons of discipline. If you want to be successful in anything you do, you have an advantage if you have played football for the University of Alabama, because you know those things and have experienced those things.

## TOMMY WILCOX, S (1979–1982)

Pro football was like vacation for me. They didn't hit anything like what we did in practice at Alabama. Practices were hard for some of the players, but not any from Alabama.

## JOEY JONES, SE (1980–1983)

Anyone who played football for Alabama is honored to have been a small part in the tradition created by hundreds of coaches and players through the years. When you are playing, it means a lot to pull on that crimson jersey; 30 years later it still means something. I have great respect for those who played before me, those I played with, and those who have played since. I also sense respect from others for those who played for the Crimson Tide. It means a lot to me to have a tie to the university, to be an alumnus. Alabama alumni and fans are everywhere, and it's always a treat to meet with them.

## PETER KIM, K (1980–1982)

I went to Alabama to become a better football player. But what I became was a better person. And I wouldn't be where I am today if I had not gone to Alabama. I have been gone for almost 30 years, but there is not a day that something doesn't take me back to my days at Alabama. Not just football, but all the teaching I had from Coach Bryant. We learned pride. We learned confidence. We learned to persevere. There have been many days running my business that I wanted to take a knee, just quit. But then I think about Coach Bryant, who told us there would be days like that in life and that you have to get it done. And those thoughts get me going.

## WALTER LEWIS, QB (1980–1983)

I never thought being black was an obstacle at Alabama. All anyone got was an opportunity, and that was all I wanted. I thought if I had the opportunity to compete, I could do the job. And that's the way it was. I got the opportunity and took advantage of it. Coach Bryant said he wanted his players to remember him as being fair. I remember a lot of things about him, and that is one of the most important.

## VAN TIFFIN, K (1983–1986)

[The game-winning field goal against Auburn in 1985] was particularly meaningful for me since I had grown up an Alabama fan. I was about nine or 10 when I went to my first Alabama-Auburn game, and in the 1970s my parents started buying season tickets. After the high school game on Friday night, we'd leave and go to the Alabama game. I was at the 1979 Sugar Bowl game against Penn State. So I was a fan.

## MIKE SHULA, QB (1983–1986)

I always pictured myself as being in football as long as I could. I had been around football all my life, seeing almost all of my father's home games and some road games. I wanted to play as long as possible and then to stay in it. There's just something different about football. It was a challenge to take the next step, whether playing in the NFL or getting into coaching. And I was fortunate enough to coach for 15 years in the NFL, and I enjoyed it very much. I have said many times I would not have left that for any college job except one—this one.

Mike Shula (11) was an exceptional quarterback as an Alabama player in the mid-1980s. He later led the Crimson Tide as head coach from 2003 to 2006 and compiled a 26–23 record.

## BOBBY HUMPHREY, RB (1985–1988)

Once you have done it, you realize it means a lot to play for the Crimson Tide. There is something special about wearing the crimson and white and knowing you are a part of the best in college football. I look back and see that it was almost lucky that I ended up at Alabama and consider myself very fortunate. Over the years I have talked with a lot of football players from many, many colleges and universities, and I am convinced that no one has better fans than the University of Alabama. Players from other schools are envious of the support that Alabama players get from Crimson Tide fans, who in my opinion also are a part of the Alabama family.

Alabama fans have great respect for the men who played football for the Crimson Tide.

## DAVID SMITH, QB (1986–1988)

Like most athletes, I don't think I appreciated the experience of being an Alabama football player as much then as I do now. But I do know it was different. I had played football all my life, every fall and practice every spring. I didn't think it was particularly special. But in my senior year at Alabama I could go out to eat or go to the mall, and I would be amazed at the number of people who would recognize me and want an autograph or want a picture made with them. And not just kids—adults, too. I guess I can understand how star pro athletes might get frustrated by it, but it was always special to me.

## ROGER SHULTZ, OL (1987–1990)

In a way it's a waste to have the opportunity to play football at Alabama when you are only 18 to 22 years old. I wish now I had paid more attention to things around me. It was so regimented—meetings, practice, meals, study halls, classes. I wish I had just taken a moment to stand in the middle of the field and look around at the full stadium. Now I realize so much more what it means to pull on that crimson jersey, what it means to be a part of the greatest tradition in college football.

## LAMONDE RUSSELL, TE/WR (1987–1990)

I had three uncles who were like father figures to me, and they were all huge Alabama fans. I was a good athlete from an early age, and it was always a dream of mine to play for Alabama. I look back on it with fond memories. I had more hair back then and I was thinner, but it boggles my mind that people still remember me the way they do.

## GARY HOLLINGSWORTH, QB (1987–1990)

I'm glad I got the opportunity and that it went the way it did. There's a satisfaction there because I could have had some opportunities probably to go play at some other schools and played earlier and maybe played more, but to look back and know that you're a part of one of the greatest traditions in college football is tremendous. It gives me great satisfaction to have been able to be a part of that and compete at that level.

## ERIC CURRY, DE (1990–1992)

Being at Alabama was all about tradition. For a player to put his hands on the grass of the practice fields or at Bryant-Denny Stadium was an unbelievable thrill, a dream. You always felt the coaches and the students and the fans were all behind you, encouraging you to be your best. That's part of the tradition. As I got older, I'd tell the younger players to realize the importance of stepping onto that field, to remember they were representing the

University of Alabama. That's prestige. That's honor. And every team that plays against Alabama knows they don't measure up to the Crimson Tide.

## Jay Barker, QB (1991–1994)

It's great to remember the wins, but there are so many things we got out of being Alabama football players. I tell my kids the same thing Coach Stallings told us: "You'll never go wrong by doing right." That sticks with you. Our coaches cared about me as a person, how I was going to measure up as a husband and a father and a worker. You hear Alabama players talk about "gut checks," that you are going to have them in life. And you learn that at Alabama. You learn about high expectations. You learn to be a team player. I can never give back to Alabama football what it has given to me. Alabama football has impacted just about everything I have done, and there is not a day in my life that passes that someone doesn't say something to me about playing at Alabama. And I think that's true for almost everyone who has pulled on that crimson jersey.

## Kareem McNeal, OT (1992–1995)

I think having been a player helps when you face tough times. You can watch a football game and see the difficulties. A player puts in a lot of hard work, and I think I have continued to have a good work ethic and a good philosophy about life—things I learned on the football field. I feel lucky to have been an Alabama football player. As I look back, I am proud to have played a part in Alabama football tradition. It is so important. And it means a lot to me that people know who I am—a kid from a small town who was able to pull on that crimson jersey. It will always be special to me.

Kareem McNeal (74) was a starter on Alabama's 1994 football team, but prior to his senior year, he was paralyzed in an automobile accident.

# ANDREW ZOW, QB (1998–2001)

It meant a whole lot to me to put on that uniform. An Alabama football player can't help but think about Coach Bryant and the great players who have gone before. A quarterback can't help but think about Joe Namath and Ken Stabler playing on the same field. When you get to Alabama, you know you are in a family atmosphere. That's players, but it's also students and fans. You feel a lot of people are behind you. When you finish playing at Alabama, the fans don't forget you. They continue to be supportive. Alabama fans make me feel that I did something that made them feel better about their school or entertained them. It's a pleasure to give autographs to fans who are so much for you and for Alabama. I talk to friends who played at other schools, and they don't get that from their fans, particularly when their playing days are over.

## WESLEY BRITT, OT (2001–2004)

What really made Alabama different was the people. I'd go to Florida on a recruiting visit, and they'd look at the tag on my shirt and say, "We'd love to have you here." When I went to Alabama, the people didn't have to look at a nametag. They looked at my face and said, "Hey, Wesley. We can't wait to have you here. We can't wait to get you. You're an Alabama boy and we have to have you." That made you feel at home.

## SHAUD WILLIAMS, RB (2002–2003)

My whole career at Alabama was very much a positive experience. I don't regret one day I spent at the University of Alabama. Some of my best friends, who will be my best friends forever, I met at Alabama. You don't realize how special a place Alabama is until you're gone. In the NFL you may play in front of 60,000 fans, as opposed to Bryant-Denny where you have more than 80,000. I am very grateful I was able to be a part of the tradition and be a part of something that was so great.

## ANTOINE CALDWELL, OL (2005–2008)

I just felt like I wanted to be a good representation, not only for the football team, but for the fans, as well. I wanted them, when they talked about me [to say], "That's a guy right there who put his best foot forward in everything he did, not just football-wise, but off the field, too." Just somebody who gave his all for Alabama, because I felt like that's what I did. I'm so proud to be associated with it.